The Beagle Handbook

BY

LINDA WHITWAM

ISBN: 979-8513874188

Copyright

I am deeply grateful to the passionate Beagle experts who have shared their extensive knowledge and love for the beautiful Beagle throughout these pages. This book, the 18th in The Canine Handbooks series, would not have been possible without them.

Specialist Contributors

RUTH DARLENE STEWART

DR SAMANTHA GOLDBERG

SALLY KIMBER

KELLIE WYNN

LORI NORMAN

Other Major Contributors

Special thanks to: Beagle Welfare, SOS Beagle Rescue. In alphabetical order: Debbie Tantrum, Georgina Armour-Langham, Karen Simkin, Kelly Diamond, Linda Forrest, Nigel Wright, Peter Sievwright, Sarah and Ben Porter, Sharon Hardisty, and holistic vet Dr Sarah Skiwski.

(Breeders' details appear at the back of the book)

Table of Contents

Author's Notes: I have alternated between "he" and "she" in chapters to make this book as relevant as possible for all owners.

The Beagle Handbook uses British English, except where Americans have been quoted, when the original US English has been preserved.

This book has been printed in black and white to make it affordable for all new owners.
The Full Colour Beagle Handbook, ISBN: 979-8514030941, is also available from Amazon.

1. Meet the Beagle

The Beagle has been popular since 1950 when Snoopy first appeared in the Peanuts comic strip. Those soulful eyes, floppy ears and velvety coat, coupled with a naturally gentle and happy temperament, have captured hearts and minds all over the world.

Beagles have established themselves as firm favourites with families and love snuggling up with their beloved humans. But don't expect a lapdog; you're getting a pure hound! Beagles are scent hounds and when their noses switch on, their ears switch off and the legs get going – usually in the opposite direction to you!

This breed is not for everyone. But owners who put in the time the Beagle needs for training and exercise are rewarded with the most loyal and affectionate friend - and a handsome, lifelong companion second to none.

A Lot of Hound in a Medium Package

There are hundreds of breeds registered with the Kennel Clubs and all of them are different, but the Beagle is truly unique - every dog is an individual.

Some love swimming, others hate rain. Some want to be constantly on the go, others are happy to spend more time chilling. Some love nothing more than baying at every blowing leaf, others bark infrequently. Some are quick to housetrain, others are stubbornly slow. But they all have strong personalities. Behind those irresistible looks, when butter wouldn't melt in their mouths, lurk the instincts of a pure hound.

The exact origin of the Beagle is shrouded in the mists of time. We do know that packs of larger hunting dogs have been around for many centuries, and it's thought that the Beagle arrived on the scene sometime in the 1800s, being bred down from larger hounds.

There are two sizes in the US, the smaller ones are up to 13" at the withers (shoulder), while the larger type is 13" to 15" at the withers. The looks and temperament are similar. Beagles aren't measured in the UK, but the ideal height is anywhere between 13" and 16."

Developed primarily for hunting hare and rabbits, the breed has an awesome sense of smell and first-rate tracking instincts. Hunting with a Beagle is called ***beagling.***

More than any other breed, they are used as detection dogs for prohibited foodstuffs in airports and quarantine around the world. This is Beagle's dream job as it combines his two favourite hobbies – sniffing and food!

Like other dogs bred to work, Beagles like a job to do. They love taking part in activities such as Barn Hunt and Agility – although if they catch a scent on the way round, don't expect them to complete the course every time! Inventing scenting games and hiding toys or treats around the home and garden is a great way to keep their busy minds occupied. A bored Beagle is a mischievous Beagle...

Beagles are first and foremost pack animals that like to be with other animals or people. They are very social creatures and do not enjoy being left alone for many hours on end. They are not "Velcro" dogs that stick to your side, they need their own quiet space but love to be involved in whatever's going on.

Creative Thinkers

They have lively, quirky minds that love problem-solving and, like all hounds, are creative thinkers with independent minds (some would say stubborn!).

Beagles involved in this book have Houdini tendencies; they can escape from just about anywhere. They can climb on top of tables, microwaves and tall fridges, they can use door handles to open fridges and forbidden rooms, one ate the top tier of her owners' wedding cake after a series of manoeuvres to reach it on a high shelf.

Restive, a UK Beagle, scrambled a wall and took herself off to the local hotel for a slap-up meal. She was found harassing the diners for scraps and was duly returned to her grateful owner!

They can also sense your mood and comfort you when sad. There are countless tales of the affection and empathy of Beagles; later in this book you'll read about 10-year-old Nala who acted as a daily nursemaid while her owner, David, recuperated in bed. Lots of them have regular conversations with their owners - and understand every word they say!

This ability to think for themselves is genetic, bred into Beagles over decades to enable them to hunt in packs at a distance from their masters.

Breeds such as the Spaniel, Labrador and other Retrievers are often easier to train than scent hounds as they were selectively bred to obey commands at their master's heel, rather than working afar using their own initiative.

Make no mistake, Beagles are smart. But these healthy, long-lived dogs approach life from their own unique perspective - don't expect yours to jump to your every command, nor be quickly housetrained (although many are).

They are intelligent and have the ability to learn quickly, but first have to be persuaded that it's in their own interests to co-operate, often with some form of bribery!

Well-socialised Beagles make super family pets, get along with everybody, form deep bonds with children and thrive with other animals in the home, especially other Beagles. Start training early and get your dog used to other people, animals and environments. An under-socialised Beagle can develop tendencies to be territorial, suspicious of new people and dogs, possessive of food and toys, or nuisance barkers.

Although they may get on very well with your pet cat in the home, once they are out and about it can be a different story.

Coupled with their incredible sense of smell, some Beagles also have a strong prey drive and will chase anything small and moving - including the kids!

Teaching the Recall is **very important** as Beagles love running free off the lead (leash) and you want yours to come back to you. Back at home the Beagle enjoys sniffing, watching passers-by, lazing in the sunshine, chasing squirrels and digging up your beautiful lawn or garden.

 Make time for your puppy. Training your Beagle to meet your expectations requires oodles of repetition and patience.

But the rewards are more than worth it. Beagles are the most affectionate and loyal of dogs. Once built, that bond with you is unbreakable.

The One and Only...

They'll make you laugh - and cry when you're trying to train them or get the stolen Sunday roast out of their mouths! But whatever life throws at you, your Beagle will be there for you through thick and thin.

A specialist Beagle trainer, two rescue organisations, leaders of the UK and American Beagle health committees and 12 dedicated breeders with hundreds of years of combined experience have added their expertise to this book. And it's fair to say that they know a thing or two about Beagles! Here is what attracted some of them to the breed, starting in the US:

Lori Norman, Lokavi Beagles, Florida: "I have bred Beagles since 1970 and shown them since I was eight years old. I love that they are a "big dog," little dog. I also adore their thinking...they know what you want in two seconds and then spend the rest of their lives trying to find ways NOT to do it! I love to laugh at their methods. They are such a happy breed - wonderful companions."

Darlene Stewart, Aladar Beagles, Alabama, and Chairperson, Health and Genetics Committee, National Beagle Club of America: "I met my first Beagle breeder in 1979, then I started showing Beagles for others and obtained my first Beagle in 1987. They are loving clowns and their antics are silly and frustrating, although not a breed for everyone. I think their popularity is due to the small size but they are sturdy enough for families with children."

Peter Sievwright, Mattily Beagles, Renfrewshire, Scotland: "My first Beagle was a tan and white girl called Mitzi. She was a beautiful, loving, energetic little thing. She was loyal, obedient and great around my children, and from that moment on I fell in love with the breed.

"It was the gorgeous eyes and big floppy ears with the sturdy short-haired frame and great personality. We now have six Beagles. We spend many hours taking time to care for each and every one of them and know them inside out - even to the point of lying on the floor with them in the whelping pens when they're in labour; being with them all night when we have to, giving them moral support and reassurance."

Sarah and Ben Porter, Puddlehill Beagles, Norfolk: "No other breed lives up to the Beagle in our eyes."

Veterinarian Dr Samantha Goldberg, Kennel Club Health Coordinator for the UK Beagle Clubs and breeder of Molesend Beagles, County Durham: "The breed is amiable, wonderful to look at, moderate in all ways, healthy, friendly and an all-round fun dog. They are also independent and stubborn in an endearing way."

Kelly Diamond, Kelcardi Beagles, Fife, Scotland: "For me it was accidental. I was only 18-years-old and took on a Beagle puppy who was needing a better home. My love for the breed started there. The Beagle's nature is second to none and their personalities are just super. I'll never not have a Beagle in my life."

Georgina Armour-Langham, Robentot Beagles, Leicester: "I love how they look, their character, sense of fun and curiosity. They are affectionate and independent. They are popular because they are perfect for active families, a good size. Little do first-time owners realise what they are getting themselves into..."

Sharon Hardisty, Blunderhall Beagles, Lancashire: "I love the size, looks and friendly, loving nature. Beagles are popular because they get on with everyone and everything. They are always happy, cheeky and tail-wagging."

A Final Few Words...

And finally, we asked our breeders to sum up their Beagles in a few words:

- 🐾 Friendly, loving, good looking, mischievous
- 🐾 Loyal, adorable, wilful, challenging
- 🐾 Tenacious, funny, happy, gorgeous
- 🐾 Loving, characterful, naughty, good looking
- 🐾 Crazy, loyal, loving and stunning
- 🐾 Lovable, friendly, loyal companions
- 🐾 They are harder than you think, don't be fooled by their cute puppy eyes!
- 🐾 Fun, infuriating, challenging, comical
- 🐾 Loving, mischievous, sociable
- 🐾 Beautiful, friendly, therapeutic and fun
- 🐾 Fun, affectionate, gentle
- 🐾 Energetic, curious, hungry, lovable

Arm yourself with lots of time, patience and a sense of humour. Then read on to learn how to understand, train and take best care of these wonderful dogs for the rest of their lives, and how to successfully build a deep bond that will become one of the most important things in your life - and certainly theirs.

2. Breed Standard

The Breed Standard is a blueprint not only for the ideal appearance of each breed, but also for character and temperament, how the dog moves and what colours are acceptable. In other words, it ensures that a Beagle looks and acts like a Beagle, preserving the breed's unique qualities. Good breeders strive to breed their dogs as close as possible to this ideal list of attributes.

If you are looking to buy a puppy, familiarise yourself with the Breed Standard and have a good look at the mother and father - or at least the mother. Purebred puppies usually resemble their parents.

....

The Breed Standard is laid down by the breed societies. In the UK it's the Kennel Club, and in the USA it's the AKC (American Kennel Club) that keeps the register of pedigree or purebred dogs. Dogs entered in conformation shows run under Kennel Club and AKC rules are judged against the Breed Standard.

The main difference between the UK and US is that there is only one type of Beagle in Europe, which is stated as being between 13 and 16 inches high at the withers (shoulders). The AKC recognises two varieties: dogs up to 13 inches at the withers and the second type from 13 to 15 inches tall.

 Stay away from any breeder who advertises *"Pocket"* Beagles, also called Miniature or Toy Beagles. They are not accepted by the Kennel Clubs and breeding solely for size (which may involve breeding for dwarfism or introducing other types of dog) can result in sickly dogs.

One breeder added: "Dwarfism is perpetuated by unscrupulous people intentionally breeding for the *"Pocket Beagle"* market. What results is a race of dwarfs complete with many related health problems."

Breeders approved by the Kennel Clubs agree to produce puppies in line with the Breed Standard and maintain certain welfare conditions. Responsible breeders select only the finest dogs for reproduction, based on the health, looks and temperament of the parents and their ancestors.

The Beagle is a scent hound bred originally to hunt hares and rabbits. It is the smallest pack hound in the *Hound Group.*

The Kennel Club says this about the Hound Group: "Breeds originally used for hunting either by scent or by sight. The scent hounds include the Beagle and Bloodhound and the sight hounds such breeds as the Whippet and Greyhound. Many of them enjoy a significant amount of exercise and can be described as dignified, aloof but trustworthy companions."

Points of Concern

In 2014 the UK Kennel Club launched its **Breed Watch Fit For Purpose** campaign. It identified potential faults that could lead to health issues. There are three categories:

1 Breeds with no current points of concern reported

2 Breeds with Breed Watch points of concern

3 Breeds where some dogs have visible conditions or exaggerations that can cause pain or discomfort

The good news is that Beagles are classed in Category 1, and they are generally regarded internationally as a healthy breed.

The UK Kennel Club says: "The Beagle is the smallest of the British pack hounds bred to hunt hare, and to be followed on foot, hence appealing to those who could not follow the larger scent hounds on horseback. The breed was established in England by the 15th century. Queen Elizabeth I kept a pack of miniature Beagles small enough to be carried in a saddle pannier or a pocket. The miniature version has fallen out of favour in the UK, but in the USA the breed is shown in two varieties."

The KC adds: SIZE – Small, EXERCISE - Up to 1 hour per day, SIZE OF HOME - Small house, GROOMING - Once a week, COAT LENGTH – Short, SHEDS – Yes, LIFESPAN - Over 12 years, VULNERABLE NATIVE BREED – No, TOWN OR COUNTRY – Either, SIZE OF GARDEN - Small/ medium garden. The AKC has this description:

Personality: Merry, friendly, and curious

Energy Level: Very Active; This quick, energetic and compact hound dog needs plenty of exercise

Good with Children: Yes

Good with other Dogs: Yes

Shedding: Seasonal

Grooming: Weekly

Trainability: Responds Well

Height: 13 inches & under, 13-15 inches

Weight: under 20 pounds (13 inches & under), 20-30 pounds (13-15 inches)

Life Expectancy: 10-15 years

Barking Level: Likes To Be Vocal

UK Breed Standard

Just like the Beagle himself, the Breed Standard is relatively straightforward - and a lot shorter than those for many other breeds:

General Appearance - A sturdy, compactly built hound, conveying the impression of quality without coarseness.

Characteristics - A merry hound whose essential function is to hunt, primarily hare, by following a scent. Bold, with great activity, stamina and determination. Alert, intelligent and of even temperament.

Temperament - Amiable and alert, showing no aggression or timidity.

Head and Skull - Fair length, powerful without being coarse, finer in the bitch, free from frown and wrinkle. Skull slightly domed, moderately wide, with slight peak. Stop well-defined and dividing length, between occiput and tip of nose, as equally as possible. Muzzle not snipy, lips reasonably well-flewed. Nose broad, preferably black, but less pigmentation permissible in lighter coloured hounds. Nostrils wide.

Eyes - Dark brown or hazel, fairly large, not deep set or prominent, set well apart with mild, appealing expression.

Ears - Long, with rounded tip, reaching nearly to end of nose when drawn out. Set on low, fine in texture and hanging gracefully close to cheeks.

Mouth - The jaws should be strong, with a perfect, regular and complete scissor bite, i.e. upper teeth closely overlapping lower teeth and set square to the jaws.

Neck - Sufficiently long to enable hound to come down easily to scent, slightly arched and showing little dewlap.

Forequarters - Shoulders well laid back, not loaded. Forelegs straight and upright well under the hound, good substance, and round in bone, not tapering off to feet. Pasterns short. Elbows firm, turning neither in nor out. Height to elbow about half height at withers.

Body - Topline straight and level. Chest let down to below elbow. Ribs well sprung and extending well back. Short in the couplings but well balanced. Loins powerful and supple, without excessive tuck-up.

Hindquarters - Muscular thighs. Stifles well bent. Hocks firm, well let down and parallel to each other.

Feet - Tight and firm. Well knuckled up and strongly padded. Not hare-footed. Nails short.

Tail - Sturdy, moderately long. Set on high, carried gaily but not curled over back or inclined forward from root. Well covered with hair, especially on underside.

Gait/Movement - Back level, firm with no indication of roll. Stride free, long-reaching in front and straight without high action; hindlegs showing drive. Should not move close behind nor paddle nor plait in front.

Coat - Short, dense and weatherproof.

Colour - Tricolour (black, tan and white); blue, white and tan; badger pied; hare pied; lemon pied; lemon and white; red and white; tan and white; black and white; all white.

With the exception of all white, all the above-mentioned colours can be found as mottle. No other colours are permissible. Tip of stern white.

Size - Desirable minimum height at withers: 33 cms (13 ins). Desirable maximum height at withers: 40 cms (16 ins).

Faults - Any departure from the foregoing points should be considered a fault and the seriousness with which the fault should be regarded should be in exact proportion to its degree and its effect upon the health and welfare of the dog and on the dog's ability to perform its traditional work.

Note - Male animals should have two apparently normal testicles fully descended into the scrotum.

US Breed Standard

Head: The *skull* should be fairly long, slightly domed at occiput, with cranium broad and full.

Ears-Ears set on moderately low, long, reaching when drawn out nearly, if not quite, to the end of the nose; fine in texture, fairly broad-with almost entire absence of erectile power-setting close to the head, with the forward edge slightly inturning to the cheek-rounded at tip.

Eyes-Eyes large, set well apart-soft and houndlike-expression gentle and pleading; of a brown or hazel color. *Muzzle*-Muzzle of medium length-straight and square-cut-the stop moderately defined. *Jaws*-Level. Lips free from flews; nostrils large and open.

Defects-A very flat skull, narrow across the top; excess of dome, eyes small, sharp and terrierlike, or prominent and protruding; muzzle long, snipy or cut away decidedly below the eyes, or very short. Roman-nosed, or upturned, giving a dish-face expression. Ears short, set on high or with a tendency to rise above the point of origin.

Body: *Neck and Throat*-Neck rising free and light from the shoulders strong in substance yet not loaded, of medium length. The throat clean and free from folds of skin; a slight wrinkle below the angle of the jaw, however, may be allowable. **Defects**-A thick, short, cloddy neck carried on a line with the top of the shoulders. Throat showing dewlap and folds of skin to a degree termed "throatiness."

Shoulders and Chest: Shoulders sloping-clean, muscular, not heavy or loaded-conveying the idea of freedom of action with activity and strength. Chest deep and broad, but not broad enough to interfere with the free play of the shoulders. Defects-Straight, upright shoulders. Chest disproportionately wide or with lack of depth.

Back, Loin and Ribs: Back short, muscular and strong. Loin broad and slightly arched, and the ribs well sprung, giving abundance of lung room. Defects-Very long or swayed or roached back. Flat, narrow loin. Flat ribs.

Forelegs and Feet: Forelegs-Straight, with plenty of bone in proportion to size of the hound. Pasterns short and straight. Feet-Close, round and firm. Pad full and hard. Defects-Out at elbows. Knees knuckled over forward, or bent backward. Forelegs crooked or Dachshund-like. Feet long, open or spreading.

Hips, Thighs, Hind Legs and Feet: Hips and thighs strong and well-muscled, giving abundance of propelling power. Stifles strong and well let down. Hocks firm, symmetrical and moderately bent. Feet close and firm. **Defects**-Cow hocks, or straight hocks. Lack of muscle and propelling power. Open feet.

Tail: Set moderately high; carried gaily, but not turned forward over the back; with slight curve; short as compared with size of the hound; with brush. **Defects**-A long tail. Teapot curve or inclined forward from the root. Rat tail with absence of brush.

Coat: A close, hard, hound coat of medium length. Defects-A short, thin coat, or of a soft quality.

Color: Any true hound color.

General Appearance: A miniature Foxhound, solid and big for his inches, with the wear-and-tear look of the hound that can last in the chase and follow his quarry to the death.

Varieties: There shall be two varieties: Thirteen Inch-which shall be for hounds not exceeding 13 inches in height. Fifteen Inch-which shall be for hounds over 13 but not exceeding 15 inches in height. **Disqualification:** Any hound measuring more than 15 inches shall be disqualified.

Packs of Beagles - Score of Points for Judging Hounds

General levelness of pack 40% - Individual merit of hounds 30% - Manners 20% - Appointments 10% - **Total 100%**

Levelness of Pack: The first thing in a pack to be considered is that they present a unified appearance. The hounds must be as near to the same height, weight, conformation and color as possible.

Individual Merit of the Hounds: Is the individual bench-show quality of the hounds. A very level and sporty pack can be gotten together and not a single hound be a good Beagle. This is to be avoided.

Manners: The hounds must all work gaily and cheerfully, with flags up-obeying all commands cheerfully. They should be broken to heel up, kennel up, follow promptly and stand. Cringing, sulking, lying down to be avoided. Also, a pack must not work as though in terror of master and whips. In Beagle packs it is recommended that the whip be used as little as possible.

Appointments: Master and whips should be dressed alike, the master or huntsman to carry horn, the whips and master to carry light thong whips. One whip should carry extra couplings on shoulder strap.

Recommendations for Show Livery: Black velvet cap, white stock, green coat, white breeches or knickerbockers, green or black stockings, white spats, black or dark brown shoes. Vest and gloves optional. Ladies should turn out exactly the same except for a white skirt instead of white breeches.

Approved September 10, 1957

Glossary:

Cow hocks – knock-kneed on the back legs

Flews – pendulous upper lips

Hock - tarsal joint of the hind leg (like the human ankle) but bending in the opposite direction

Occiput - bony bump seen at the top rear of the skull on some breeds

Pastern – the area below the wrist or hock but above the foot

Self color – base colour of hair nearest the body of the dog (not the tip)

Snipy – Weak muzzle, pointed or lacking depth or width

Stop - area between a dog's eyes, below the skull

Withers - the ridge between the shoulder blades

3. Finding Your Puppy

Finding a good puppy can be a minefield. If you haven't got yours yet, read this chapter before you commit to anything; it will help you find a healthy, happy puppy with a good temperament

The best way to select a puppy is with your HEAD - not your heart! You'll soon find dozens of Beagle puppies advertised, but it requires a bit more time and research to find a first-rate breeder. If you already have your puppy, skip to the next chapter.

....

With their beautiful soulful eyes, loving expressions, floppy ears and velvety skin, there are few more appealing things on this Earth than Beagle puppies. If you go to view a litter, the pups are sure to melt your heart and it is extremely difficult – if not downright impossible - to walk away without choosing one.

If you haven't yet chosen your pup and take only one sentence from this entire book, it is this:

FIND AN ETHICAL BREEDER WHO PRODUCES PUPPIES FROM HEALTH-SCREENED PARENTS WITH GOOD TEMPERAMENTS

– even if that means paying a bit more. It will be worth it.

FACT > Although the Beagle is regarded as a healthy breed, there are still genetic disorders that can be passed down from the parents. So, a main priority should be to buy a puppy whose parents have been health-screened for the relevant diseases.

Find a breeder who knows Beagles inside out and who does not breed lots of different types of dogs.

After all, apart from getting married or having a baby, getting a puppy is one of the most important, demanding, expensive and life-enriching decisions you will ever make.

Beagles will love you unconditionally - but there is a price to pay. In return for their devotion - you have to fulfil your part of the bargain.

In the beginning, you have to be prepared to devote much of your day to your new puppy. You have to feed her several times a day and housetrain virtually every hour, you have to give her your attention and start to gently introduce the rules of the house. You also have to be prepared to part with hard cash for regular healthcare and pet insurance.

If you are unable to devote the time and money to a new arrival, if you have a very young family, a stressful life or are out at work all day, then now might not be the right time to consider getting a puppy. Beagles love their families and thrive on being involved.

If left alone too long, behaviour issues often result. This is a natural reaction and is not the dog's fault; she is simply responding to an environment that is failing to meet her needs. Pick a healthy pup and she should live 12 to 15 or 16 years if you're lucky - so this is certainly a long-term commitment. Before taking the plunge, ask yourself some questions:

Do I Have Enough Time for a Puppy?

Even an independent Beagle puppy will feel lonely and possibly even a little afraid after leaving her mother and littermates. Spend time with your new arrival to make her feel safe and sound. Ideally, for the first few days you will be around all the time to help her settle and to start bonding.

If you work, book time off if you can - although this is more difficult for some of our working American readers who get short vacations - but don't just get a puppy and leave her all alone in the house a couple of days later. Leave her a few minutes a day and gradually build up the time so she doesn't over-bond with you and develop separation anxiety.

Housetraining (potty training) starts the moment your pup arrives home. Then, after the first few days and once she's feeling more settled, make time for short sessions of a few minutes of behaviour training. Beagle puppies are very lively, curious, greedy and have an incredible sense of smell, and these traits can lead to mischief if not channelled.

You'll also have to find time to slowly start the socialisation process by taking her out of the home to see new places, strangers, other animals, loud noises, busy roads, etc. - but make sure you CARRY her until the vaccinations have taken effect.

FACT ❯ The importance of socialising Beagles cannot be over-emphasised. Start socialisation as soon as possible, as that critical window up to four months of age is when she is at her most receptive to all things new.

Beagles are scent hounds and hounds use their voices to alert that they are on to a scent. Under-socialised Beagles can bark at the slightest thing and may become too noisy; some may become too protective of their food, toys or humans.

The more positive experiences a Beagle is introduced to, the better. Get into the habit of taking your pup for a short walk every day - five minutes once fully vaccinated, increasing gradually to around 10 minutes at four months. While the garden or yard is fine, new surroundings stimulate interest and help to stop puppies becoming bored.

Gently introducing her to different people will help her to become more relaxed around people. Initially, get people to sit on the floor at her level. Make time right from the beginning to get your pup used to being handled by all the family and dog-friendly visitors, gently brushed, ears checked, and later having her teeth touched and cleaned.

 We recommend you have your pup checked out by a vet within a couple of days of arriving home – many good breeders insist on it - but don't put your puppy on the clinic floor where she can pick up germs from other dogs.

Factor in time to visit the vet's surgery for annual check-ups as well as vaccinations, although most now last several years – check with your vet.

How Long Can I Leave My Puppy?

This is a question we get asked a lot and one that causes much debate among new owners. All dogs are pack animals; their natural state is to be with others. So being alone for long periods is not normal for them - although many have to get used to it.

Another issue is the toilet; Beagle puppies have really tiny bladders. Forget the emotional side of it, how would you like to be left for eight hours without being able to visit the bathroom? So how many hours can you leave a dog alone?

FACT In the UK, canine rescue organisations will not allow anybody to adopt if they are intending to regularly leave the dog alone for more than four or five hours a day.

The Beagle was originally bred to perform a task as a working hound, and leaving a Beagle alone for too long can trigger unwanted behaviour. A bored or lonely Beagle may display signs of unhappiness such as nuisance barking, resource guarding, chewing, getting into things she shouldn't, digging, stubbornness, aggression, disobedience, eliminating or just plain switching off.

Tip In terms of housetraining, a general rule of thumb is that a puppy can last without urinating for one hour or so for every month of age, sometimes longer.

So, provided your puppy has learned the basics, a three-month-old puppy should be able to last for around three hours without needing to go. Of course, until housetraining kicks in, young puppies just pee at will!

Family and Children

Beagles really do make excellent family pets - with one or two provisos, and our breeders have some advice on this. With their tiny bodies and bones, Beagle puppies may not be suitable for families with very young children. Toddlers and young kids are uncoordinated and there can be a risk of injury if not well supervised.

Beagles can and do form extremely strong and loving bonds with children - once both have learned respect for each other.

Tip Children (and adults) should be taught how to correctly handle Beagle puppies. Encourage youngsters to interact with the dog on the floor, rather than constantly picking them up to cuddle.

Here's what breeders have to say about Beagles and families, starting in the UK: Kelly Diamond, Kelcardi Beagles, Fife, Scotland, says: "Most definitely I would place a puppy with a family with young children, but as a breeder I would place a puppy whose personality best suited that type of environment. I think it's important to match families and puppies as best we can."

Sarah Porter, Puddlehill Beagles, Norfolk: "Yes, I place Beagles with families, but only if the parents and new owners are sensible. Incidences only happen if people are lazy and don't keep an eye on both the child or children and dog and become complacent. I still worry about my dogs with my 12-year-old, just because sometime common sense can sometimes be lacking."

Sharon Hardisty, Blunderhall Beagles, Lancashire: "Beagles are excellent with children. I would, however, be cautious about very young children and a young puppy as Beagle puppies can be boisterous."

Debbie Tantrum, Debles Beagles, Shropshire: "All of our puppies are brought up with children. Currently we have two grandchildren, one aged two-and-a-half and the other aged two. Beagles

are a family dog and love the fuss and attention, but I would never dream of putting any dog in front of children if I did not feel safe."

Karen Simkin, Simeldaka Beagles, London: "Beagles are brilliant with children. I place with children, but really interview hard to see how they react to my Beagles first."

Butter wouldn't melt in their mouths! Photo of this beautiful litter courtesy of Karen.

Georgina Armour-Langham, Robentot Beagles, Leicester: "Older children are best with Beagles, but I encourage all new owners to follow Kellie Wynn (The Beagle Lady) on Facebook, to encourage sleep and rest and consistent behaviour."

Darlene Stewart, of Aladar Beagles, Alabama, said: "Beagles and children are usually good for each other. Beagles love activity and usually children can be their pack members. I do place most of mine in homes with older children. If young children under the age of four are in the home I usually suggest an adult Beagle, unless it is a very experienced dog home. My rule is: *"The younger the children, the older the Beagle."*

The excellent booklet **Beagle as Pets**, available free online at www.beaglewelfare.org.uk/wp-content/uploads/2020/04/Beagles-as-Pets.pdf and reproduced in this book with kind permission of the authors, states: "Beagles are tough and love being with a family, but children must be taught to respect all dogs and not treat them like toys.

"Your hound should be provided with a special place of its own (like the folding metal crates described later in this leaflet) where children are not allowed to go or disturb the dog. Bringing a Beagle into your home is a great commitment in time and patience and some people have found that they are unable to cope with a very young family at the same time."

Puppies regard children as playmates - just like a child regards a puppy as a playmate. Both are playful and excitable, so it's important to teach them both the boundaries of play. A Beagle puppy would never intentionally harm a child, or vice versa, but either could cause injury if they get over-excited.

Your children will naturally be delighted about your new arrival, but kids and puppy should not be left unsupervised until each has learned to respect the other - no matter how well they get along in the beginning.

 Teach your children to be gentle with your dog and your dog to be gentle with your children.

Lively behaviour and nipping are not aggression; it is normal play for puppies. Put the time in to teach your pup what is acceptable and what is not – and any nipping should be dealt with straight away. See **training chapters 8 and 9** for more detailed information.

Your dog's early experiences with children should all be positive. If not, a dog may become nervous or mistrustful - and what you want around children is most definitely a relaxed dog that does not feel threatened by a child's presence. Take things steady in the beginning and your Beagle will undoubtedly form a deep, lifelong bond your children will remember throughout their lives.

Single People

Many singles own dogs, but if you live alone, getting a puppy will require a lot of dedication on your part. There is nobody to share the responsibility, so taking on a people-loving dog like the Beagle requires a commitment and a lot of your time if the dog is to have a decent life.

If you are out of the house all day, a Beagle is NOT a good choice. They thrive on being involved and get bored quite easily, which can lead to mischief - typical of dogs originally bred to do a job. Being alone all day is not much of a life for a dog as intelligent and active as the Beagle. However, if you can spend considerable time with the pup, then a Beagle will definitely become your best friend.

Older People

Dogs can be a great tonic for fit, older people. In his mid-80s my father still walked his dog for an hour to 90 minutes every day – even in the rain or snow. He grumbled occasionally, but it was good for him and it was good for the dog - helping to keep them both fit and socialised! They got fresh air, exercise and the chance to communicate with other dogs and their humans.

You're never alone when you've got a dog. Many older people get a canine companion after losing a loved one - a husband, wife or previous much-loved dog. A pet gives them something to care for and love, as well as a constant companion.

Bear in mind that dog ownership is not cheap, so budget for annual pet insurance, veterinary fees, a quality pet food, etc. The RSPCA in the UK has estimated that owning a dog costs an average of around £1,300 ($1,700) a year!

Other Pets

However friendly your puppy is, other pets in your household may not be too happy at a new arrival. Socialised Beagles usually get on well with other animals, but it might not be a good idea to leave your hamster or pet rabbit running loose. The Beagle was bred to hunt and some have strong prey instincts. The pup has first to learn to fit in alongside other pets and if introduced slowly, they will probably become best friends.

Beagle puppies are naturally extremely curious and playful and will sniff and investigate other pets. They may even chase them in the beginning. Depending on how lively your pup is, you may have to separate them initially, or put the pup into a pen or crate for short periods to allow the cat to investigate without being pestered by a hyperactive pup who thinks the cat is a great playmate.

This will also prevent your puppy from being injured. If the two animals are free and the cat lashes out, your pup's eyes could get scratched. A timid Beagle might need protection from a bold cat - or vice versa. A bold cat and a timid Beagle will probably settle down together quickest!

If things seem to be going well with no aggression, then let them loose together after one or two supervised sessions. Take the process slowly; if your cat is stressed or frightened, he may decide to leave. Our feline friends are notorious for abandoning home because the board and lodgings are better down the road...

More than One Dog

Well-socialised Beagles have no problem sharing their home with other dogs. Introduce your puppy to other dogs and animals in a positive, non-frightening manner that will give her confidence. Supervised sessions help everyone to get along and for the other dog or dogs to accept your new pup.

If you can, introduce them for the first time outdoors on neutral ground, rather than in the house or in an area that one dog regards as her own. You don't want the established dog to feel he has to protect his territory, nor the puppy to feel she is in an enclosed space and can't get away.

Photo of George (left) and Martina courtesy of Biao Li and Lori Norman, Lokavi Beagles, Florida.

If you are thinking about getting more than one pup, consider waiting until your first puppy is a few months old or an adult before getting a second. Waiting means you can give your full attention to one puppy; get housetraining, socialisation and the basics of obedience training out of the way before getting your second. Another benefit is that an older well-trained dog will help teach the new puppy some manners.

 Think carefully before getting two puppies from the same litter. Apart from the time and expense involved, you want your new Beagle to learn to focus on YOU, and not her littermate.

Owning two dogs can be twice as nice; they will be great company for each other, but bear in mind that it's also double the training, food and vet's bills.

....

Plan Ahead

Choosing the right breeder is one of the most important decisions you will make. Like humans, your puppy will be a product of her parents and will inherit many of their characteristics. Size, appearance, natural temperament and how healthy your puppy is depends to a large extent on the genes of her parents.

Responsible breeders test their dogs; they check the health records and temperament of the parents and only breed from suitable stock. Sound Beagle puppies are not cheap – health screening, socialisation and first-rate care come at a cost.

The price of puppies of all breeds has shot up, so it's hard to say what a fair price is for a pedigree pup from **fully health-screened** parents. Factors such as colour, markings and region also affect price, and you'll pay more for a Beagle with show prospects than for a pet Beagle. Avoid *"bargains,"* these are not top-quality pups. Instead, spend the time to find a reputable breeder and read **Chapter 11. Beagle Health** to discover what health certificates to look for before buying.

BE PATIENT. Start looking months or even a year before your planned arrival. Good Beagle breeders with health-screened breeding dogs often have a waiting list for their pups, so get your name on a list in good time.

Phone or email your selected breeder or breeders to find out about future litters and potential dates, but don't commit until you've asked lots of questions.

Photo of this new-born litter courtesy of Peter Sievwright, Mattily Beagles.

A healthy Beagle will be your irreplaceable companion for over a decade so why buy one from a pet shop or general ad? Would you buy an old car or a house with potential structural problems just because it looked pretty in a website photo or was cheap? The answer is probably no, because you know you'd have stress and expense at some point in the future.

Visit the breeder personally at least once – this should be an absolute-must in the UK.

NOTE: Many American breeders do not allow the public on to their properties when they have unvaccinated pups. Also, when vast distances are involved, personal visits are not always possible. In these cases speak at length on the phone to the breeder, video call, ask lots of questions and ask to see photos and videos of the pups. Reputable breeders will be happy to answer all your questions - and will have lots for you too.

Beagles should be eight weeks to 12 or 13 weeks old before they leave the breeder. Puppies need this time to physically develop and learn the rules of the pack from their mothers and littermates. In some US states it is illegal to sell a puppy younger than eight weeks.

....

Buyer Beware

Good breeders do not sell their dogs on general purpose websites, Gumtree, Craig's List or Freeads, in car parks or somebody else's house. In 2020, the UK Government passed *Lucy's Law* saying:

"*'Lucy's Law'* means that anyone wanting to get a new puppy or kitten in England must now buy direct from a breeder, or consider adopting from a rescue centre instead. Licensed dog breeders are required to show puppies interacting with their mothers in their place of birth. If a business sells puppies or kittens without a licence, they could receive an unlimited fine or be sent to prison for up to six months. The law is named after Lucy, a Cavalier King Charles Spaniel who was rescued from a puppy farm."

There is no such law in the US. And if you are looking at dogs on Pets4Homes in the UK, follow their guidelines carefully, check the health screening and see the pup with the mother.

There is a difference between *a hobby breeder* and a *backyard or backstreet breeder*. Both may breed just one or two litters a year and keep the puppies in their homes, but that's where the similarity ends. In the UK there are many good *hobby breeders.* They often don't have a website and you will probably find out about them via word of mouth.

Good hobby breeders are usually breed enthusiasts or experts; sometimes they show their pedigree dogs. They carry out health tests and lavish care and love on their dogs. They are not professional dog breeders.

NOTE: While it is often a good sign in the UK, the term *"hobby breeder"* can have negative implications in the USA.

Backyard breeders are often breeding family pets. They have less knowledge about the breed, pay little attention to the health and welfare of their dogs and are doing it primarily for extra cash. They may be very nice people, but avoid buying a dog from them.

FACT All GOOD breeders, professional or hobby, have in-depth knowledge of the Beagle. They take measures to prevent potential health issues being passed on to puppies, and are passionate about the breed. www.beaglehealth.info

Here are four reasons for buying from a good breeder:

1. **HEALTH:** Like all breeds, Beagles have potentially inheritable health issues. Screening breeding stock and NOT breeding from those that fail the health tests is the best way of preventing genetic disorders from being passed on to puppies.

2. **SOCIALISATION:** Scientists and dog experts now realise that the critical socialisation period for dogs is up to the age of four months. An unstimulated puppy is likely to be less well-adjusted and more likely to have fear or behaviour issues as an adult. Good breeders start this process, they don't just leave the puppies in an outbuilding for two or three months. Socialisation is important for Beagles.

3. **TEMPERAMENT:** Good breeders select their breeding stock based not only on sound structure and health, but also on temperament. They will not breed from an aggressive or overly timid dog.

4. **PEACE OF MIND:** Most good breeders agree to take the dog back at any time in her life or rehome her if things don't work out - although you may find it too hard to part with your beloved Beagle by then.

Spotting Bad Breeders

Getting a puppy is such an emotional decision - and one that should have a wonderfully positive impact on you and your family's life for over a decade. Unfortunately, the high price of puppies has resulted in unscrupulous people producing litters for the money.

This section helps you avoid the pitfalls of getting a puppy from a puppy mill, a puppy importer, broker (somebody who makes money from buying and selling puppies) or a backyard breeder. You can't buy a Rolls Royce or a Corvette for a couple of thousand pounds or dollars - you'd immediately suspect that the *"bargain"* on offer wasn't the real deal. No matter how lovely it looked, you'd be right – well, the same applies to Beagles.

Become Breeder Savvy

- Avoid websites where there are no pictures of the owners' home or kennels

- If the website shows lots of photos of cute puppies with little information about the family, breeding dogs, health tests and environment, click the X button

- Don't buy a website puppy with a shopping cart symbol next to her picture

- See the puppies with their mother face-to-face. If this is not possible due to distances, speak at length on the phone with the breeder and ask lots of questions

- You hear: "You can't see the parent dogs because......" ALWAYS ask to see the parents and, as a minimum, see the mother and how she looks and behaves with the pups, *pictured.* If the pups are really hers, she will interact with them

- Good breeders are happy to provide lots of information and at least one reference before you commit

- If the breeder is reluctant to answer your questions, look elsewhere

- Pressure selling: on the phone, the breeder doesn't ask you many questions and then says: "There are only X many puppies left and I have several other buyers interested." Walk away

- You hear "Our Beagle puppies are cheaper because...." Walk away

- At the breeder's, ask to see where the puppy is living. If the breeding dogs are not housed in the family home, they should be in clean kennels, not too hot or cold, with access to grass and time spent with humans

- Ask to see the other puppies from the litter

- The mother is not with the puppies, but brought in to meet you

- The puppies look small for their stated age

- If the breeder says that the dam and sire are Kennel Club or AKC registered, ask to see the registration papers

- Photographs of so-called "champion ancestors" do not guarantee the health of the puppy

 Look beyond the cute, fluffy exterior. The way to look INSIDE the puppy is to see the parents and, most importantly, check what health screening has been carried out. *"Vet checked"* does NOT mean the pup or parents have passed any genetic health tests

- The person you are buying the puppy from did not breed the dog themselves. Deal with the breeder, not an intermediary

- The only place you meet the puppy seller is a car park, somebody else's house or place other than the puppies' home

- The seller tells you that the puppy comes from top, caring breeders from your own or another country. Good breeders don't sell their puppies through brokers

- Ask to see photos of the puppy from birth to present day

- Be wary of "rare colours" or "rare markings"

- Avoid "pocket Beagles"

- Price – if you are offered a very cheap puppy, there is a reason. The price reflects the time, money and expertise invested in the puppy

- If you get a rescue Beagle, make sure it is from a recognised rescue group and not a "puppy flipper" who may be posing as a do-gooder, but is in fact getting dogs (including stolen ones) from unscrupulous sources

- NEVER buy a puppy because you feel sorry for it; you are condemning other dogs to a life of misery

- If you have any doubt, go with your gut instinct and WALK AWAY - even if this means losing your deposit. It will be worth it in the long run

 Bad breeders do not have two horns coming out of their heads! Most will be friendly when you phone or visit - after all, they want to make the sale. It's only later that problems develop.

Puppy Mills and Farms

Unscrupulous breeders are everywhere. That's not to say there aren't some excellent Beagle breeders out there; there certainly are. You just have to do your research.

While new owners might think they have bagged a cheap puppy, it often turns out to be false economy and emotionally disastrous when the puppy develops health problems or behavioural problems due to poor temperament or lack of socialisation. The UK's Kennel Club says as many as one in four puppies bought in the UK may come from puppy farms - and the situation is no better in North America. The KC Press release states: "As the popularity of online pups continues to soar:

- Almost one in five pups bought (unseen) on websites or social media die within six months

- One in three buys online, in pet stores and via newspaper adverts - outlets often used by puppy farmers – this is an increase from one in five in the previous year

- The problem is likely to grow as the younger generation favour mail order pups, and breeders of fashionable breeds flout responsible steps

"We are sleepwalking into a dog welfare and consumer crisis as new research shows that more and more people are buying their pups online or through pet shops, outlets often used by cruel puppy farmers, and are paying the price with their pups requiring long-term veterinary treatment or dying before six months old."

The KC research found that:

- One third of people who bought their puppy online, over social media or in pet shops failed to experience "overall good health"

- Some 12% of puppies bought online or on social media end up with serious health problems that require expensive on-going veterinary treatment from a young age

The Kennel Club said: "Whilst there is nothing wrong with initially finding a puppy online, it is essential to then see the breeder and ensure that they are doing all of the right things. This research clearly shows that too many people are failing to do this, and the consequences can be seen in the shocking number of puppies that are becoming sick or dying."

Marc Abraham, TV vet and founder of Pup Aid, added: "Sadly, if the *"buy it now"* culture persists, then this horrific situation will only get worse. There is nothing wrong with sourcing a puppy online, but people need to be aware of what they should then expect from the breeder.

"For example, you should not buy a car without getting its service history and seeing it at its registered address, so you certainly shouldn't buy a puppy without the correct paperwork and health certificates and without seeing where it was bred."

"However, too many people are opting to buy directly from third parties, such as the internet, pet shops, or from puppy dealers, where you cannot possibly know how or where the puppy was raised. Not only are people buying sickly puppies, but many people are being scammed into paying money for puppies that don't exist, as the research showed that 7% of those who buy online were scammed in this way."

I hear these stories all the time. In fact a friend of mine was scammed out of a £350 ($460) deposit on a puppy just last month.

Beagle Welfare (www.beaglewelfare.org.uk) adds: "Welcoming a new puppy into your home should be a joyous occasion, but if you buy from the wrong source the buying process can sometimes be upsetting, and in some cases end in the puppy's death. This may sound overly dramatic, but at Beagle Welfare we are very aware of the high numbers of puppy farmers, pet shops and commercial breeders who are only interested in making money out of dogs.

"Puppy farmers have no concern for the physical or mental well-being of either their breeding stock or the puppies they produce. They will make no effort to breed for good temperament or with regard to possible hereditary defects.

"Cheap puppies can easily be found on the internet, but unfortunately many of these pups will have been bred in appalling conditions on puppy farms. The puppies themselves may have health problems and only had the very minimum human contact, resulting in them having long-term behavioural problems. The adult breeding stock at these establishments live lives of total misery. Their lives are spent producing puppies for the 'cheap' end of the market. They will be destroyed once their useful production days are over.

"If you buy from a puppy farm, a pet shop, or other retail outlet, you may think that you're getting a bargain, but somewhere down the line a terrible price has been paid."

Visit www.thekennelclub.org.uk/paw for the Kennel Club's tips on buying a puppy.

Advice From The Experts

Our breeders have LOTS of advice about what to look for and what to avoid! Darlene Stewart says: "Most US breeders will not let just anyone visit for the health and safety of the puppies prior to vaccinations. With the use of internet, videos of puppy, littermates, mother and living conditions should be sent to prospective owners.

"As a responsible breeder I also ask for video of the home my puppy may be living in. I ask for vet references and I have no problem with prospective owner asking any questions.

"I go over not only all the health testing and research I have done, but also the problems I have encountered and how I have worked to breed away from them. Often the sire will not be on premise as many breeders look for best mate for the female, and he may be in another city, or even use frozen semen from an older male that is deceased."

Photo of CH Aladars Something Wild (Joker) aged two years courtesy of Darlene.

"The puppies should be raised in the home and the breeder should be as concerned about making sure the puppy will go to a responsible home as you should be making sure you are buying from a responsible breeder. Responsible breeders should always provide a contract and health guarantee, and take back, if needed, any puppy bred by them for the life of that dog."

Georgina Armour-Langham, UK: "A healthy puppy, alongside its litter mates and parent(s) should be bright-eyed, friendly, well-fed, not overweight, with a shiny coat. The environment should be clean with food and water and an area to exercise in. The breeder should be able to answer questions about the dogs, health tests, vet contact, and parent(s) available to see.

"The buyer should also be able to see the puppy's pedigree on the Kennel Club website. A breeder should not ask for money until the puppies have been seen at the age of at least four weeks."

Karen Simkin: "Puppies should be in a clean, warm environment with their dam (mother). They should be alert, moving around and interested in everything. ALWAYS see the pups with their dam."

Sarah Porter: "Since Covid there have been lots and lots of horror stories about unscrupulous breeders and people jumping on the bandwagon to make quick money. Signs of a healthy well-bred pup would be soft fluffy coat, bright eyes, inquisitive, happy, funny, ears that are alert, listening, not too leggy, good head carriage, good tail carriage - just a well-rounded healthy-looking pup. A badly bred pup would be lethargic, not willing to engage, shying away from people and what is going on, dull and sad eyes, tail down."

Sharon Hardisty: "Signs of a bad breeder are: no parents to be seen, no health tests, timid pups, underweight, dull coats, lethargic. Never buy a puppy without seeing it in the home environment with its mum."

Peter Sievwright, Mattily Beagles, Renfrewshire, Scotland: "One of the things I have noticed over the years is how many people are just breeding for money. They know nothing about the Beagle and can't answer any questions on how to look after a Beagle. Other things that differentiate good breeders from bad breeders are how many times the pups have been wormed and if they have been microchipped and had first vaccinations.

"Other warning signs are if the mother is not present with pups at time of viewing or purchase, and the overall condition of the mother, puppies and surroundings. Does it look like that puppy has lived there - pups are very destructive when not supervised? Is the puppy's surrounding destroyed? Does the puppy have a safe place to sleep and play in a clean, sanitary manner? Are the pup's surroundings dirty and smelly? What paperwork do you get with your pup?

"I have been to various other Beagle kennels. They were all completely fine, apart from one where the person's house was chewed and run down in a bad state of repair. When I decided not to buy the pup, the person started throwing the pup from one hand to the other in a juggling motion."

Photo of this hungry litter courtesy of Peter.

Where to Find a Good Breeder

1. The Kennel Club in your country. Look for Assured Breeders in the UK at www.thekennelclub.org.uk/search/find-an-assured-breeder and an AKC Breeder of Merit or a Bred with H.E.A.R.T. breeder in the US: https://marketplace.akc.org/puppies/beagle

2. Breed clubs. In the UK search for *Puppy Enquiries* at The Beagle Club www.thebeagleclub.org or visit The Beagle Association at http://beagleassociation.org.uk/puppies.html The National Beagle Club of America has an excellent resource page listing all member breeders and their email addresses by city at https://www.nationalbeagleclub.org/Breeders

3. Visit dog shows or canine events where Beagles are participating and talk to competitors and breeders.

4. Get a recommendation from somebody who has a Beagle that you like - but make sure the breeder health screens her dogs.

5. Ask your vet for details of local, ethical Beagle breeders.

6. Search the internet - there are hundreds of breeders out there; use the advice in this chapter to find the right one.

7. If you are in the UK, visit the Beagle stand at Discover Dogs during the annual Crufts dog show in early March or Discover Dogs at Excel in London, normally held during November. www.thekennelclub.org.uk/events-and-activities/events/

Questions to Ask a Breeder

Here's a list of the questions you should be asking. The Kennel Club also has a three-minute video entitled *The Dos and Don'ts of Buying a Puppy* at: www.youtube.com/watch?v=1EhTu1TQcEc

1. **Have the parents been health screened?** Ask to see certificates and what guarantees the breeder is offering in terms of genetic illnesses.

2. **What veterinary care have the pups had so far?** Ask to see records of flea treatments, wormings and vaccinations, microchipping.

3. **Are you registered with the Kennel Club (UK), AKC (US) or a member of a Beagle breed club?** Not all good Beagle breeders are members, but this is a good place to start.

4. **How long have you been breeding Beagles?** You are looking for someone who has a track record with the breed.

5. **Can you put me in touch with someone who already has one of your puppies?** ALWAYS contact at least one owner.

6. **How many litters has the mother had?** Females are better waiting until they are 18 months or two years old, and The UK Kennel Club will not register puppies from a dam that has had more than four litters or is over the age of eight. Check the age of the mother.

7. **What happens to the mother once she has finished breeding?** Are they kept as part of the family, rehomed in loving homes, sent to animal shelters or auctioned off? Do you see any old Beagles at the breeder's home?

8. **Do you breed any other types of dog?** Buy from a specialist, preferably one who does not breed lots of other types of dog - unless you know they have a particularly good reputation.

9. **What is so special about this litter?** You are looking for a breeder who has used good breeding stock and his or her knowledge to produce handsome, healthy dogs with good temperaments.

10. **What is the average lifespan of your dogs?** Generally, pups bred from healthy stock tend to live longer.

11. **How socialised and housetrained is the puppy?** Good breeders usually start the socialisation and potty training process before they leave.

12. **How would you describe the temperament of the parents?** Temperament is extremely important; try to interact with both parents, or at least the mother.

13. **What do you feed your adults and puppies?** A reputable breeder will feed a top-quality dog food and advise that you do the same.

14. **Why aren't you asking me any questions?** A good breeder is committed to making a good match between the new owners and their puppies. If the breeder spends more time discussing money than the welfare of the puppy, draw your own conclusions as to what his or her priorities are – they probably don't include improving the breed. Walk away.

Choosing a Healthy Beagle

Once you've selected your breeder and a litter is available, you then have to decide WHICH puppy to pick, unless the breeder has already earmarked one for you after asking lots of questions. Here are some pointers on puppy health:

1. Your chosen Beagle puppy should have **a well-fed appearance.** She should not have a distended abdomen (pot belly) as this can be a sign of worms or other illnesses. The ideal puppy should not be too thin either - you should be able to feel her ribs, but not see them.

2. **The pup's eyes should be bright and clear** with no discharge or tear stain. Steer clear of a puppy that blinks a lot. (Bordetella and Kennel Cough vaccines can sometimes cause runny eyes and nose for up to 10 days – ask when the litter was vaccinated for these).

3. **Her nose should be cool, damp and clean** with no discharge.

4. **The pup's ears should be clean** with no sign of discharge, soreness or redness and no unpleasant smell.

5. **Check the puppy's rear end** to make sure it is clean and there are no signs of diarrhoea.

6. **The pup's coat should look clean,** feel soft and velvety, not matted - and puppies should smell good! The coat should have no signs of ticks or fleas. Red or irritated skin or bald spots could be a sign of infestation or a skin condition. Also, check between the toes of the paws for signs of redness or swelling.

7. **The puppy should be alert,** and curious about you and her surroundings, not timid.

8. **Gums should be clean and pink.**

9. **Choose a puppy that moves freely** without any sign of injury or lameness. It should be a fluid movement, not jerky or stiff, and the pup should have a straight back, not arched.

10. When the puppy is distracted, clap or make a noise behind her - not so loud as to frighten her - to **make sure she is not deaf.**

11. Finally, **ask to see veterinary records** to confirm your puppy has been wormed and had her first vaccinations and a vet check.

If you get the puppy home and things don't work out for whatever reason, good breeders will either take the puppy back or find them a suitable home.

Breeder Debbie Tantrum sums up the love and care that good breeders put into a litter: "We are proud to say that our puppies are brought up with the upmost care. We treat them as our babies; they have plenty of puppy fat, good shiny coat, and are kept clean at all times. We always say to our prospective buyers that they are free to ask whatever they want and always make sure our puppies are safe and handled with care.

"You can tell how a puppy is by their general behaviour: if they come up to you of their own free will then they are comfortable, if they cower away then there's a problem. Look for healthy gums and the general state of the puppy and both mum and, if possible, dad are available to be seen."

Kelly Diamond said: "Look for how the puppies interact with you and the breeder. A healthy well-raised puppy will have bundles of energy, be confident and happy, and eager to get your attention. A litter of puppies that are none of the above is a huge red flag.

"The breeder should be willing and able to answer any questions you may have. I for one don't mind being interrogated! Also the breeder should show interest in you and your suitability for one of their puppies. You should also be able to see the mother of the puppies - the father isn't always available."

Lori Norman added: "Chunky, solid, pups are what you seek, happy, energetic, and full of mischief. Avoid thin, fearful, puppies. They should come bouncing over to see you."

Take your puppy to a vet to have a thorough check-up within 48 hours of purchase. If your vet is not happy with the pup's condition, return her - no matter how painful it may be. Keeping an unhealthy puppy will only lead to further distress and expense.

Puppy Contracts

Most good breeders provide their puppy parents with an official Puppy Contract. This protects both buyer and seller by providing information on the puppy until he or she leaves the breeder. A Puppy Contract will answer such questions as whether the puppy:

- Is covered by breeder's insurance and can be returned if there is a health issue within a certain time period
- Has been micro-chipped (compulsory in the UK) and/or vaccinated and details of worming treatments
- Has been partially or wholly toilet-trained
- Has been socialised and where he or she was kept
- What health conditions the pup and parents have been screened for
- What the puppy is currently being fed and if any food is being supplied
- Was born by Caesarean section
- And details of the dam and sire

It's not easy for caring breeders to part with their puppies after they have lovingly bred and raised them, and so many supply extensive care notes for new owners, which may include details such as:

- The puppy's daily routine
- Feeding schedule
- Vet and vaccination schedule
- General puppy care
- Toilet training
- Socialisation

The Royal Society for the Prevention of Cruelty to Animals (RSPCA) has a downloadable puppy contract, *pictured*, endorsed by vets and animal welfare organisations; you should be looking for something similar from a breeder. Type *"RSPCA Puppy Contract"* into a search engine, or *"AKC Preparing a Puppy Contract"* if you're in the US.

A good course of action would be something like this:

1. Decide to get a Beagle.
2. Do your research and find a good breeder whose dogs are health screened.
3. Decide on a male or female.
4. Register your interest - and WAIT until a puppy becomes available.
5. Pick one with a suitable temperament to fit in with your family.
6. Enjoy 12 or more years with a beautiful, healthy Beagle.

Some people pick a puppy based on how the dog looks. If coat colour or size, for example, is very important to you, make sure the other boxes are ticked as well.

4. Bringing Puppy Home

Getting a new puppy is so exciting; you can't wait to bring him home. Before that happens, you probably dream of all the things you are going to do together; going for walks, snuggling down on the couch, playing games, and maybe even taking part in activities or shows.

Your pup has, of course, no idea of your big plans, and the reality when he arrives can be a big shock! Puppies are wilful little critters with minds of their own and sharp teeth. They leak at both ends, chew anything in sight, constantly demand your attention, nip the kids or anything else to hand, cry and don't pay a blind bit of notice to your commands... There is a lot of work ahead before the two of you develop that unique bond!

Your pup has to learn what you require from him before he can start to meet some of your expectations - and you have to learn what your pup needs from you.

....

Once your Beagle puppy lands in your home, your time won't be your own, but you can get off to a good start by preparing things before the big day. Here's a list of things to think about getting beforehand - your breeder may supply some of these:

Puppy Checklist

- ✓ A dog bed or basket
- ✓ Bedding – a Vetbed or Vetfleece is a good choice
- ✓ A piece of cloth (remove buttons, etc) that has been rubbed on the puppy's mother to put in the bed
- ✓ A puppy gate or pen
- ✓ A crate if you decide to use one
- ✓ A collar or puppy harness with ID tag and a lead (leash)
- ✓ Food and water bowls, preferably stainless steel
- ✓ Puppy food – find out what the breeder is feeding and stick with that to start with
- ✓ Puppy treats, healthy ones, carrot and apple pieces are good, no rawhide
- ✓ Newspapers or pellet litter, and a bell if you decide to use one, for potty training
- ✓ Poop bags
- ✓ Toys and chews suitable for puppies
- ✓ A puppy coat if you live in a cool climate or it's winter
- ✓ Old blanket for cleaning and drying and partially covering the crate

AND PLENTY OF TIME!

Later on, you'll also need grooming brushes, flea and worming products and maybe a car grille or travel crate. Many good breeders provide Puppy Packs to take home; they contain some or all of the following items:

- ✓ Pedigree certificate
- ✓ Puppy contract
- ✓ Information pack with details of vet's visits, vaccinations and wormings, parents' health certificates, diet, breed clubs, etc.
- ✓ Puppy food
- ✓ ID tag/microchip info
- ✓ Blanket that smells of the mother and litter
- ✓ Soft toy that your puppy has grown up with, possibly a chew toy as well
- ✓ A month's free insurance

FACT ❱ By law, all UK puppies have to be microchipped BEFORE they leave the breeder and they must be at least eight weeks old — many Beagle breeders keep their puppies for up to 12 or 13 weeks.

Puppy Proofing Your Home

Some adjustments will be needed to make your home safe and suitable. Beagle puppies are small bundles of curiosity, instinct and energy when they are awake, with little common sense and even less self-control. They have bursts of energy before running out of steam and spending much of the rest of the day sleeping. As one breeder says: "They have two speeds — ON and OFF!"

They also have an incredible sense of smell and love to investigate with their noses and mouths. Fence off or remove all poisonous or low plants with sharp leaves or thorns, such as roses, that could cause eye injuries.

There are literally dozens of plants harmful to a puppy if ingested, including azalea, daffodil bulbs, lily, foxglove, hyacinth, hydrangea, lupin, rhododendron, sweet pea, tulip and yew. The Kennel Club has a list of some of the most common ones, type *"Kennel Club poisonous plants"* into Google or visit: http://bit.ly/1nCv1qJ The ASPCA has an extensive list for the USA at: http://bit.ly/19xkhoG or Google *"ASPCA poisonous plants."*

Make sure any fencing planks are extremely close together and that EVERY LITTLE GAP has been plugged; Beagle puppies can get through almost anything and they have no road sense whatsoever. Don't leave your new puppy unattended in the garden or yard.

FACT ❱ Dognapping is on the increase. Some 2,000 dogs are now being stolen each year in the UK. The figures are much higher for the US, where the AKC reports increasing dog thefts and warns owners against leaving dogs unattended.

Puppies are little chew machines and puppy-proofing your home involves moving anything sharp, breakable or chewable - including your shoes. Lift electrical cords, mobile phones and chargers, remote controls, etc. out of reach and block off any off-limits areas of the house with a child gate or barrier, especially as he may be shadowing you for the first few days.

Create an area where your puppy is allowed to go, perhaps one or two rooms, preferably with a hard floor that is easy to clean. Keep the rest of the house off-limits, at least until the pair of you have mastered potty training.

This area should be near the door to the garden or yard for toileting. Restricting the puppy's space also helps him to settle in. He probably had a den and small space at the breeder's home. Suddenly having the freedom of the whole house can be quite daunting - not to mention messy!

You can buy a purpose-made dog barrier or use a sturdy baby gate, which may be cheaper, to confine a puppy to a room or prevent him from going upstairs.

Choose one with narrow vertical gaps or mesh, and check that your puppy can't get his head stuck between the bars, or put a mesh over the bottom of the gate initially. You can also make your own barrier, but bear in mind that cardboard, fabric and other soft materials will definitely get chewed.

A puppy's bones are soft, and studies have shown that if pups go up and down stairs regularly, or jump on and off furniture before their growth plates are fully formed, they can develop joint problems later in life.

Don't underestimate your puppy! Young Beagles are lively and determined - they can jump and climb, so choose a barrier higher than you think necessary.

The puppy's designated area or room should not be too hot, cold or damp and free from draughts. Little puppies can be sensitive to temperature fluctuations; if you live in a hot climate, your new pup may need air conditioning in the summertime.

 Just as you need a home, so a puppy needs a den; a haven where your pup feels safe. One of the most important things you can do for your young Beagle puppy is to ALLOW HIM LOTS AND LOTS OF SLEEP – as much as 18 or 20 hours a day!

Your puppy doesn't know this and will play until he drops, so make sure you put him in his quiet place regularly - even if he doesn't want to go, he will fall asleep and get the rest he needs. The importance of enough sleep for Beagle pups cannot be overemphasised - trainer Kellie Wynn has more to say on this in **Chapter 9.** Lack of sleep can lead to unwanted behaviour traits developing and make your Beagle harder to train.

The time any young children spend with the puppy should be limited to a few short sessions a day and supervised. You wouldn't wake a baby every hour or so to play, and the same goes for puppies.

You have a couple of options when it comes to sleeping arrangements: you can get a dog bed or basket, or you can use a crate, which can also speed up potty training. **See Chapter 5. Crate and Housetraining** for getting your Beagle used to - and then to enjoy - being in a crate.

It may surprise American readers to learn that common practice in the UK is to contain the puppy in the kitchen or utility room until he's housetrained, and then to allow the dog to roam around the house at will. There are owners who do not allow their dogs upstairs, but many do. Some owners prefer to create a safe penned area for their pup, rather than a crate, while others use both a pen and a crate. You can make your own barriers or buy a manufactured playpen.

Wait a day or two before inviting friends round to see your handsome new puppy. However excited you are, your new arrival needs a few days to get over the stress of leaving mother and siblings and start bonding with you.

While confident, well-socialised puppies may settle in right away, other puppies may feel sad and a little afraid. Make the transition as gentle and unalarming as possible.

After a few sleep-deprived nights followed by days filled with entertaining your little puppy and dealing with chewed shoes, nipping and a few housetraining "accidents," your nerves might be a tiny bit frayed! Try to remain calm and patient... your Beagle puppy is doing his best... it just takes a little time for you both to get on the same wavelength.

FACT > This early period is a very important time for your puppy - how you react and interact with each other during these first few days and weeks will help to shape your relationship and your Beagle's character for the rest of his life.

Beagles are scent hounds and they explore the world with their noses. Once they have found something interesting, they put it in their mouths, so chew treats and toys are a must. Beagles, like other dogs bred to work, tend to be "mouthy," so don't scold a pup for chewing; it's instinct.

Instead, put objects you don't want chewed out of reach and replace them with chew toys. There are some things you can't move out of puppy's way, like kitchen cupboards, doors, sofas, fixtures and fittings, so try not to leave your pup unattended for any length of time where he can chew something that is hard to replace.

Tip Avoid giving old socks, shoes or slippers, or your pup will naturally come to think of your footwear as fair game!

You can give a Beagle puppy *a raw bone* to gnaw on - NEVER cooked bones as these can splinter. Avoid poultry and pork bones, and ribs - especially pork ribs - are too high in fat. Knuckle bones are a good choice and the bone should be too big for the puppy to swallow. Puppies should be supervised and the bone removed after an hour or so. Don't feed a puppy a bone if there are other dogs around, it could lead to food aggression.

FACT > Raw bones contain bacteria, and families with babies or very young children shouldn't feed them indoors. Keep any bones in a fridge or freezer and always wash your hands after handling them.

Alternatives to real bones or plastic chew bones include natural *reindeer antler* chew toys which have the added advantage of calcium, although they are hard and have been known to crack teeth. Natural chews preferred by some breeders include ears, dried rabbit pelt and tripe sticks – all excellent for teething puppies - once you have got over the smell!

Tip Rawhide chews are not recommended as they can get stuck in a dog's throat or stomach, but bully sticks *(pictured)* are a good alternative.

Made from a bull's penis(!) they can be a good distraction from chewing furniture, etc. and help to promote healthy teeth and gums. *Bully sticks* are highly digestible, break down easily in the stomach and are generally considered safe for all dogs. They are made from 100% beef, normally contain no additives or preservatives, come in different sizes and dogs love 'em. NOTE: Puppies should be supervised while eating bully sticks or any other treats.

Dental sticks are good for cleaning your dog's teeth, but many contain preservatives and don't last very long with a determined chewer. One that does last is the **Nylabone Dura Chew Wishbone, pictured,** made of a type of plastic infused with flavours appealing to dogs. Get the right size and throw it away if it starts to splinter with sharp edges.

Another long-lasting treat option is the **Lickimat (pictured),** which you smear with a favourite food. This inexpensive mat will keep your puppy occupied for some time – although they can leave a bit of a mess.

Other choices include **Kong toys,** which are pretty indestructible, and you can put treats (frozen or fresh) or smear peanut butter inside to keep your dog occupied while you are out. All of these are widely available online, if not in your local pet store.

As far as toys go, the **Zogoflex Hurley** and the **Goughnut** are both strong and float, so good for swimmers – and you'll get your money back on both if your Beagle destroys them! For safety, the Goughnut has a green exterior and red interior, so you can tell if your dog has penetrated the surface - as long as the green is showing, you can let your dog "goughnuts."

A **natural hemp** or cotton tug rope is another option, as the cotton rope acts like dental floss and helps with teeth cleaning. It is versatile and can be used for fetch games as well as chewing.

> **FACT** ❯ Puppies' stomachs are sensitive, so be careful what goes in. Even non-poisonous garden plants can cause intestinal blockages and/or vomiting. Like babies, pups can quickly dehydrate, so if your puppy is sick or has watery poop for a day or two, seek medical advice.

Collecting Your Puppy

- ❧ Let the breeder know what time you will arrive and ask her not to feed the pup for a couple of hours beforehand - unless you have a very long journey, in which case the puppy will need to eat something. He will be less likely to be car sick and should be hungry when he lands in his new home. The same applies to an adult dog moving to a new home

- ❧ Ask for an old blanket or toy that has been with the pup's mother – you can leave one on an earlier visit to collect with the pup. Or take one with you and rub the mother with it to collect her scent and put this with the puppy for the first few days. It will help him to settle

- ❧ Get copies of any health certificates relating to the parents and a Contract of Sale or Puppy Contract – see **Chapter 3. Finding Your Puppy** for details. It should also state that you can return the puppy if there are health issues within a certain time frame. The breeder will also give you details of worming and any vaccinations, as well as an information sheet

- ❧ Find out exactly what the breeder is feeding and how much; dog's digestive systems cannot cope with sudden changes in diet - unless the breeder has deliberately been feeding several different foods to her puppies to get them used to different foods. In the beginning, stick to whatever the pup is used to; good breeders send some food home with the puppy

The Journey Home

Bringing a new puppy home in a car can be a traumatic experience. Your puppy will be sad at leaving his mother, brothers and sisters and a familiar environment. Everything will be strange and frightening and he may whimper and whine or even bark on the way home.

If you can, take somebody with you on that first journey – some breeders insist on having someone there to hold and cuddle the pup to make the journey less stressful for the pup. Under no circumstances have the puppy on your lap while driving. It is simply too dangerous - a Beagle puppy is extremely cute, wriggly and far too distracting. Have an old towel between your travel companion and the pup as he may quite possibly pee - the puppy, not the passenger!

If you have to travel any distance, take a crate – a canvas or plastic travel crate with holes in for air flow, or a wire crate he'll use at home. Cover the bottom of the crate with a waterproof material and then put a comfortable blanket on top. You can put newspapers in half of the crate if the pup is partly housetrained.

Don't forget to allow the pup to relieve himself beforehand, and if your journey is more than a couple of hours, take water to give him en route. He may need the toilet, but don't let him outside on to the ground as he is not yet fully vaccinated. As soon as you arrive home, let your puppy into the garden or yard, and when he "performs," praise him for his efforts.

These first few days are critical in getting your puppy to feel safe and confident in his new

surroundings. Spend time with the latest addition to your family, talk to him often in a reassuring manner. Introduce him to his den and toys, slowly allow him to explore and show him around the house – once you have puppy-proofed it.

If you've got other animals, introduce them to each other slowly and in supervised sessions on neutral territory - or outdoors where there is space so neither feels threatened - preferably once the pup has got used to his new surroundings, not as soon as you walk through the door. Gentleness and patience are the keys to these first few days, so don't over-face your pup.

Tip Have a special, gentle puppy voice and use his new name frequently - and in a pleasant, encouraging manner. Never use his name to scold or he will associate it with bad things. The sound of his name should always make him want to pay attention to you as something good is going to happen - praise, food, playtime, and so on.

Settling In

We receive emails from worried new owners. Here are some of their most common concerns:

- 🐾 My puppy won't stop crying or whining
- 🐾 My puppy is shivering
- 🐾 My puppy won't eat
- 🐾 My puppy is very timid
- 🐾 My puppy follows me everywhere, he won't let me out of his sight
- 🐾 My puppy sleeps all the time, is this normal?

These behaviours are quite common at the beginning. They are just a young pup's reaction to leaving his mother and littermates and entering into a strange new world. It is normal for puppies to sleep most of the time, just like babies. It is also normal for some puppies to whine during the first couple of days.

Tip If you constantly pick up a crying pup, he will learn that your attention is the reward for his crying. Wait until your puppy STOPS crying before giving him your attention.

If your puppy is shivering, check that he's warm enough, as he is used to the warmth of his siblings. If he's on the same food as he was at the breeder's and won't eat, then it is probably just nerves. If he leaves his food, take it away and try it later, don't leave it down all of the time or he may get used to turning his nose up at it.

Make your new pup as comfortable as possible, ensuring he has a warm (but not too hot), quiet den away from draughts, where he is not pestered by children or other pets. Handle him gently, while giving him plenty of time to sleep. Avoid placing him under stress by making too many demands. If your puppy whines or cries, it is usually due one of the following reasons:

- He is lonely
- He is hungry
- He is cold
- He needs to relieve himself
- He wants attention from you

If it is none of these, then physically check him over to make sure he hasn't picked up an injury. Try not to fuss too much! If he whimpers, reassure with a quiet word. If he cries and tries to get out of his allotted area, he may need to go to the toilet. Take him outside and praise him if he performs.

FACT ❯ Beagle puppies from breeders who have already started socialisation and training are often more confident and less fazed by new things. They often settle in quicker than those reared with less human contact.

A puppy will think of you as his new mother, and if you haven't decided what to call him yet, "Shadow" might be apt as he will follow you everywhere! But after a few days start to leave your pup for periods of a few minutes, gradually building up the time. A puppy unused to being left alone can grow up to have separation anxiety - see **Chapter 7. Beagle Traits** for more information.

Helping a new pup to settle in is virtually a full-time job. If your routine means you are normally out of the house for a few hours during the day, get your puppy on a Friday or Saturday so he has at least a couple of days to adjust to his new surroundings. A far better idea is to book time off work to help your puppy to settle in, if you can. (Easier to do in the UK than the US). If you don't work, leave your diary free for the first couple of weeks.

Your puppy's arrival at your home coincides with his most important life stage for bonding, so the first few weeks are very important. The most important factors in bonding with your puppy are TIME and PATIENCE, even if he makes a mess in the house or chews something. Spend time with your Beagle pup and you will have the most loyal lifelong friend. This emotional attachment may grow to become one of the most important aspects of your life – and certainly his.

Where Should the Puppy Sleep?

Where do you want your new puppy to sleep? In the beginning, you cannot simply allow a pup to wander freely around the house. Ideally, he will be in a contained area, such as a pen or crate, at night. While it is not acceptable to shut a dog in a cage all day, you can keep your puppy in a crate at night until housetrained. Many adult Beagles prefer to sleep in a crate.

Some breeders recommend putting the puppy in a crate (or similar) next to your bed for the first two or three nights before moving him to the permanent sleeping place. Knowing you are close and being able to smell you may help overcome initial fears. Others recommend starting the puppy off in his permanent sleeping place - ask your own breeder's advice on this one.

It's normal for most puppies to cry for the first night or two. Resist the urge to get up to hold and comfort the pup, who learns that crying equals attention. Invest in a pair of silicone earplugs; they soon settle down.

Young puppies can't go through the night without needing to pee (and sometimes poo); their bodies simply aren't up to it. As you will read, opinion is divided as to whether you should get up in the night to let your pup out to the toilet.

Some breeders recommend putting newspapers or pellets in the pup's crate or confined area that he can use without soiling his bedding. Then set your alarm for an early morning wake-up call and take him out first thing, even before you are dressed - unless you live in a high-rise apartment!

We don't recommend letting new puppies sleep on the bed. They are not housetrained. They need to learn their place in the household and have their own quiet place for resting. It's up to you whether to let yours on the bed or not once housetrained.

Beagles can sleep almost anywhere and anyhow. They don't need your comfy bed, as these photos of Skittles (left) and Maggie bred by Lori Norman, Lokavi Beagles, Florida, show.

If your Beagle is to be allowed upstairs, don't let him race up and down stairs as it's bad for his joints. And be aware that dogs snuffle, snore, fart and - if not in a crate - pad around the bedroom in the middle of the night and come up to the bed to check you are still there - or see if you want to play! None of this is conducive to a good night's sleep.

While it is not good to leave a dog alone all day, it is also not healthy to spend 24 hours a day together, as a dog can become too dependent. Although this is very flattering for you, it actually means that the dog is nervous and less sure of himself when you are not there. The last thing you want on your hands is an anxious Beagle.

 A Beagle puppy used to being on his own every night is less likely to develop attachment issues such as separation anxiety, so consider this when deciding where he should sleep.

Breeders' Advice

We asked breeders where puppy should sleep and whether to get up in the night at the beginning. This is what they said:

Lori Norman: "I always recommend an exercise pen with his water, food, toys, litter box, and bedding. It has everything he needs so you can be free to go about your day. When you are watching TV, the puppy can be loose in the room where you can watch him, but when you can't watch him, he can be in his playpen. If you attach a crate to it with an open door, with bedding, you will find that he will go in the crate to sleep. This gets him used to sleeping in the crate and when he gets older and is freed from his playpen, he will still sleep comfortably in his crate.

"I don't recommend getting up in the night. I use a litter box with cedar shavings, pine pellets, or paper pellets from about four weeks old. They are very used to having their "toilet" in their playpen. At eight to ten weeks old they are dealing with separation from their litter and quite needy. If you go to them every time they cry, thinking they have to go out, you will be up all night.

"First, they don't know to cry when they have to potty, they just potty.... what they do know is they do so in their litter box. Second, they will quickly learn that the cry summons you and they will have company. They will have successfully trained you to come to them!

"I recently sold a puppy to a nice family who wanted to do the best for their puppy. I explained about the litter box and playpen and they got everything set up and ready. Then they went to their veterinarian for a check-up and were told not to do that. Instead, they were instructed to put the puppy in a crate and take him out when he whined during the night, so he will learn to hold it.

"Well, it didn't take long for the family to get sleep deprived. It overwhelmed them! The puppy would whine, he would go take him out, the puppy would play and be happy to see him. This was repeated throughout the night. This puppy was nine weeks old. There is no way possible for the puppy to hold it, or even learn to hold it, that young. They are babies!

"They wanted to return the pup, but I was out of town. I begged them to go back to what the pup knew to do, and what we had discussed until I got home. When I got home four days later, they called and told me they no longer wanted to return the pup. Going back to what the puppy knew allowed him to sleep and the puppy to do what he needed to do, when he needed to do it. The puppy has settled in just fine.

"I will always suggest to new owners that they turn off the lights at night. So many people think they need a night light. They don't. When I have puppies, they spend their time doing all the heathen things that litters do. When the light goes off, they go to sleep and not a sound is heard all night.... until the sun peeks out in the morning. Then the ruckus begins again! Dark means sleep, so if you want a puppy to settle down, turn off the lights. You might leave a low volume radio or playlist, on, to soothe them and to drown out other noises that may wake them up."

Darlene Stewart, Aladar Beagles, Alabama: "Having to get up at night with puppy has to be individualized. I know by the time my puppies go to their new home at 12 weeks, the majority are on a schedule and do sleep from about 10pm to 6am in their crate without accidents. If younger and needs to go out at night, new owners can even have a potty/litter area in part of house or elect to go outside with puppy. I would never just let a puppy out alone."

Peter Sievwright, Mattily Beagles, Renfrewshire, Scotland: "We say to potential puppy owners that if they don't want to deal with the pup's mess in the morning, they do have to get up in the middle of the night to let their pup out to relieve itself. But realistically this is not always possible."

Photo courtesy of Peter.

"Other alternatives are using a puppy toilet tray, which is like a cat litter tray but without the cat litter. Your pup will use it once they get used to it and these can then be cleaned in the morning. We provide these with every puppy, and although not an ideal solution, it does work. You also don't have to worry about the pup shredding alternatives like newspaper or puppy pads, which can be potential choking hazards and worse than cleaning up dog mess.

"We recommend that your pup should be kept in a crate in a dark, quiet place away from drafts and direct sunlight. Crates are like cots for puppies and should be used for your pup's safety. Other alternatives include puppy pens."

Sharon Hardisty, Blunderhall Beagles, Lancashire: "I personally don't recommend getting up in the night, I use paper or puppy pads in the playpen a short distance from the crate.

"Having any puppy is like having a new baby, they are completely dependent on you for everything. A puppy needs a safe place, plenty of sleep, toys and safe chews. A crate is a safe place to sleep and that can be forever or can progress to a normal pet bed when older."

Kelly Diamond, Kelcardi Beagles, Fife, Scotland, says: "There is no right or wrong place; the most common place is often the kitchen. I personally feel a crate is a useful tool when used correctly, and for the first few nights we recommend the puppy sleeps in a crate closer to you, so you are more aware when the puppy wakes and able to take them outside.

"An element of crying at night is normal. If the puppy cries for attention, ignore this, but if he or she really needs out, get up when the puppy cries, take it straight out to do the toilet, but no other interactions (cuddling, playing). The owner needs to use their own initiative. For example, if the puppy has just been out to the toilet, then he is crying for attention and obviously this needs to be ignored.

"This training method teaches the puppy to use this unwanted behaviour in a more positive way, i.e. to alert us to needing to toilet. So, you're toilet training and eliminating unwanted night-time behaviour at once. We do this with all our puppies and advise our new owners to do the same, and always get good results."

Georgina Armour-Langham, Robentot Beagles, Leicester: "I recommend a crate. You may consider a bedside bed for the first few days then move them to a safe, contained area where you want them to sleep permanently."

Sarah Porter, Puddlehill Beagles, Norfolk: "Personally, I think it's a crate and in the room that will be his or hers. There obviously needs to be lots of positivity assigned to that area such as naps, feeding, play etc. so that this is its safe place. I would always cover the crate (but not right to the bottom, air needs to flow) so that it muffles out sounds and is dark to initiate sleep. Occasionally a puppy pen around the crate will help if owners do not want to close the crate entirely.

"I don't recommend getting up in the night at the beginning. If you are concerned about your puppy needing the toilet, make sure there is an area in the sleeping area - whether a crate or within a puppy pen - where this can take place."

Karen Simkin, Simeldaka Beagles, London: "A crate is essential in my opinion. I always put a small crate in the puppy pen so they get used to it."

Photo of this young litter courtesy of Karen.

Debbie Tantrum, Debles Beagles, Shropshire: "All our puppies are crate-trained, and their crate is their safe space when they need naps throughout the day. Puppies need these naps as they are crucial whilst training, and their final resting place at night.

"Sometimes they will be much better with the door open, while others will be OK with the door shut. It's like having a new baby, some may need a light on or some background music. We ask new owners to continue with the routine that we give them as it will benefit the puppies in the future."

Vaccinations and Worming

We recommend having your Beagle checked out by a vet soon after picking him up. In fact, some Puppy Contracts stipulate that the dog should be examined by a vet within a few days. This is to everyone's benefit and, all being well, you are safe in the knowledge that your puppy is healthy, at least at the time of purchase.

NOTE: Keep your pup on your lap away from other dogs in the waiting room as he will not yet be fully protected against canine diseases.

Vaccinations

All puppies need immunisation and currently the most common way of doing this is by vaccination. They usually receive their first dose while still with the breeder at six, or more commonly, eight weeks old. The second vaccination is done two to four weeks later, and a week after this the puppy is considered to have protection – so, at around 13 weeks. A booster is normally given six months to a year later.

An unimmunised puppy is at risk every time he meets other dogs as he has no protection against potentially fatal diseases – and it is unlikely a pet insurer will cover an unvaccinated dog.

It should be stressed that vaccinations are generally safe and side effects are uncommon. If your Beagle is unlucky enough to be one of the *few* that suffers an adverse reaction, here are some signs to look out for; a pup may exhibit one or more of these:

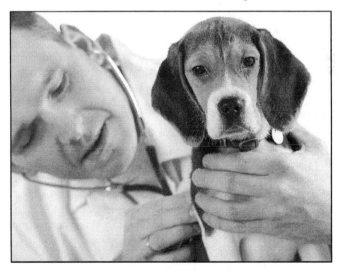

MILD REACTION - Sleepiness, irritability and not wanting to be touched. Sore or a small lump at the place where he was injected. Nasal discharge or sneezing. Puffy face and ears.

SEVERE REACTION - Anaphylactic shock. A sudden and quick reaction, usually before leaving the vet's, which causes breathing difficulties. Vomiting, diarrhoea, staggering and seizures.

A severe reaction is rare. There is a far greater risk of your Beagle either being ill or spreading disease if he does not have the injections.

BSAVA (British Small Animal Veterinary Association) recommends the following core vaccinations in the UK: CDV (Distemper, although this is now rare), CPV (Parvo) and CAV (Adenovirus or Infectious Canine Hepatitis) and Leptospirosis. Many vets also recommend vaccinating against Kennel Cough (Bordetella). Rabies is very rare in the UK; it's more commonly seen in Europe. When deemed necessary, Rabies vaccines start at 12 weeks.

Dr Samantha Goldberg BVSc MRCVS, Kennel Club Health Coordinator for the UK Beagle Clubs, adds: *"I also recommend puppies have at least one course of Fenbendazole (marketed here as Panacur) as it also covers Giardia, which we see commonly in puppies with diarrhoea."*

Core vaccinations in the US can be found on the World Small Animal Veterinary Association website, search online for *"WSAVA dog vaccinations"* or visit: https://wsava.org/wp-content/uploads/2020/01/WSAVA-Vaccination-Guidelines-2015.pdf

"Core vaccines for dogs are those that protect against canine distemper virus (CDV), canine adenovirus (CAV) and the variants of canine parvovirus type 2 (CPV-2)... with the final dose of these being delivered at 16 weeks or older and then followed by a booster at six or 12 months of age."

Puppies in the US also need vaccinating separately against Rabies after 16 weeks, but this varies by state. There are optional vaccinations for Coronavirus (C) and - depending on where you live and if your dog is regularly around woods or forests - Lyme Disease. Bordetella (Kennel Cough) is another non-core vaccine. It can be given intranasally, by tablet or injection, with boosters recommended for dogs deemed to be at high risk, e.g. when boarding or showing.

- 🐾 Boosters for Distemper, Parvo and Canine Hepatitis are recommended no more often than every three years
- 🐾 Boosters for Leptospirosis are every year

The current Lepto vaccine only protects against certain types of the many different variants of the Leptospira bacteria. However, having your dog vaccinated does decrease their risk of becoming sick with Lepto.

NOTE: Beagles have been known to have bad reactions to the Lepto vaccination.

Alabama breeder Darlene Stewart, who is also chairperson of the Health and Genetics Committee, National Beagle Club of America, says: *"There are many reports of adverse reactions to the Lepto vaccination in Beagles. Lepto is now a non-core vaccination in the US and an owner needs to discuss the risk factors for their particular environment.*

"IF it is decided the Beagle needs the vaccination, the suggestion from many breeders is to NOT give Lepto as a combo vaccination - give it as single vaccination. Do not give it until after 16 weeks. Do not give it at the same time as the Rabies vaccination."

Diseases such as Parvo and Kennel Cough are highly contagious and you should not let your new arrival mix with other dogs - unless they are your own and have already been vaccinated - until a week after his last vaccination, otherwise he will not be fully immunised. Parvovirus can also be transmitted by the faeces of many animals, including foxes.

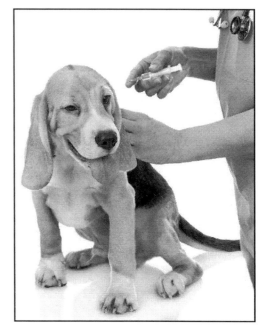

The vaccination schedule for the USA is different, depending on which area you live in and what diseases are present. Full details can be found by typing *"AKC puppy shots"* into Google, which will take you to this page: www.akc.org/content/health/articles/puppy-shots-complete-guide

 Avoid taking your new puppy to places where unvaccinated dogs might have been, like the local park. This does not mean that your puppy should be isolated - far from it.

This is an important time for socialisation. It is OK for the puppy to mix with other dogs that you absolutely know are

up-to-date with their vaccinations and annual boosters. Perhaps invite a friend's dog round to play in your garden or yard to begin the socialisation process.

The vet should give you a record card or send you a reminder when a booster is due, but it's also a good idea to keep a note of the date in your diary. Tests have shown that the Parvovirus vaccination gives most animals at least seven years of immunity, while the Distemper jab provides immunity for five to seven years. In the US, many vets now recommend that you take your dog for a titre test once he has had his initial puppy vaccinations and one-year booster.

The Diseases

Vaccinations protect your puppy and adult dog against some nasty diseases, so it's important to keep your Beagle up to date with protection.

Canine Distemper (CDV) is a contagious disease that affects different parts of the body, including the gastrointestinal and respiratory tracts, spinal cord and brain. Common symptoms include a high fever, eye inflammation, eye and/or nose discharge, struggling for breath, coughing, vomiting, diarrhoea, loss of appetite and lethargy, and hardening of nose and footpads. It can also result in bacterial infections and serious neurological problems.

Canine parvovirus (CPV) is a highly contagious viral disease that commonly causes acute gastrointestinal illness in puppies commonly aged six to 20 weeks old, although older dogs are sometimes also affected. Symptoms include lethargy, depression and loss or lack of appetite, followed by a sudden onset of high fever, vomiting, and diarrhoea.

Infectious Canine Hepatitis (ICH), also called Canine Adenovirus or CAV, is an acute liver infection. The virus is spread in the poop, urine, blood, saliva, and nasal discharge of infected dogs, and other dogs pick it up through their mouth or nose. The virus then infects the liver and kidneys. Symptoms include fever, depression, loss of appetite, coughing and a tender abdomen. Dogs can recover from mild cases, but more serious ones can be fatal.

Leptospirosis (Lepto) is a bacterial disease that causes serious illness by damaging vital organs such as the liver and kidneys. Leptospirosis bacteria can spread in urine and can enter the body through the mouth, nose or wounds. Symptoms vary but include fever, jaundice (yellow gums and eyes), muscle pain and limping, weakness, reduced appetite, drinking more, vomiting, bloody diarrhoea, mouth ulcers and difficulty breathing.

Bordetella (Kennel Cough) - Dogs catch Kennel Cough when they breathe in bacteria or virus particles. The classic symptom of is a persistent, forceful cough that often sounds like a goose honk (and different from a reverse sneeze). Some dogs may show other symptoms, including sneezing, a runny nose or eye discharge, but appetite and energy levels remain the same. It is not usually a serious condition and most dogs recover without treatment.

Rabies is a fatal virus that attacks the brain and spinal cord. All mammals, including dogs and humans, can catch rabies, which is most often contracted through a bite from an infected animal. Rabies usually comes from exposure to wild animals like foxes, bats and raccoons. An infected dog may quickly become restless and irritable, even showing aggression – or excessive affection. Rabid animals may also be uncharacteristically affectionate. One of the most well-known symptoms is foaming at the mouth, a sign that the disease is progressing.

Lyme Disease gets into a dog's or human's bloodstream via a tick bite. Once there, the bacteria travels to different parts of the body and causes problems in organs or specific locations such as joints. These ticks are often founds in woods, tall grasses, thick brush and marshes – all places that Beagles love. Lyme Disease can usually be treated if caught early enough. It can be life-threatening or shortening if left untreated.

Giardia is an infection caused by a microscopic parasite that attaches itself to a dog's intestinal wall causing a sudden onset of foul-smelling diarrhoea. It may lead to weight loss, chronic intermittent diarrhoea, and fatty poop. The disease is not usually life threatening unless the dog's immune system is immature or compromised. Treated dogs usually recover, although very old dogs and those with compromised immune systems have a higher risk for complications.

....

Titres (Titers in the USA)

Some breeders and owners feel strongly that constantly vaccinating our dogs is having a detrimental effect on our pets' health. Many vaccinations are now effective for several years, yet some vets still recommend annual "boosters." One alternative is titres. The thinking behind them is to avoid a dog having to have unnecessary repeat vaccinations for certain diseases as he already has enough antibodies present. Known as a *VacciCheck* in the UK, they are still relatively new here; they are more widespread in the USA.

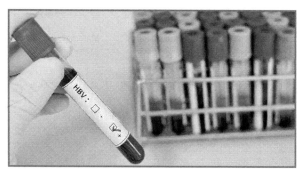

Not everybody agrees with titres. One vet I spoke to said that the titre results were only good for the day on which the test was taken, and it is true that many boarding kennels do NOT accept titres.

To *"titre"* is to take a blood sample from a dog (or cat) to determine whether he has enough antibodies to guarantee immunity against a particular disease, usually Parvovirus, Distemper and Adenovirus (Canine Hepatitis).

If so, then an annual injection is not needed. Titering is NOT recommended for Leptospirosis, Bordetella or Lyme Disease, as these vaccines provide only short-term protection. Many US states also require proof of a Rabies vaccination.

The vet can test the blood at the clinic without sending off the sample, thereby keeping costs down for the owner. A titre for Parvovirus and Distemper currently costs around $100 in the US, sometimes more for Rabies, and a titre test in the UK costs as little as £40.

Titre levels are given as ratios and show how many times blood can be diluted before no antibodies are detected. So, if blood can be diluted 1,000 times and still show antibodies, the ratio would be 1:1000, which is a strong titre, while a titre of 1:2 would be "weak."

A *strong (high) titre* means that your dog has enough antibodies to fight off that specific disease and is immune from infection. A *weak titre* means that you and your vet should discuss revaccination - even then your dog might have some reserve forces known as *"memory cells"* that will provide antibodies when needed. If you are going on holiday and taking your dog to kennels, check whether the kennel accepts titre records; many don't as yet.

Sharon Hardisty, Blunderhall Beagles, Lancashire, UK, said: "I titre test periodically rather than do annual boosters. They have all still had a full level of immunity on the tests - that's from their initial puppy vaccinations as I don't do any further ones."

Another UK breeder said: "When my puppies go to their new homes, I tell all my owners to follow their vet's advice about worming and vaccinating, as the last thing new owners require is to be at odds with their vets. All dogs must have their puppy vaccinations; it is now thought that the minimum duration of immunity is between seven and 15 years.

"However, a few owners do express concern about all the chemicals we are introducing into our puppies' lives and if they do, I explain how I try to give my dogs a chemical-free life, if possible, as adult dogs.

"Instead of giving my adult dogs their core vaccinations for Canine Distemper, Parvovirus and Adenovirus (Hepatitis) every three years, I just take my dogs down to the local vet and ask them to do something called a titre test, also known as a VacciCheck. They take a small amount of blood and send it to a lab and the lab checks for antibodies to the diseases. If they have antibodies to the diseases, there is no reason to give dogs a vaccination.

"However, you should note that there is a separate vaccination for Leptospirosis and Canine Parainfluenza, which is given annually. Leptospirosis is recommended by the BSAVA (British Small Animal Veterinary Association). Leptospirosis is more common in tropical areas of the world and not that common in England. In order to make a decision about whether to give this to your dog annually, you need to talk to your vet and do some research yourself so you can make an informed decision.

"We vaccinate our children up to about the age of 16. However, we don't vaccinate adults every one to three years, as it is deemed that the vaccinations they receive in childhood will cover them for a lifetime. This is what is being steadily proved for dogs and we are so lucky that we can titre test our dogs so we don't have to leave it to chance."

Another breeder added: "I do not vaccinate my dogs beyond the age of four to five years, I now have them titre-tested. Every dog I have titre tested aged five to 10 years has been immune to the diseases vaccinated against when younger. I believe many vets over-vaccinate."

The (UK) Kennel Club now includes titre testing information into its Assured Breeder Pack, but has yet to include it under its general information on vaccines on its website. In the US, type *"titer test Embrace Pet Insurance"* into Google for more info.

Worming

All puppies need worming (technically, deworming). A good breeder will give the puppies their first dose of worming medication at around two weeks old, then probably again at five and eight weeks before they leave the litter – or even more often. Get the details and inform your vet exactly what treatment, if any, your pup has already had.

The main worms affecting puppies are roundworm and tapeworm. In certain areas of the US, the dreaded heartworm can also pose a risk. If you live in an affected area, discuss the right time to start heartworm medication when you visit your vet for puppy vaccinations – it's usually from a few months old.

The pill should be given every month when there is no heavy frost (frost kills mosquitos that carry the disease); giving it all year round gives the best protection. The heartworm pill is by prescription only and deworms the dog monthly for heartworm, round, hook, and whip worm.

Roundworm can be transmitted from a puppy to humans – often children - and can in severe cases cause blindness, or miscarriage in women, so it's important to keep up to date with worming.

Tip Worms in puppies are quite common, usually picked up through their mother's milk. If you have children, get them into the habit of washing their hands after they have been in contact with the puppy – lack of hygiene is the reason why children are susceptible.

Most vets recommend worming a puppy once a month until he is six months old, and then around every two to three months. If your Beagle is regularly out and about running through woods and fields, it is important to stick to a regular worming schedule, as he is more likely to pick up worms than one that spends more time indoors.

Fleas can pass on tapeworms to dogs, but a puppy would not normally be treated unless it is known for certain he has fleas - and then only with caution. You need to know the weight of your puppy and then speak to your vet about the safest treatment to get rid of the parasites.

NOTE: Buy age-appropriate worming treatments.

Breeders worm their puppies. However, there are ways to reduce worming treatments for adult dogs.

Following anecdotal reports of some dogs experiencing side effects with chemical wormers, more owners are looking to use natural wormers on their dogs. If you go down this route, check exactly which worms your chosen herbal preparation deals with – it may not be all of them.

A method of reducing worming medication by testing your dog's stools is becoming more popular. You send a small sample of your dog's poo(p) off in an envelope every two to three months. If the result is positive, your dog needs worming, but if negative, no treatment is necessary.

In the UK this is done by veterinary labs like Wormcount www.wormcount.com and similar options are available in the USA – there is even a *"fecal worm test"* available at just over $20 from Amazon.com.

5. Crate and Housetraining

Crates are becoming more popular year on year. Used correctly, they speed up housetraining (potty training), give you and your puppy short breaks from each other and keep him safe at night or when you are out. Many adult Beagles grow to love their crates. Breeders, trainers, behaviourists, and people who show, compete or train dogs all use them.

Using A Crate

A crate should always be used in a humane manner. If you decide to use one, spend time getting your puppy or adult dog used to it, so he comes to regard the crate as his own safe haven and not a punishment cell or prison.

Crates may not be suitable for every dog – or owner. Dogs are social animals; they thrive on interaction. Being caged for long periods is a miserable existence for any dog, but particularly a hunting breed like the Beagle.

We prefer a wire crate that allows air to pass through, although some breeders like the plastic ones. A crate should never be used as a means of confinement while you are out of the house for six, eight or more hours every day.

 Dogs can suffer from joint problems if confined in a small space for too long.

1. Always remove your dog's collar before leaving him inside when you are not there. Sadly, dogs have been known to die after panicking when their collars or tags got caught.

2. If the door is closed, your dog must have access to water while inside during the day. Non-spill water bowls are available from pet shops and online, as are bowls to attach to the bars.

Crates are ideal for giving you or the puppy some down time. You cannot watch a puppy 24/7 and a crate is a safe place for him while you get on with doing other things. Beagle puppies need LOTS OF SLEEP - see **Chapter 9. Specialist Training** for more information – but they don't know this, so a crate (or puppy pen) is an excellent place for resting without distractions. Your puppy first has to get used to the crate so he looks forward to going in there - some breeders may have already started the process.

NOTE: An eight-week-old puppy should not be in a crate for longer than two hours at a time.

Not every owner wishes to use a crate, but used correctly they:

- 🐾 Are a useful housetraining tool
- 🐾 Create a canine den
- 🐾 Give you a break
- 🐾 Limit access to the rest of the house until potty trained

- 🐾 Are a safe place for the dog to nap or sleep at night
- 🐾 Provide a safe way to transport your dog in a car

Another very good reason to crate-train is that if your dog has to visit the vet or be confined for an illness, he will not have the added stress of getting used to a crate. Confining a Beagle NOT used to a crate is very stressful for both dog and owner.

Which Crate and Where?

The crate should be large enough to allow your dog to stretch out flat on his side without being cramped, and he should be able to turn around easily and sit up without hitting his head on the top.

A 30" (76cm) crate is a good size for most adult Beagles

If the crate is too big for your pup, it can slow down housetraining. Some owners use a crate divider *(pictured)* or block off a part of the crate while the pup is growing. A smaller area also helps him to feel more secure.

 Partially covering the crate with an old blanket creates a den for your new puppy at night. Only cover on three sides - leave the front uncovered - you can cover half or part of the crate to make it cosier for the pup.

Place the crate in the kitchen or another room where there are people during the day, preferably one with a hard, easy-to-clean floor. Puppies are curious pack animals and like to see and smell what is going on. If you have children, strike the balance between putting the crate in a place where the pup won't feel isolated, yet allowing him some peace and quiet from the kids.

Avoid putting the crate in a closed utility room or garage away from everybody, or he will feel lonely and sad. If you are using a room off the kitchen, allow the pup free run of the room and use a pet gate or baby gate with narrowly-spaced bars so his head can't get stuck but he can still see what's going on. You can also buy or create a puppy playpen to use as well as (or instead of) a crate.

The chosen location should be draught-free, not too hot and not in bright sunshine.

Some breeders recommend putting the crate right next to the bed for the first night or two – even raised up next to the bed - to help the puppy settle in quicker. A few owners have even been known to sleep downstairs on the sofa or an air mattress next to the crate for the first one or two nights! After that, you might put the crate in a place where the dog can hear or smell you during the night, e.g. the landing, or leave it in the same place downstairs all the time. Put the following items inside the crate:

- 🐾 Bedding – Vet Bed *(pictured)* or other bedding your puppy won't chew in a few days
- 🐾 A blanket or similar item that has been rubbed with the mother's scent
- 🐾 A non-spill water bowl
- 🐾 A healthy chew to stop him gnawing the crate and bedding
- 🐾 A toy to keep him occupied

At night, remove the water and chew. Add an extra blanket if you think he might get cold overnight; he has been used to the warmth of his littermates and mother. Puppies are little chew machines so, at this stage, don't spend a lot of money on a fluffy floor covering for the crate, as it is likely to get destroyed.

The widely available and washable "Vet Bed" is a good choice for bedding. Made from double-strength polyester, they retain extra heat, allow air to flow through and are widely used in vets' clinics to make dogs feel warm and secure. They also have drainage properties, so your pup will stay dry if he has an accident.

Vet Beds are also a good option for older dogs, as the added heat is soothing for aging muscles and joints. You can buy "Vet Bedding" by the roll, which keeps costs down.

One breeder added: "Don't use beds with stuffing at this age, as once they learn to de-stuff a bed, it may become a lifelong habit and possibly graduate into de-stuffing furniture or pillows later!"

 Consider putting a Snuggle Puppy in the crate with the new puppy. The Snuggle Puppy *(pictured)* is a safe soft toy with a heartbeat. (Remove it if your dog chews it and exposes the internal mechanism).

Whining

If your puppy is whining or whimpering in the crate, make sure:

A. He doesn't need the toilet.

B. He is warm.

C. He is physically unharmed.

Then the reason he is whimpering is because he doesn't want to be alone. He has come from the warmth and security of his mother and litter, and the Brave New World can be a very daunting place for a few-weeks-old puppy all alone in a new home. He is not crying because he is in a cage. He would cry if he had the freedom of the room - he is crying because he is separated. Beagles are pack animals and being alone is not a natural state for them.

However, with patience and the right training, he will get used to being alone and being in the crate. Some owners make the crate their dog's only bed, so he feels comfortable and safe in there, and many adult Beagles love their crates.

Here are some other tips to help your puppy settle in his crate:

❖ Leave a ticking clock next to the crate

❖ Leave a radio on softly nearby

❖ Lightly spray DAP on a cloth or small towel and place in the crate

FACT ❯ DAP, or Dog Appeasing Pheromone, is a synthetic form of the pheromone that nursing Beagles (and other breeds) give off after giving birth and then again after weaning to reassure their puppies that everything is fine.

DAP has been found to help reduce fear in young puppies, as well as separation anxiety, phobias and aggression caused by anxiety in adult dogs. According to one French study: "DAP has no toxicities or side effects and is particularly beneficial for sick and geriatric dogs." Google *"Canadian Veterinary Journal Dog Appeasing Pheromone"* for more details of the study.

NOTE: There is also an ADAPTIL collar with slow-release DAP, which is designed to reduce fear in anxious adult dogs. It gets good reports from many, not all, owners.

Travel Crates

Special travel crates are useful for the car, or for taking your dog to the vet's or a show or competition. Choose one with holes or mesh in the side to allow free movement of air, rather than a solid one in which a dog can soon overheat. You can also use your regular crate in the car.

These puppies bred by Debbie Tantrum, Debles Beagles, Shropshire, are already used to a crate at 10 weeks old. They're pictured in the car heading to the vet's for their second set of vaccinations.

Put the crate on the shady side of the interior and make sure it can't move around and put the seatbelt around it. If it's very sunny and the top of the crate is wire mesh, cover part of it so your dog has some shade and put the windows up and the air conditioning on.

 Don't leave your Beagle unattended in a vehicle. They can overheat, be targeted by thieves or get into mischief.

We recommend using a crate fastened with a seatbelt, rather than a metal grille in the back of the car. And allowing your dog to roam freely inside the car is simply too dangerous as he is likely to get thrown around and injured.

Avoid letting your Beagle ride with his head out of the window - even if his Easy Rider look does make you smile! Wind pressure can cause ear infections or bits of dust, insects, etc. to fly into unprotected eyes. Your dog will fly forward if you suddenly hit the brakes.

....

Getting your Puppy Used to a Crate

Once you've got your crate, you'll need to learn how to use it properly so that it becomes a safe, comfortable den for your dog. Many breeders will have already started the process but, if not, here's a tried-and-tested method of getting your dog firstly to accept a crate, and then to actually want to spend time in there. These are the first steps:

1. Drop a few puppy treats around and then inside the crate.

2. Put your puppy's favourite toy in there.

3. Keep the door open.

4. Feed your puppy's meals inside the crate. Again, keep the door open.

 Place a chew or treat INSIDE the crate and close the door while your puppy is OUTSIDE the crate. He will be desperate to get in there! Open the door, let him in and praise him for going in. Fasten a long-lasting chew inside the crate and leave the door open. Let your puppy wander inside to spend some time eating the chew.

5. After a while, close the crate door and feed him some treats through the mesh. At first just do it for a few seconds at a time, then gradually increase the time. If you do it too fast, he may become distressed.

6. **Slowly build up the amount of time he's in the crate.** For the first few days, stay in the room, then gradually leave first one minute, then three, then 10, 30 and so on.

Next Steps

7. Put your dog in his crate at regular intervals during the day - maximum two hours.

8. **If your pup is not yet housetrained, make sure he has relieved himself BEFORE you put him in the crate.** Putting him in when he needs to eliminate will slow down training.

9. **Don't crate only when you are leaving the house.** Put him in the crate while you are home as well. Use it as a *"sleep zone"* or *"safe zone."* By using the crate both when you are home and while you are gone, your dog becomes comfortable there and not worried that you won't come back, or that you are leaving him alone. This helps to prevent separation anxiety.

10. **If you are leaving your dog unattended, give him a chew and remove his collar, tags and anything else that could become caught in an opening or between the bars.**

Beagle puppies need tons of sleep, as ably demonstrated by 11-week-old Benji, bred by Lori Norman, Lokavi Beagles, Florida.

11. **Make it very clear to any children that the crate is NOT a den for them,** but a *"special room"* for the dog.

12. **Although the crate is your dog's haven and safe place, it must not be off-limits to humans.** You should be able to reach inside at any time.

13. **Try and wait until your dog is calm before putting him in the crate.** If he is behaving badly and you grab him and shove him in the crate straight away, he will associate the crate with punishment. Try not to use the crate if you can't calm him down, instead either leave the room or put the dog in another room until he calms down.

14. **The crate should ALWAYS be associated with a positive experience in your dog's mind.**

15. **Don't let your dog out of the crate when he is barking or whining, or he'll think that this is the key to opening the door.** Wait until he has stopped whining for at least 10 or 20 seconds before letting him out.

 Reminder:

- ❧ During the day the crate door should not be closed until your pup is happy with being inside

- ❧ At night-time it is OK to close the door

- ❧ Consider keeping the pup right next to you for the first one or two nights

- ❧ If you don't want to use a crate, use a pet gate, section off an area inside one room, or use a puppy pen to confine your pup at night

Housetraining

A Beagle is a hound, and all hounds have an independent streak running through them. Some, particularly males, can be a bit reluctant to pee and poop in the right place.

Although very smart, Beagles can also be independent-minded so the right approach is essential. Lots of repetition with bribes (praise, treats and toys) are key, but scolding and making a fuss about accidents are counter-productive.

The good news is that a puppy's instinct is not to soil his own den. From about the age of three weeks, a pup will leave his sleeping area to go to the toilet. The bad news is that when you bring your little pup home, he doesn't realise that your whole home is not his den – and off-limits for making a mess!

He may think that a corner of the crate, the kitchen, behind the sofa or anywhere else in the house is an acceptable place for him to relieve himself. The aim of housetraining (potty training) is to teach him exactly WHERE this space starts and finishes.

It could take a couple of weeks - or many months if neither of you is vigilant.

FACT ❯ The speed and success of housetraining depends to some degree on the individual dog and how much effort the breeder has already put in. However, the single most important factor in success is undoubtedly the owner.

Like all dogs, Beagles are creatures of routine - not only do they like the same things happening at the same times every day, but establishing a regular routine with your dog also helps to speed up housetraining.

Dogs are tactile creatures, so they pick a place to eliminate which feels good under their paws. Many dogs like to go on grass - but this will do nothing to improve your lawn, so think carefully about what area to encourage your Beagle to use as a toilet. Consider a small patch of gravel, or a dog litter tray if you live in an apartment.

Clear your schedule and make housetraining your No.1 priority - it will be worth it. I get complaints from some American readers for advising: "Book a week or two off work to housetrain your dog." I know Americans get much shorter vacation time than almost anybody else, but honestly, if you can take time off to monitor housetraining at the beginning, it will undoubtedly speed up the results.

If you've rescued a Beagle, he may have picked up some unwanted habits before arriving at your home. In such cases, extra time, patience and vigilance are essential to gently teach your dog the new ways.

A general rule of thumb is that puppies can last for one hour per month of age without urinating, sometimes a bit longer. So:

- 🐾 An eight-week pup can last for two hours
- 🐾 A 12-week-old pup can last for three hours
- 🐾 A 16-week pup can last for four hours
- 🐾 A six-month-old can last for six hours

NOTE: This only applies when the puppy is calm and relaxed.

 **FACT** If a puppy is active or excited, he will urinate more often, and if he is excited to see you, he may urinate at will.

As you have read in the previous chapter, some breeders recommend setting your alarm clock to get up in the night to let the pup out to relieve himself for the first week or two. Ask your own breeder's advice on this one.

Housetraining Tips

Follow these tips to speed up housetraining:

1. Constant supervision is essential for the first week or two if you are to housetrain your puppy quickly. If nobody is there, he will learn to pee or poop inside the house.

2. Take your pup outside at the following times:

   a) As soon as he wakes – every time
   b) Shortly after each feed
   c) After a drink
   d) When he gets excited
   e) After exercise or play
   f) Last thing at night
   g) Initially every hour or two - whether or not he looks like he wants to go

You may think that the above list is an exaggeration, but it isn't! Housetraining a pup is almost a full-time job in the beginning. If you are serious about toilet training your puppy quickly, then clear your diary for a week or two and keep your eyes firmly glued on your pup...learn to spot that expression or circling motion just before he makes a mess on your floor.

1. Take your pup to **the same place** every time, you may need to use a lead (leash) in the beginning - or tempt him there with a treat. Some say it is better to only pick him up and dump him there in an emergency, as it is better if he learns to take himself to the chosen toilet spot.

   Dogs naturally develop a preference for going in the same place or on the same surface. Take or lead him to the same patch every time so he learns this is his toilet area.

   Photo courtesy of Peter Sievwright, Mattily Beagles, Renfrewshire.

2. **No pressure – be patient. Beagles do not perform well under pressure.** You must allow your distracted little darling time to wander around and have a good sniff before performing his duties – but do not leave him, stay around a short distance away. Unfortunately, puppies are not known for their powers of concentration, so it may take a while for him to select the perfect bathroom spot!

3. **Housetraining a Beagle should ALWAYS be reward-based, never negative or aggressive.** Give praise and/or a treat IMMEDIATELY after he has performed his duties in the chosen spot. Persistence, praise and rewards are best for quick results.

4. **Share the responsibility.** It doesn't have to be the same person who takes the dog outside all the time. In fact, it's easier if there are a couple of you, as this is a very time-demanding business. Just make sure you stick to the same principles, command and patch of ground.

5. **Stick to the same routine.** Sticking to the same times for meals, exercise, playtime, sleeping and toilet breaks will help settle him into his new home and housetrain him quicker.

6. **Use the same word** or command when telling your puppy to go to the toilet – or while he is in the act. He will gradually associate this phrase or word with toileting.

7. **Use your voice ONLY if you catch him in the act indoors.** A short sharp sound is best - ACK! EH! It doesn't matter, as long as it is loud enough to make him stop. Then either pick him up or run enthusiastically towards your door, calling him to the chosen place and wait until he has finished what he started indoors. Only use the ACK! sound if you actually catch him MID-ACT.

8. **No punishment, no scolding, no smacking or rubbing his nose in it.** Beagles hate it. He will become either more stubborn or afraid to do the business in your presence, so may start going secretly behind the couch or under the bed.

   Accidents will happen. He is a baby with a tiny bladder and bowels and little self-control. Housetraining a Beagle takes time - remain calm, ignore him (unless you catch him in the act) and clean up the mess.

   FACT ❯ Beagles are scent hounds. If there's an "accident" indoors, use a special spray from your vet or a hot washing powder solution to completely eliminate the smell, which will discourage him from going there again.

9. **Look for the signs.** These may be:
   a. Whining
   b. Sniffing the floor in a determined manner
   c. Circling and looking for a place to go
   d. Walking uncomfortably - particularly at the rear end!

   Take him outside straight away, and try not to pick him up all the time. He has to learn to walk to the door himself when he needs to go outside.

10. **Use a crate at night-time** with the door closed.

Troubleshooting

Don't let one or two little accidents derail your potty training - accidents WILL happen! Here is a list of some possible scenarios and action to take:

   ❖ **Puppy peed when your back was turned -** Don't let him out of his crate or living space unless you are prepared to watch his every move

- 🐾 **Puppy peed or pooped in the crate** - Make sure the crate isn't too big; it should be just enough for him to stand up and turn around, or divided. Also, make sure he is not left in the crate for too long

- 🐾 **Puppy pooped without warning** - Observe what he does immediately beforehand. That way, you'll be able to scoop him up and take him outside next time before an accident happens

- 🐾 **Puppy pees on the same indoor spot daily** - Make sure you get rid of the smell completely and don't give your puppy too much indoor freedom too soon. Some breeders use *"tethering"* where the puppy is fastened to them on a lead indoors. That way they can watch the puppy like a hawk and monitor his behaviour. They only do this for a short time - a week or so – but it can speed up housetraining no end

- 🐾 **Puppy not responding well -** Increase the value of your treats for housetraining and nothing else. Give a tiny piece of meat, chicken etc. ONLY when your Beagle eliminates outdoors in the chosen spot.

Even after all your hard work, some dogs continue to eliminate indoors, often males, even though they understand housetraining perfectly well. This is called "marking" and they do it to leave a scent and establish your home as their territory. This can take time to cure - although neutering generally reduces the urge to mark indoors.

Other reasons for peeing indoors when housetrained include a urinary tract infection, or an older dog losing continence or forgetting housetraining,

Apartment Living

If you live in an apartment, housetraining can be a little trickier, as you don't have easy access to the outdoors. One method is to indoor housetrain your puppy.

Most dogs can be indoor housetrained fairly easily, especially if you start early. Stick to the same principles already outlined, the only difference is that you will be placing your Beagle on puppy pads or newspaper instead of taking him outdoors.

Start by blocking off a section of the apartment for your pup. Use a baby gate or make your own barrier, but make sure you choose a chew-proof material! You will be able to keep a better eye on him than if he has free run of the whole place, and it will be easier to monitor his "accidents."

Select a corner away from his eating and sleeping area that will become his permanent bathroom area – a carpeted area is to be avoided if at all possible.

At first, cover a larger area than is actually needed - about 3x3 or 4x4 feet - with puppy pads or newspapers and gradually reduce the area as training progresses. Take your puppy there as indicated in the **Housetraining Tips** section.

Praise him enthusiastically when he eliminates on the puppy pad or newspaper. If you catch him doing his business out of the toilet area, pick him up and take him back there. Correct with a firm voice - never a hand. With positive reinforcement and close monitoring, he will learn to walk to the toilet area on his own.

Owners attempting indoor housetraining should be aware that it does generally take longer than outdoor training. Some dogs will resist. Also, once a dog learns to go indoors, it can be difficult to train them to go outdoors on their walks. If you don't monitor your puppy carefully enough in the beginning, indoor housetraining will be difficult. The first week or two is crucial to your puppy learning what is expected of him.

NOTE: While some breeders use puppy pads in homes with gardens or yards, others believe they can actually they can slow down potty training by encouraging a pup to soil inside the house. Because dogs are tactile, and puppy pads are soft and comfy - dogs like going on them! When you remove the pads, the puppy may be tempted to find a similar surface - like a carpet or rug. Ask your breeder's advice then make your own decision.

....

Bell Training

Bell Training is a method that works well with some dogs. There are different types of bells, the simplest are inexpensive and widely available, consisting of a series of adjustable bells that hang on a nylon strap from the door handle.

Another option is a small metal bell attached to a metal hanger that fixes low down on the wall next to the door with two screws. As with all puppy training, do bell training in short bursts of five to 10 minutes or your easily-distracted little student will switch off!

1. Show your dog the bell, either on the floor, before it is fixed anywhere or by holding it up. Point to it and give the command *"Touch," "Ring,"* or whatever word you decide.

2. Every time he touches it with his nose, reward with praise.

3. When he rings the bell with his nose, give him a treat. You can rub on something tasty, like peanut butter, to make it more interesting.

4. Take the bell away between practice sessions.

5. Once he rings the bell every time you show it to him, move on to the next step.

6. Take the bell to the door you use for housetraining. Place a treat just outside the door while he is watching. Then close the door, point to the bell and give the command.

7. When he rings the bell, open the door and let him get the treat outside.

8. When he rings the bell as soon as you place a treat outside, fix the bell to the door or wall.

9. The next time you think he needs to relieve himself, walk to the door, point to the bell and give the command. Give him a treat or praise if he rings it, let him out immediately and reward him again with enthusiastic praise when he performs his duty.

(Tip) **In between training sessions, ring the bell yourself EVERY time you open the door to let him outside.**

Some dogs can get carried away by their own success and ring the bell any time they want your attention, fancy a wander outdoors or see a squirrel!

Make sure that you ring the bell every time your puppy goes out through the door to relieve himself, but DON'T ring the bell if he is going out to play. And if he starts playing or dawdling around the garden or yard, bring him in!

Breeders on Crates and Housetraining

Lori Norman, Beagle breeder for over 50 years: "Housetraining depends on the consistency of the trainer/owner. If someone pays close attention and doesn't let the pup create bad habits, then it will go quickly. A puppy left to make their own rules will do what is easy for them.

"I always like to use a litter box with cedar shavings, pine pellets, or paper pellets and keep it in their play pen. That way they have a "bail out," or something to use when you aren't around to take them out. Still take them outside and condition them to that, but don't just accept that they should potty wherever they want. They need to potty, so give them a solution, this allows you to sleep through the night. When they outgrow the play pen, they outgrow the need for the litter box. Puppies trained using pee pads sometimes view throw rugs as alternatives, so look at things from their perspective.

"Make sure they have good access to water. Puppies between about three to five months are very susceptible to UTI's (urinary tract infections), especially little girl pups. It has to do with how they are built...the vulva is carried high and indented when they are young. The result is that some don't drain well when they urinate, and it will collect bacteria. As they mature, the problem mitigates itself.

Pictured (top) is 15" faded tri-colour CC, bred by Emily Cloudman, and (bottom) 13" bi-colour Karen, bred by Lori and Jessica Brigante.

"Sometimes the problem with housetraining is physical, so be extra vigilant. Again, consistency is the key. You have a schedule and they need to understand that schedule. They aren't born knowing it – it is up to you to teach them it.

"Take them outside using the same door, the same phrase, like: *"Let's go outside!"*, and same relative times. Reward them for good results. You will notice, through time, that Beagles do wear imaginary wristwatches and will soon let you know what time it is...dinnertime, bedtime, and outside time.

"This a joke that breeders share and it makes me smile: Tell the owners to get a newspaper and roll it up. Set it on the coffee table, and when your puppy potties on the floor, pick up the newspaper and hit YOURSELF on the head while repeating, "I wasn't watching my puppy. I wasn't watching my puppy!"

"I definitely think crates are your friend. Dogs are instinctively cave-dwelling animals. They want somewhere safe to rest. I always start with a crate, either attached to the play pen or inside the pen, so the puppy discovers it to be a great place to sleep. I leave the door open so they can go in or out. They will naturally turn to sleeping in the crate, so when the pup gets a bit older and you are ready to have him sleep in the crate with the door closed, it won't be a shock. Dogs who are used to crates view it as their bedroom. Sometimes we joke that they wish we'd give them curtains so they can shut us out!"

Darlene Stewart, Aladar Beagles, Alabama, has bred and shown Beagles for over 40 years and is Chairperson of the National Beagle Club of America's Health and Genetics Committee: "Crate training is VITAL in my opinion. I usually use the plastic Vari Kennel type *(pictured)*.

"Every vet will tell you having a dog that knows to settle in crate and relax makes any stay at the vet's much less stressful. There are many circumstances where having a crate-trained Beagle will be so advantageous: storms, evacuations, travel - motel stays, visits to other family homes, safety if in a car wreck. Travel with a dog in a crate is safer than traveling with one in the back seat in harness.

"A responsible breeder will have started training puppy to a crate. Also housetraining should have been started, even when in the whelping box, with pad training and litter training. The breeder should tell you how the puppy is sleeping thru the night. I usually recommend letting a puppy sleep in a crate in the bedroom at first for security, but I suggest another crate in a room where the family spends most of their time.

"Always feed in the crate with the door closed, and always use the crate as positive place the puppy can seek out. When cooking, put puppy in the crate where they can see you. When eating, put the puppy in the crate away from the table. If watching TV and puppy is tired, put him in the crate with a toy. A crate should be a positive thing.

"A crate is not for all-day confinement. Puppy day care, a doggie door to secure smaller area, and a dog walker can all be used to break up crate time for those owners that work long hours."

Photo: CH Aladar Longlake's Just Mischievous, Bubba, aged six, 15", enjoying the snow.

Peter Sievwright's notes to new owners outline the schedule when the puppy leaves Peter: "The routine your puppy has been used to for the last three weeks is: Breakfast, then outside to play and relieve itself for 30 minutes to an hour, back to bed for a snooze. Then at 10.30am out again for 30 minutes to an hour, then back to bed again.

"Up at about 12.30pm for lunch, then out to play and relieve itself for about an hour, and back to bed for a third time. Then up at 3pm for more play and relieving for 30 minutes to an hour, back to bed for the fourth time, then up at 5.30 for dinner, play and toilet until 7pm. At 7-9 pm your pup goes back to their pen and to bed for the final time.

"To make your puppy sleep through the night, all lights are turned out in the living room as well as shutting the room door and this encourages him or her to sleep quietly through the night. This doesn't mean you have to go to bed! You can still be sitting in the room quietly watching TV, although we do recommend that you finish this at 9pm and then vacate the room.

"If you find that your puppy wakes up after this time, say 9pm-12 midnight, its best to avoid talking or playing with your pup as this will teach him or her to get up at this time regularly for a play. The key to a pup is the routine. The routine I've set is what works for me, this is not to say this is your routine and you can change it to suit your lifestyle."

He added: "We do use a crate; we look at it as a cot for puppies. We believe this is the safest way to house your puppies when you are not able to be with them for whatever reason, plus your dog feels safe in its own safe place.

"We have never had to crate train our pups as our routine is at three weeks the whelping box is removed and the pups and mum sleep in a crate together. So by the time the pups leave for their new homes, they have been living and sleeping in a crate inside our puppy pen for five weeks, so the pups regard the crate as a safe space."

Karen Simkin, Simeldaka Beagles, London, agrees: "A crate is essential in my opinion. I always put a small crate in the puppy pen so they are used to it. I advise new owners to start as you mean to go on; put the pup in its bed or crate from Day 1. You may have a few disturbed nights, but must be consistent.

"Pups differ so much; housetraining can be from a couple of weeks going into months! I put newspaper in the puppy pen for them to toilet on. When they come into the kitchen or hall, I place a sheet of paper near the door to allow them to toilet. I also place paper outside in an enclosed area (before going into big garden) for them to use. I think as the pups have just paper in the pen with their siblings it becomes a natural progression.

"Take them outside often using the command you've chosen and give lots of praise. Patience is essential, I never scold a pup. You don't scold a toddler for wetting his pants so why a pup?"

Debbie Tantrum, Debles Beagles, Shropshire, had a Beagle as a child and has bred them for 15 years. She crate trains all her puppies: "By the time our puppies leave they are sleeping through the night. We don't advise waking them as this sets the puppy back a stage or two. We ask that they take them for a wee before bedtime and then let them out as early as possible in the morning. Unless puppy is in distress, leave them to sleep."

Pictured is Debles Miss Honey aged four weeks.

"Housetraining depends on the puppy and also the time of year. We advise new owners to let puppy have a good sniff around when they arrive home, then show them to their bed, which would be their crate or basket. They put the scent blanket we provide in there. Then shake some food in the dog bowl and get the puppy to follow you outside to the toilet the way in which you'd like puppy to go. We ask owners to do this constantly for the first couple of days.

"As soon as puppy wakes up, has food or a drink, go straight outside. We don't advise the use of puppy pads as pups tend to chew and rip them up, and newspaper is putting a scent down, so it leads the puppy to do it wherever paper is. We ask that they do not shout at the puppy, but reward with play and love. Most puppies are toilet-trained by six months of age."

Kelly Diamond, Kelcardi Beagles, Fife, Scotland, is a "relative newcomer," but still has a decade of experience behind her: "A Beagle puppy can be housetrained in respect to knowing to go to the toilet outside very quickly - within a week. However, a puppy has a very small bladder so if not taken outside at regular intervals or left for too long, they will still have accidents.

"The best bit of advice I can give is to take them out after they do ANYTHING: after they eat/drink/wake up/play - take them outside immediately. The more work you put in early, the better. It does speed the process up."

6. Feeding a Beagle

Providing the right nutritional fuel helps keep your dog's biological machine in excellent working order. And while it is important for all breeds to have a healthy diet, it is especially important for Beagles, because:

1. Many are obsessed with food — and won't stop eating even when full.

2. They are prone to obesity if their calorie intake is not monitored.

3. Good nutrition can have a beneficial effect on health.

4. The right food can help reduce or eliminate food sensitivities and skin issues.

The topic of feeding can be a minefield; owners are bombarded with advertisements and numerous choices. There is not one food that gives every single Beagle the strongest bones, the most energy, the best coat, the easiest digestion, the least gas and the longest life.

You could feed a high-quality food to a group of Beagles and find that most of them thrive on it, some do not so well, while a few might put weight on, get an upset stomach or itchy skin. The question is: *"Which food is best for MY Beagle?"*

We don't recommend one brand of dog food over another, but we do have lots of tips to help you decide, and several Beagle breeders share their thoughts on nutrition.

Life Stages

Beagle puppies should stay with the litter until at least eight to 12 weeks old, to give the mother enough time to teach her offspring important rules about life. Initially, pups get all their nutrients from their mother's milk and then are gradually weaned (put on to a different food by the breeder) from three or four weeks of age.

Unless the puppy has had an extremely varied diet at the breeder's, continue feeding the same puppy food and at the same times as the breeder when you bring your puppy home. It is always a good idea to find out what the breeder feeds, as she knows what her bloodlines do well on. If you decide to switch foods, do so gradually, as dogs' digestive systems cannot handle sudden changes of diet. (By the way, if you stick to the identical brand, you can change flavours in one go). These ratios are recommended by Doctors Foster & Smith Inc:

*   Days 1-3 add 25% of the new food

*   Days 4-6 add 50%

*   Days 7-9 add 75%

*   Day 10 feed 100% of the new food

Feed your puppy three or four times a day up to the age of 12-16 weeks. If at any time your puppy starts being sick, has loose stools or is constipated, slow the rate at which you are switching the food. Puppies soon dehydrate, so seek veterinary advice if vomiting or diarrhoea continues for more than a day. Some breeders purposely feed their pups lots of different foods over the first few weeks of life to reduce the risk of them developing sensitive stomachs or becoming fussy eaters.

 If you live far away from the breeder, fill a large container with water from the breeder's house and mix it with your own water back home. Different types of water, e.g. moving from a soft to a hard water area or vice versa, can upset a sensitive pup's stomach.

During the first six months, puppies grow quickly and it is important that they grow at **a controlled rate.** Giving your puppy more or less food will not affect his adult size, it will only affect his weight and rate of growth.

 Beagle puppies should look well-covered, not fat. Overfeeding leads to excess weight, which makes them vulnerable to lots of health issues in later life.

Pictured at the perfect weight is River (Kelcardi Chasing Rainbows), aged six weeks, bred by Kelly Diamond.

There are three **Life Stages** to consider when feeding: **Puppy, Adult, Senior,** also called **Veteran.**

Some manufacturers also produce a Junior feed for adolescent dogs. If you decide on a commercially-prepared food, choose one approved either for **Puppies** or for **All Life Stages.** An **Adult** feed won't have enough protein, and the balance of calcium and other nutrients will not be right for a pup. Puppy food is very high in calories and nutritional supplements.

Look at switching to an Adult food when your pup is around 10 to 14 months old and consider reducing feeds from three to two a day at this time.

 Because Beagles are medium-sized dogs with relatively fast metabolisms, we recommend feeding your adult twice a day, rather than once.

NOTE: Feeding elderly dogs is covered in **Chapter 16. Caring for Older Beagles.**

Reading Dog Food Labels

A NASA scientist would have a hard job understanding some manufacturers' labels, so it's no easy task for us lowly dog owners. Here are some things to look out for on the manufacturers' labels:

* The ingredients are listed by weight and the top one should always be the main content, such as chicken or lamb. Don't pick one where grain is the first ingredient; it is a poor-quality feed. If your Beagle has a food allergy or intolerance to wheat, check whether a food is gluten free; all wheat contains gluten

* Chicken meal (dehydrated chicken) has more protein than fresh chicken, which is 80% water. The same goes for beef, fish and lamb. So, if any of these "meals" are No. 1 on the ingredient list, the food should contain enough protein

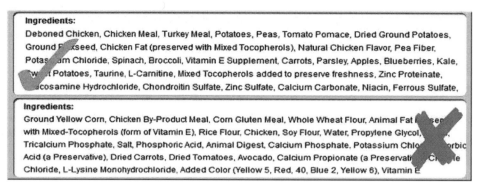

Ingredients:
Deboned Chicken, Chicken Meal, Turkey Meal, Potatoes, Peas, Tomato Pomace, Dried Ground Potatoes, Ground Flaxseed, Chicken Fat (preserved with Mixed Tocopherols), Natural Chicken Flavor, Pea Fiber, Potassium Chloride, Spinach, Broccoli, Vitamin E Supplement, Carrots, Parsley, Apples, Blueberries, Kale, Sweet Potatoes, Taurine, L-Carnitine, Mixed Tocopherols added to preserve freshness, Zinc Proteinate, Glucosamine Hydrochloride, Chondroitin Sulfate, Zinc Sulfate, Calcium Carbonate, Niacin, Ferrous Sulfate,

Ingredients:
Ground Yellow Corn, Chicken By-Product Meal, Corn Gluten Meal, Whole Wheat Flour, Animal Fat (preserved with Mixed-Tocopherols (form of Vitamin E), Rice Flour, Chicken, Soy Flour, Water, Propylene Glycol, Tricalcium Phosphate, Salt, Phosphoric Acid, Animal Digest, Calcium Phosphate, Potassium Chloride, Ascorbic Acid (a Preservative), Dried Carrots, Dried Tomatoes, Avocado, Calcium Propionate (a Preservative), Choline Chloride, L-Lysine Monohydrochloride, Added Color (Yellow 5, Red, 40, Blue 2, Yellow 6), Vitamin E

- Anything labelled **"human-grade"** is higher quality than normal dog food ingredients. E.g. Human-grade chicken includes the breast, thighs and other parts of the chicken suitable for human consumption. Human-grade chicken complies with United States Department of Agriculture (USDA) welfare standards

- A certain amount of flavouring can make a food more appetising for your dog. **Choose a food with a specific flavouring,** like *"beef flavouring"* rather than a general *"meat flavouring,"* where the origins are not so clear

- **Find a food suitable for the Beagle breed and your dog's age and activity level.** Talk to your breeder or vet, or visit an online Beagle forum to ask other owners' advice

- **Natural is best.** Food labelled *'natural'* means that the ingredients have not been chemically altered, according to the FDA in the USA. However, there are no such guidelines governing foods labelled **"holistic"** – so check ingredients and how they have been prepared

- In the USA, dog food that meets American Feed Control Officials' (AAFCO) minimum nutrition requirements has a label that states: **"[food name] is formulated to meet the nutritional levels established by the AAFCO Dog Food Nutrient Profiles for [life stage(s)]"**

Tip
If you live in the USA, we recommend looking for a food "as fed" to real pets in an AAFCO-defined feeding trial. The AAFCO label is the gold standard, and brands that do costly feeding trials indicate so on the package.

Dog food labelled *'supplemental'* isn't complete and balanced. Unless you have a specific, vet-approved need for it, it's not something you want to feed your dog long term. The *Guaranteed Analysis* listed on a sack or tin legally guarantees:

- Minimum percentages of crude protein and crude fat, and

- Maximum percentages of crude fibre and moisture

While it is a start, don't rely on it too much. One pet food manufacturer made a mock product with a guaranteed analysis of 10% protein, 6.5% fat, 2.4% fibre, and 68% moisture (similar to what's on some canned pet food labels) – the ingredients were old leather boots, used motor oil, crushed coal and water!

- **Protein** – found in meat and poultry, protein should be the first ingredient and is very important. It helps build muscle, repair tissue and contributes to healthy hair and skin. According to AAFCO, a growing puppy requires a diet with minimum 22% **protein,** while an adult requires 18% minimum

- **Fats** – these are a concentrated form of energy that give your dog more than twice the amount of energy that carbohydrates and proteins do. Common fats include chicken or pork fat,

GUARANTEED ANALYSIS	
Crude protein (min.)	28.00 %
Crude fat (min.)	12.00 %
Crude fiber (max.)	4.50 %
Moisture (max.)	11.00 %
Docosahexaenoic acid (DHA) (min.)	0.05 %
Calcium (min.)	1.20 %
Phosphorus (min.)	1.00 %
Omega-6 fatty acids* (min.)	2.20 %
Omega-3 fatty acids* (min.)	0.30 %
Glucosamine* (min.)	500 mg/kg
Chondroitin sulfate* (min.)	500 mg/kg

* Not recognized as an essential nutrient by the AAFCO Dog Food Nutrient Profiles.

cottonseed oil, vegetable oil, soybean oil, fish oil, safflower oil, and many more. They are highly digestible and are the first nutrients to be used by the body as energy. AAFCO recommends minimum 8% fat for puppies and 5% for adults

- ❧ **Fibre** – found in vegetables and grains. It aids digestion and helps prevent anal glands from becoming impacted. The average dry dog food has 2.5%-4.5% crude fibre, but reduced-calorie feeds may be as high as 9%-10%

- ❧ **Carbohydrates** typically make up anywhere from 30%-70% of a dry dog food. They come mainly from plants and grains, and provide energy in the form of sugars

- ❧ **Vitamins and Minerals** – have a similar effect on dogs as humans. Glucosamine and chondroitin are good for joints

- ❧ **Omegas 3 and 6** – fatty acids that help keep Beagles' skin and coat healthy. Also good for inflammation control, arthritic pain, heart and kidneys

Well-formulated dog foods have the right balance of protein, fat, carbohydrates, vitamins, minerals and fatty acids. If you're still not sure what to choose for your Beagle, check out these websites: www.dogfoodadvisor.com/best-dog-foods/german-Beagles run by Mike Sagman in the USA and www.allaboutdogfood.co.uk run by UK canine nutritionist David Jackson.

How Much Food?

Maintaining a healthy body weight is all about balancing calories taken in with calories burned. If a dog is exercised two or three times a day or taking part in a physical competition, he will need more calories than a relatively inactive or older Beagle.

- ❧ Breed
- ❧ Gender
- ❧ Age
- ❧ Natural energy levels
- ❧ Metabolism
- ❧ Amount of daily exercise
- ❧ Health
- ❧ Environment
- ❧ Number of dogs in the house or kennel
- ❧ Quality of the food
- ❧ Whether your Beagle is competing, hunting or simply a pet

Beagles are generally active dogs, but energy levels vary from one dog to the next. Dogs that have been spayed may be more likely to put on weight. Certain health conditions, e.g. underactive thyroid, diabetes, arthritis or heart disease, can lead to dogs putting on weight. And just like us, a dog kept in a very cold environment will need more calories to keep warm than a dog in a warm climate, as he burns extra calories in keeping warm.

 A Beagle kept on his own is more likely to be overweight than one kept with other dogs, as he receives all of the food-based attention.

Manufacturers of cheap foods may recommend feeding more than necessary, as a major ingredient is cereal, which is not doing much except bulking up the weight of the food – and possibly triggering allergies. The daily recommended amount listed on dog food sacks or tins can be too high – after all, the more your dog eats, the more they sell!

 Tip There is an excellent leaflet that clearly explains each component of a dog's diet and how much to feed your dog based on weight and activity level. It can be found by searching for *"Your Dog's Nutritional Needs National Academies"* online.

Feeding Options

We are what we eat. The right food is a very important part of a healthy lifestyle for dogs as well as humans. Here are the main options explained:

Dry dog food – or kibble, is a popular and relatively inexpensive way of providing a balanced diet. Millions of dogs thrive on kibble. It comes in a variety of flavours and with differing ingredients to suit the different stages of a dog's life. Cheap kibble is often false economy.

Canned food – dogs love the taste and it generally comes in a variety of flavours. Some owners feed kibble mixed with some canned food. These days there are hundreds of options, some are high quality made from natural, organic ingredients with herbs and other beneficial ingredients.

Read the label closely, the origins of cheap canned food are often somewhat dubious. Some dogs can suffer from stomach upsets with too much soft food. Avoid fillers and preservatives and brands with lots of grain or recalls.

Semi-Moist – this food typically has a water content of around 60%-65%, compared to 10% in dry food, making it easier to digest. It also has more sugar and salt, so is not suitable for some dogs. Semi-moist treats are shaped like pork chops, bacon *(pictured)*, salamis, burgers, etc. They are the least nutritional of all dog foods, full of sugars, artificial flavourings and colourings, so avoid giving them regularly.

Home-Cooked - some owners want the ability to be in complete control of their dog's diet and to know exactly what their dog is eating. Feeding a home-cooked diet can be time-consuming and expensive. The difficult thing (as with the raw diet) is sticking to it once you have started out with the best of intentions, but your dog will love it and he won't be eating preservatives or fillers. Some high-end dog food companies now provide boxes of freshly-prepared meals with natural ingredients.

Dehydrated - this dried food *(pictured)* is becoming increasingly popular. It looks similar to kibble, but is only minimally processed. It offers many of the benefits of raw feeding, including lots of nutrients, but with none of the mess or bacteria.

Gentle heating slowly cooks proteins and helps start the digestive process, making it easier on the digestive tract of older Beagles, or those with sensitive stomachs. Owners just add water and let it stand for a minute or two to reconstitute the meal.

Freeze-Dried – this is usually raw, fresh food that has been freeze-dried by frozen food manufacturers. It's a more convenient, hygienic and less messy option than raw, and handy if you're going on a trip. It contains healthy enzymes but no preservatives, is highly palatable and keeps for six months to a year.

It says *"freeze-dried"* on the packet, but the process bumps up the cost. A good option for owners who can afford it.

The Raw Diet

Opinions are divided on a raw diet. There is anecdotal evidence that some dogs thrive on it, particularly those with food intolerances or allergies, although scientific proof is lagging behind. Claims made by fans of the raw diet include:

- Reduced symptoms of - or less likelihood of - allergies, and less scratching
- Better skin and coats
- Easier weight management
- Improved digestion
- Less doggie odour and flatulence
- Higher energy levels
- Reduced risk of bloat
- Helps fussy eaters
- Fresher breath and improved dental health
- Drier and less smelly stools, more like pellets
- Overall improvement in general health and less disease
- Most dogs love a raw diet

If your Beagle is not doing well on a dry dog food or has skin issues, you might consider a raw diet. Some commercial dog foods contain artificial preservatives, grains and excessive protein and fillers – causing a reaction in some dogs. Dry, canned and other styles of processed food were mainly created as a means of convenience – for humans, not dogs!

Some nutritionists believe there are inherent beneficial enzymes, vitamins, minerals and other qualities in meats, fruits, vegetables and grains in their natural, uncooked state. However, critics of a raw diet say that the risks of nutritional imbalance, intestinal problems and food-borne illnesses caused by handling and feeding raw meat outweigh any benefits.

It is true that owners must pay strict attention to hygiene when preparing a raw diet and it may not be a suitable option if you have small children. The dog may also be more likely to ingest bacteria or parasites such as Salmonella, E. Coli and Ecchinococcus - although freeze-dried meals reduce the risk. If you do switch your dog over to raw feeding, do so over a period of at least a week.

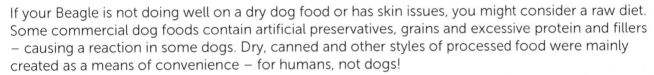 **FACT** ❯ Raw is not for every dog; it can cause loose stools, upset stomach and even vomiting in some, and there are other dogs who simply don't like the taste.

There are two main types of raw diet, one involves feeding raw, meaty bones and the other is known as the BARF diet *(Biologically Appropriate Raw Food or Bones And Raw Food),* created by Dr Ian Billinghurst.

Raw Meaty Bones

- Raw meaty bones or carcasses form the bulk of the diet. **Cooked bones should NOT be fed, as they can splinter**
- Table scraps both cooked and raw, such as vegetables
- Australian veterinarian Dr Tom Lonsdale is a leading proponent of the raw meaty bones diet. He believes the following foods are suitable:

- Chicken and turkey carcasses, after the meat has been removed for human consumption
- Poultry by-products, e.g. heads, feet, necks and wings
- Whole fish and fish heads
- Sheep, calf, goat, and deer carcasses sawn into big pieces of meat and bone
- Pigs' trotters and heads, sheep heads, brisket, tail and rib bones
- A certain amount of offal can be included in the diet, e.g. liver, lungs, trachea, hearts, tripe
- Table scraps and some fruit and vegetable peelings, but should not make up more than one-third of the diet

Low-fat game animals, fish and poultry are the best source of food. If you feed meat from farm animals (cattle, sheep and pigs), avoid excessive fat and bones too large to be eaten. It depends on price and what's available locally - start with your local butcher or farm shop.

FACT > Dogs are more likely to break their teeth eating large knuckle bones and bones sawn lengthwise than when eating meat and bone together.

You'll also need to think about WHERE and WHEN you are going to feed. A dog takes some time to eat a raw bone and will push it around the floor, so the kitchen may not be the most hygienic place. Outside is one option, but what do you do when it's raining? If you live in a hot climate, evening feeding may be best to avoid flies. Establishing the right quantity is based on your dog's activity levels, appetite and body condition. A very general guide of raw meaty bones for the average dog is:

15%-20% of body weight per week, or 2%-3% a day.

Dr Lonsdale says: "Wherever possible, feed the meat and bone ration in one large piece requiring much ripping, tearing and gnawing. This makes for contented pets with clean teeth." More information is available from www.rawmeatybones.com

NOTES: Pregnant or lactating females and growing puppies need more food. This diet may not be suitable for old dogs used to a processed diet or those with dental issues, or in households with children due to the risk of bacterial infection from raw meat.

Monitor your dog while he eats, especially in the beginning. Don't feed bones with sharp points, and remove any bone before it becomes small enough to swallow. Raw meaty bones should be kept separate from human food and any surface the uncooked meat or bones have touched should be thoroughly cleaned afterwards

Tip Puppies can and do eat diets of raw meaty bones, but consult your breeder or vet before embarking on raw with a young dog.

The BARF diet - A variation of the raw meaty bones diet is the BARF created by Dr Ian Billinghurst, who owns the registered trademark "Barf Diet." A typical BARF diet is made up of 60%-75% of raw meaty bones - with about 50% meat, such as chicken neck, back and wings - and 25%-40% of fruit and vegetables, offal, meat, eggs or dairy foods. There is lots of information on the BARF diet online.

Beagle Feeding Tips

1. If you choose a manufactured food, pick one where meat or poultry (or meat or poultry meal) is the first item listed. Many Beagles do not do well on cheap cereals or sugar, so choose a high quality one.

2. If a Beagle has sensitive skin, "hot spots" or allergies, a cheap food bulked up with grain will only make this worse. A dry food described as *"hypoallergenic"* on the sack means *"less likely to cause allergies."*

3. Consider feeding a probiotic, such as a spoonful of natural, live yoghurt, to each meal to help maintain healthy gut bacteria.

4. Feed your adults twice a day, rather than once. Smaller feeds are easier to digest, and reduce the risk of Bloat as well as gas.

5. Establish a feeding regime and stick to it. Dogs like routine. Stick to the same times, morning and tea-time. Feeding too late won't give your dog's body time to process the food before bed. Feeding at the same times also helps your dog establish a toilet regime.

6. Take away uneaten food between meals. Most Beagles love their food, but any dog can become fussy if food is constantly available. Remove the bowl after 15-20 minutes – even if there is some left. A healthy, hungry dog will look forward to the next meal and should soon stop leaving food. If he's off his food for a couple of days or more, it could be a sign of illness.

7. Feeding time is a great training opportunity - particularly for the commands **SIT** and **STAY** and the release.

8. Use stainless steel or ceramic bowls. Plastic bowls don't last as long and can trigger an allergic reaction around the muzzle in some sensitive dogs.

9. Use apple or carrot slices, or other healthy alternatives, as training treats for puppies.

10. If you feed dried animal product treats, check the country of origin. Some use toxic chemicals that can damage kidneys. Dried jerky-type treats can be very good for teeth, but read the labels carefully.

11. Don't feed too many tidbits or treats between meals as they throw a balanced diet out of the window and cause obesity. Feed leftovers in the bowl as part of a meal, rather than from the table, as this encourages attention-seeking behaviour, begging and drooling.

12. Don't feed cooked bones, as these can splinter and cause choking or intestinal problems. And avoid rawhide, as a dog can gulp it without chewing, causing an internal blockage.

13. These are poisonous to dogs: grapes, raisins, chocolate, onions, Macadamia nuts, any fruits with seeds or stones, tomatoes, avocados, rhubarb, tea, coffee and alcohol.

14. Obesity leads to all sorts of health issues, such as joint problems, diabetes, high blood pressure and organ disease. Your Beagle's tummy should be higher than his rib cage - if his belly is level or hangs down below it, reduce his food.

15. Check your dog's faeces (aka stools, poo or poop)! If the diet is suitable, the food should be easily digested and produce dark brown, firm stools. If your dog is producing light or sloppy poo or lots of gas, his diet may well need changing. Consult your vet or breeder for advice.

16. And finally, always make sure that your dog has access to clean, fresh water. Change the water and clean the bowl every day or so – it gets slimy!

 If your dog is not responding well to a particular family member, get him or her to give the feeds - the way to a Beagle's heart is often through his stomach!

Food Allergies

Dog food allergies are a reaction to food that involves the body's immune system and affect about one in 10 dogs. They are the third most common canine allergy after atopy (inhaled or contact allergies) and flea bite allergies.

Food allergies affect males and females in equal measure as well as neutered and intact pets. They can start when your dog is five months or 12 years old - although the vast majority start when the dog is between two and six years old. It is not uncommon for dogs with food allergies to also have other types of allergies. Here are some common symptoms of food causing problems:

- 🐾 Itchy skin (this is the most common). Your dog may lick or chew his paws or legs and rub his face with his paws or on the furniture, carpet, etc.

- 🐾 Excessive scratching

- 🐾 Hair loss

- 🐾 Hot patches of skin – *"hot spots"*

- 🐾 Redness and inflammation on the chin and face

- 🐾 Increased bowel movements (maybe twice as often as usual)

- 🐾 Recurring ear or skin infections that clear up with antibiotics but recur when the antibiotics run out

The problem with food allergies is that the symptoms are similar to symptoms of other issues, such as environmental or flea bite allergies, intestinal problems, mange and yeast or bacterial infections. There's also a difference between dog food *allergies* and dog food *intolerance*:

ALLERGIES = SKIN PROBLEMS AND/OR ITCHING

INTOLERANCE = DIARRHOEA AND/OR VOMITING

Dog food intolerance can be compared to people who get an upset stomach from eating spicy curries. Symptoms can be cured by changing to a milder diet. With dogs, certain ingredients are more likely to cause a reaction than others. Unfortunately, these are also the most common ingredients in dog foods! In order of the most common triggers in dogs in general, they are:

Beef - Dairy Products – Chicken – Wheat – Eggs – Corn - Soya (Soy in the US)

Dr Samantha Goldberg, veterinarian and breeder of Molesend Beagles, County Durham, has some excellent information for owners: "Many meats are triggers for Beagles - chicken is a common one that is flagged. However, cooked meats may trigger differently than raw, due to protein denaturing at cooking. Not all diets are equal!

"Always aim for the highest quality diet you can afford with a high meat content. Also look at the process of production - some can appear good in theory, but if they have been processed within an inch of their life they won't have many nutrients left.

"Grains per se are not all "bad," but finely-milled grains tend to produce glucose spikes when digested; rolled or whole grains are digested more slowly. Look at the composition of the fat content.

"The balance of Omega 3 and 6 oils can be very important for a Beagle's health. Omega 6 can be good for the skin and Omega 3 for joints, but too much or an imbalance is not good. I feed my adult beagles on a mixture of Blunderhall's Grain Free, mostly the fish-based diet, and raw from DAF. They get raw chicken wings and raw beef shanks to keep their teeth clean.

"My puppies are reared on a mix of Royal Canin and Blunderhall Puppy kibble mixed with Betsy's raw diets. Their dam gets the same as the puppies. We don't get bad poops very often and they grow nicely. I aim for a good body covering to allow growth, but not pot-bellied," *as shown here with this healthy Molesend puppy.*

 A dog is allergic or sensitive to an <u>ingredient</u>, not to a particular brand, so it's important to read the label. If your Beagle reacts to beef, for example, he'll react to any food containing beef, regardless of how expensive it is or how well it has been prepared.

AVOID corn, corn meal, corn gluten meal, artificial preservatives (BHA, BHT, Propyl Gallate, Ethoxyquin, Sodium Nitrite/Nitrate and TBHQBHA), artificial colours, sugars and sweeteners, e.g. corn syrup, sucrose and ammoniated glycyrrhizin, powdered cellulose, propylene glycol.

Food Trials

The only way to completely cure a food allergy or intolerance is complete avoidance, which is not as easy as it sounds. First you have to determine your dog DOES have an allergy to food - and not pollen, grass, etc. - and then you have to discover WHICH food is causing the reaction.

A **food trial or exclusion diet** involves feeding one specific food for 12 weeks, something the dog has never eaten before.

Before you embark on one, know that they are a real pain-in-the-you-know-what! You have to be incredibly vigilant and determined, so only start one if you are prepared to see it through to the end or you are wasting your time.

The chosen food must be the **only thing** eaten during the trial. During the trial, your dog shouldn't roam freely, as you can't control what he is eating or drinking when out of sight.
Don't give:

- 🐾 Treats
- 🐾 Rawhide (not recommended anyway)
- 🐾 Pigs' ears
- 🐾 Cows' hooves
- 🐾 Flavoured medications (including heartworm treatments) or supplements
- 🐾 Flavoured toothpastes
- 🐾 Flavoured plastic toys

A more practical, less scientific approach is to eliminate ingredients one at a time by switching diets over a period of a week or so. If you switch to home-cooked or raw, you know exactly what your dog is eating; if you choose a commercial food, a hypoallergenic one is a good place to start.

They all have the word *"hypoallergenic"* in the name and do not include wheat protein or soya. They are often based around less common ingredients.

Grain Intolerance

Although beef is the food most likely to cause allergies in the general dog population, there is plenty of anecdotal evidence to suggest that GRAIN can also be a problem. *"Grain"* is wheat or any other cultivated cereal crop. Some dogs also react to starch, which is found in grains and potatoes, as well as bread, pasta, rice, etc.

Dogs have short digestive tracts and don't process grains as well as humans. Foods high in grains and sugar can cause increases in unhealthy bacteria and yeast in the stomach, which crowds out the good bacteria and allows toxins to affect the immune system. They also cause lots of GAS!

The itchiness related to food allergies can then cause secondary bacterial and yeast infections, which may show as hot spots, ear or bladder infections, excessive shedding, reddish or dark brown tear stains. You may also notice a musty smell.

FACT ❯ Drugs like antihistamines and steroids will help temporarily, but they do not address the root cause.

Before you automatically switch to a grain-free diet, a recent study by University of California, Davis, vets found a link between a form of heart disease called ***taurine-deficient dilated cardiomyopathy*** and some popular grain-free dog foods where legumes (e.g. beans, lentil, peas, soy) or potatoes were the main ingredients.

Lead author Joshua Stern said that while many owners may not want to see *"by products"* listed in their dog's food, they often contain organ meat like heart and kidney, which are good sources of taurine.

Some food allergy symptoms - particularly the scratching, licking, chewing and redness - can also be a sign of environmental allergies or flea bites. See **Chapter 12. Beagle Skin and Allergies** for more details.

 If you've switched diet to little effect, it's time to see a vet. Many vets promote specific dog food brands, which may or may not be the best option for your Beagle. Do your own research.

Bloat

Bloat occurs when there is too much gas in the stomach. It is known by several different names: *twisted stomach, gastric torsion* or *Gastric Dilatation-Volvulus (GDV)* and occurs mainly in larger breeds with deep chests, such as the Doberman. Although it is uncommon in Beagles, they have been known to suffer from it after stealing food, and overeating. Bloat is statistically more common in males than in females and in dogs over seven years old.

As the stomach swells with gas, it can rotate 90° to 360°. The twisting stomach traps air, food and water inside and the bloated organ stops blood flowing properly to veins in the abdomen, leading to low blood pressure, shock and even damage to internal organs.

The causes are not fully understood, but there are some well-known risk factors. One is the dog taking in a lot of air while eating - either because he is greedy and gulping the food too fast, or stressed, e.g. in kennels where there might be food competition.

A dog that is fed once a day and gorges himself could be at higher risk; another reason why most owners feed twice a day. Exercising straight after eating or after a big drink also increases the risk - like colic in horses.

Another potential cause is diet. Fermentable foodstuffs that produce a lot of gas can cause problems for the stomach if the gas is not burped or passed into the intestines. Symptoms are:

- Swollen belly
- Standing uncomfortably or hunched
- Restlessness, pacing or looking for a place to hide
- Rapid panting or difficulty breathing
- Dry retching, or excessive saliva or foam
- White or colourless gums
- Excessive drinking
- Licking the air
- General weakness or collapse

Tips to Avoid Canine Bloat:

- Some owners buy a frame for food bowls so they are at chest height for the dog, other experts believe dogs should be fed from the floor – do whichever slows your Beagle down
- Avoid dog food with high fats or those using citric acid as a preservative, also avoid tiny pieces of kibble
- If your Beagle is a gulper, invest in a bowl with nobbles *(pictured)* and moisten your dog's dry food – both of these slow down a gulper
- Feed twice a day rather than once
- Don't let your dog drink too much water just before, during or after eating
- Stress can possibly be a trigger, with nervous and aggressive dogs being more susceptible. Maintain a peaceful environment, particularly around his mealtimes
- Avoid vigorous exercise before or after eating, allow one hour either side of mealtimes before strenuous exercise

FACT Bloat can kill a dog in less than one hour. If you suspect your Beagle has it, get him into the car and off to the vet IMMEDIATELY. Bloat is one of the leading killers of dogs after cancer.

Overweight Beagles

Many Beagles are obsessive about food - which is great for training, but not so good for maintaining a healthy weight. According to VCA (Veterinary Centers of America):

"In North America, obesity is the most common preventable disease in dogs. Approximately 25-30% of the general canine population is obese, with 40-45% of dogs aged 5-11 years old weighing in higher than normal." And the Beagle is one of the breeds most prone to putting on the pounds.

You may think you are being kind to your beloved Beagle by giving him extra treats and scraps, but the reality is that you are shortening his life.

The extra weight puts huge strain on his short legs, back and organs, often resulting in a reducing lifespan. It is far easier to regulate your dog's weight and keep it at a healthy level than to slim down a pleading Beagle once he becomes overweight. Overweight dogs are susceptible to:

IVDD – a study by the Royal Veterinary College found that dogs that were fat or obese were more likely to suffer from IVDD than fitter, slimmer ones.

Joint disease – excessive body weight increases joint stress, which then tends to lead to a vicious circle of less exercise and weight gain, further reducing exercise.

Heart and lung problems – fatty deposits within the chest cavity and too much circulating fat contribute to cardio-respiratory and cardiovascular disease.

Diabetes – is a major risk factor for overweight Beagles.

Tumours – obesity increases the risk of mammary tumours in female dogs.

Liver disease – fat degeneration can result in liver insufficiency.

Reduced Lifespan - one of the most serious proven findings in obesity studies is that obesity in both humans and dogs reduces lifespan.

Most Beagles are extremely loyal companions and very attached to their humans. They are a part of our family. However, beware of going too far.

FACT Studies show that dogs regarded as "family members" by the owner (anthropomorphosis) are at greater risk of becoming overweight. This is because attention given to the dog often results in food being given as well.

To see diagrams and descriptions of overweight, underweight and correct weight Beagles, type *"Beagle health UK body condition and weight"* into an online search engine.

If you have to put your dog on a diet, be aware that a reduced amount of food will also mean reduced nutrients, so he may need a supplement during this time.

Don't despair if your Beagle is overweight. Many problems associated with being overweight are reversible with weight loss.

What the Breeders Feed

We asked a number of breeders what they give their dogs. This is what they said, starting with the UK breeders, who are all Kennel Club Assured Breeders.

Sharon Hardisty, who has the small Blunderhall Beagles show kennel in Lancashire: "I feed a dry complete food mainly due to ease and convenience with having a large number to feed. It's our own brand called Blunderhall.

"It is high quality with a large fresh meat/fish percentage and uses human-grade ingredients. If I didn't have so many dogs, I would feed raw."

Stepping out in style in the show ring is Blunderhall Fleur Tayshuss (Martha), aged 18 months.

Debbie Tantrum, Debles Beagles, Shropshire: "Ours are all fed on Purina, from puppy to adult. It has an optimum digest system that allows the food to be digested easily, they are fed twice a day as it's easier to digest, and given just water. It gives them a lovely shiny coat, they look healthy and their poop is solid, we know when we have a poorly dog if poop's not right.

"I do not use raw or BARF diet, it is too costly, and we have found that the dogs end up fighting due to the smell of blood."

Kelly Diamond: I feed my dogs and puppies a complete dry food according to age. I have not fed raw as I'm aware there is little science behind it and I'm happy with the diet mine have."

Karen Simkin, Simeldaka Beagles, London: "We feed Royal Canine Beagle breed dry food. We start our pups with their 'Starter' food and then the puppy food. I have never fed raw, it doesn't appeal to me to handle it, etc.... Yet the things I pick up! I like the convenience of dry, especially at shows or when going away."

Georgina Armour-Langham, Robentot Beagles, Leicester: "Kibble is easiest, but they always get vegetable trimmings, particularly cabbage and carrot. Mine love to graze on grass!

"Our dogs' teeth are all good with minimal signs of decay; they all have calm personalities and are very rarely bothered by ill health. The most common comment we get about our Beagles is how young they look - we are even asked how old our puppies are when, in fact, the oldest are nearly nine and seven years old!"

Peter Sievwright, Mattily Beagles, Renfrewshire, Scotland: "We start our dogs on high energy dry kibble from Royal Canin as we feel this gives our pups the best start in life. This is then supplemented with puppy meat mixed in with the dry food.

"Pups need a lot of energy food and we feel that our dry kibble, wet food mixture covers all the dogs' needs and allows them to grow at the rate their development requires.

"Our adult dogs are then transferred onto low energy adult dry kibble, supplemented now and again with puppy food to keep their weight and overall health at the optimum for the breed."

Sarah Porter, Puddlehill Beagles, Norfolk: "I feed a BARF diet and have done this exclusively. When we first got our first Beagle pup he was on kibble and his behaviour was hyperactive. As soon has he was changed over to BARF, his personality changed; he was far calmer and far more amenable."

Photo of this relaxed trio courtesy of Sarah.

Lori Norman, Lokavi Beagles, Florida: "I feed Royal Canin because I find it keeps them in great condition. I don't feed raw for a variety of reasons, but I have no problem with puppy owners feeding it, as long as it is a good, balanced raw diet and not just table scraps."

Darlene Stewart, Aladar Beagles, Alabama: "I have found that wheat, corn and soy will set off some of my Beagles with yeasty ears. I feed mostly a kibble with rice or pea base. I also supplement with other veggies and cooked meat. I have fed raw at times and have used raw chicken backs - never give cooked chicken bones!

"I have found for me a kibble-based food with extras added works best for me. I add meat, vitamins, joint supplement and some veggies on regular basis."

7. Beagle Traits

With a Beagle you are getting a full-on scent hound and a free spirit. And if you've decided to share your life with one, it helps to have an insight into what is going on in that maverick mind of his or hers!

You have to learn what makes a Beagle tick before you can develop a stress-free relationship that makes both of you happy. This chapter helps you to do just that, and to bring out the best in your Beagle.

Just as with humans, a dog's personality is made up of a combination of temperament and character – or **Nature and Nurture.**

Temperament is the nature – or inherited characteristics - a dog is born with; it's the predisposition to act or react to the world around him. The amount of natural hound instinct your Beagle has is dominated by genetics and varies greatly from one Beagle to the next.

One bred from generations of hunting dogs will have the drive and nose of a scent hound, whereas one bred from generations of companion dogs is likely to be content with less physical and mental exercise and scent work. Good breeders not only produce puppies from physically healthy dams and sires, but they also consider temperament when choosing which dogs to breed.

Character is what develops through the dog's life and is formed by a combination of temperament and environment. How you treat your dog will have a huge effect on his personality and behaviour.

Start off on the right foot with your puppy by establishing the rules of the house and good routines, while making time to teach the all-important Recall while your puppy is very young and still wants to follow you.

Treat him well and make lots of time for socialisation, training and, as his body matures, exercise.

FACT Socialisation means "learning to be part of society." With dogs, it means helping them learn to be comfortable living within a human society which includes many different types of people, environments, buildings, sights, noises, smells and other animals.

All dogs need different environments and experiences to keep them stimulated and well-balanced. As hounds, Beagles enjoy activities that challenge their minds as well as their bodies. They also enjoy running free off the lead.

Typical Beagle

Every Beagle is unique, while they share some characteristics, no two Beagles are alike in looks or temperament. They all have their own special ways – it's part of their appeal.

However, to give you an idea of why yours acts like he does, here are some typical traits common within the breed:

- The good news is that the Beagle is considered a healthy and fairly robust breed

- They are naturally mild-mannered dogs that tend to be friendly with everybody

- Beagles have a reputation for being very good with children, provided they and the kids are both well trained and socialised

- The Beagle is not an aggressive breed; most Beagles get on well with other dogs and pets. (Occasionally, a dog may show signs of aggression if he has not been well socialised or taught to share)

- They are both handsome AND smart – but you need to know that their intelligence doesn't necessarily mean "easy to train"

- They have a smooth, short coat that sheds a lot, so not suitable for allergy sufferers. They are considered low-maintenance when it comes to grooming, although you'll have to bath them every now and again as they enjoy rolling in/paddling through wet and smelly things!

- They were bred to work alongside Man and are extremely loyal dogs

- Never forget they are first and foremost scent hounds with an incredible sense of smell. They are ruled by their nose and a desire to hunt

- Beagles are pack animals. They LOVE the companionship of other dogs or humans – even cats sometimes - and do not do well when left alone for long periods

- Packs of working Beagles are kennelled outdoors, but pet Beagles should be kept indoors

- All Beagles need their own quiet space - a basket, bed or crate where they can relax

- Beagle puppies need LOTS of sleep or they can become overstimulated and naughty

- Beagles work in packs away from their masters when hunting and are able to act on their own initiative. Because of this, they have a reputation for being creative thinkers with minds of their own

- Without proper training and channelling of these natural traits, a Beagle can become mischievous or stubborn; lots of time and patience are required to train them properly

- An adult Beagle requires at least an hour a day exercise

- Mental stimulation is just as important as physical activity for working and hunting breeds. Activities and games involving scent work can be as effective as a long walk for tiring out a Beagle

- Because of their amazing sense of smell and hunting instinct, the Beagle is one of the hardest breeds to teach the Recall. With their nose to the ground on a scent they become completely deaf to your commands...

- Don't let your Beagle off the lead until they have learned the Recall. And even then, they have absolutely no road sense - so keep yours on a lead at ALL times near roads. Consider using a GPS tracker collar any time you let yours off-lead in an unfenced area

- They are escape artists! Make sure every little gap is plugged in any fencing

- Some love to chase small animals and birds. Whether your Beagle is like this depends on his genes and how much natural hunting instinct is in them

- Hunting dogs have "drive." Again, whether your dog is naturally mellow or a ball of fire depends to some extent on his genes, but all Beagles need exercise and mental stimulation to be happy

- They are a very affectionate breed; their tendency is to bond with the whole family - and especially with the person who feeds them

- Beagles can give Labradors a run for their money in the title race for World's Greediest Dog! They can sniff out even the tiniest morsel and are constantly on the lookout for opportunities to get more food – no matter what the consequences

- They don't know when they've had enough and are prone to putting on weight, which is bad for lots of reasons. It's up to you to monitor your dog's calorie intake

- While not the easiest breed to train, Beagles are very smart and tenacious. They don't give up easily and enjoy problem-solving, so bolt down or move out of reach (which is higher than you think) anything you don't want yours to get into – Beagles are thieves!

- Resource guarding can become an issue with some when they won't let go of the stolen item. Right from puppyhood and using rewards, teach your dog to hand things back when you tell him to, and train him to allow you to put your hand in or near his food bowl whenever you want

- Due to their independent-mindedness, the trick to successful training or housetraining is to persuade them that what YOU want them to do is really what THEY want to do – this usually involves bribery!

- A bored Beagle is a mischievous Beagle

- Some are excellent watch dogs; they alert their owners to somebody approaching the house from quite a distance. However, while they will (or can be trained to) bark, they are quite happy to watch intruders make off with your prize family heirlooms in return for a tasty treat or two

- Beagles have a distinctive "bay" when excited – a howling bark with nose and tail up in the air. They also have a surprising array of other sounds, including, whining, deep barking, snoring, yapping, squeaking - some owners even say they "talk"

- Beagles are very curious and interested in anything new or different. They love to have a purpose or a challenge, especially playing with their owners and scent work

- They are quirky, affectionate freethinkers who make you laugh and are completely lovable!

Canine Emotions

As pet lovers, we are all too keen to ascribe human characteristics to our dogs; this is called **anthropomorphism** – "the attribution of human characteristics to anything other than a human being."

Most of us dog lovers are guilty of that, as we come to regard our pets as members of the family - and Beagles certainly regard themselves as members of the family.

An example of anthropomorphism might be that the owner of a male dog might not want to have him neutered because he will "miss sex," as a human might if he or she were no longer able to have sex. This is simply not true.

A male dog's impulse to mate is entirely governed by his hormones, not emotions. If he gets the scent of a bitch in heat, his hormones (which are just chemicals) tell him he has to mate with her. He does not stop to consider how attractive she is or whether she is *"the one"* to produce his puppies.

No, his reaction is entirely physical, he just wants to head on over there and get on with it!

It's the same with females. When they are in heat, a chemical impulse is triggered in their brain making them want to mate – with any male, they aren't at all fussy. So, don't expect your little Princess to be all coy when she is in heat, she is not waiting for Prince Charming to come along - the tramp down the road or any other scruffy pooch will do! It is entirely physical, not emotional.

Food is another issue. A Beagle's greatest desire is to get that delicious-smelling treat or food – you have to count the calories.

Beagles are incredibly loyal and loving. They are amusing characters and if yours doesn't make you smile from time to time, you must have had a humour by-pass. All of this adds up to one thing: a beloved family member that is all too easy to spoil.

 Beagles form deep bonds with their humans and respond well to the right motivation - usually treats and/or toys. Teach yours to respect the authority figure, which is you - not him! In the beginning, think of yourself as a kindly but firm teacher with a slightly stubborn young student.

Learn to understand his mind, patiently train him to be comfortable with his place in the household, teach him some manners and household rules – like not jumping up, stealing things or constantly barking - and you will be rewarded with a companion who is second to none and fits in beautifully with your family and lifestyle.

Dr Stanley Coren is well known for his work on canine psychology and behaviour. He and other researchers believe that in many ways a dog's emotional development is equivalent to that of a young child. Dr Coren says: "Researchers have now come to believe that the mind of a dog is roughly equivalent to that of a human who is two to two-and-a-half years old. This conclusion holds for most mental abilities as well as emotions.

"Thus, we can look to human research to see what we might expect of our dogs. Just like a two-year-old child, our dogs clearly have emotions, but many fewer kinds of emotions than found in adult humans.

"At birth, a human infant only has an emotion that we might call excitement. This indicates how excited he is, ranging from very calm up to a state of frenzy. Within the first weeks of life the excitement state comes to take on a varying positive or a negative flavour, so we can now detect the general emotions of contentment and distress.

"In the next couple of months, disgust, fear, and anger become detectable in the infant. Joy often does not appear until the infant is nearly six months of age and it is followed by the emergence of shyness or suspicion. True affection, the sort that it makes sense to use the label "love" for, does not fully emerge until nine or ten months of age."

So, our Beagles can truly love us — but we knew that already!

According to Dr Coren, dogs can't feel shame. So, if you are housetraining your puppy, don't expect him to feel ashamed if he makes a mess in the house, he can't; he simply isn't capable of feeling shame. But he will not like it when you ignore him when he's behaving badly, and will love it when you praise or reward him for relieving himself outdoors.

FACT ❯ **He is simply responding to you with his simplified range of emotions.**

Although Beagles can sometimes be stubborn, they can also be sensitive and show empathy - *"the ability to understand and share the feelings of another."* They can pick up on the mood and emotions of the owner.

One emotion that all dogs can experience is jealousy. It may display itself by being overly-protective of humans, food or toys. An interesting article was published in the PLOS (Public Library of Science) Journal in 2014 following an experiment into whether dogs get jealous.

Building on research that shows that six-month old infants display jealousy, the scientists studied 36 dogs in their homes and videoed their actions when their owners showed affection to a realistic-looking stuffed canine *(pictured).*

Over three-quarters of the dogs pushed or touched the owner when they interacted with the decoy. The envious mutts were more than three times as likely to do this for interactions with the stuffed dog, compared to when their owners gave their attention to other objects, including a book.

Around a third tried to get between the owner and the plush toy, while a quarter of the put-upon pooches snapped at the dummy dog!

Professor Christine Harris from University of California in San Diego said: "Our study suggests not only that dogs do engage in what appear to be jealous behaviours, but also that they were seeking to break up the connection between the owner and a seeming rival."

The researchers believe that the dogs thought that the stuffed dog was real. The authors cite the fact that 86% of the dogs sniffed the toy's rear end during and after the experiment!

Professor Harris said: "We can't really speak of the dogs' subjective experiences, of course, but it looks as though they were motivated to protect an important social relationship. Many people have assumed that jealousy is a social construction of human beings - or that it's an emotion specifically tied to sexual and romantic relationships.

"Our results challenge these ideas, showing that animals besides ourselves display strong distress whenever a rival usurps a loved one's affection."

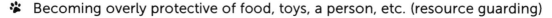

Cause and Effect

When treated well, socialised and trained, Beagles make wonderful canine companions. Once you've had one, no other dog seems quite the same. But sometimes they, just like other breeds, can develop behaviour problems. Poor behaviour may result from a number of factors, including:

- Lack of socialisation
- Lack of training
- Poor breeding
- Boredom, due to lack of exercise or mental challenges, *pictured*
- Being left alone too long
- Being badly treated
- A change in living conditions
- Anxiety, insecurity or fear
- Being spoilt

Bad behaviour may show itself in different ways:

- Becoming overly protective of food, toys, a person, etc. (resource guarding)
- Excessive barking
- Chewing or destructive behaviour
- Stealing things
- Excessive digging
- Nipping, biting
- Aggression or excitability on the lead
- Jumping up
- Soiling or urinating inside the house
- Constantly demanding your attention
- Aggression towards people or other dogs, fortunately this is relatively rare in Beagles

 Avoid poor behaviour by devoting lots of time early on to socialise and train your Beagle, and to nip any potential problems in the bud.

If you are rehoming a Beagle, you'll need extra time and patience to help your new arrival unlearn some bad habits.

10 Ways to Avoid Unwanted Behaviour

Here are some tips to help you start out on the right foot:

1. **Buy from a good breeder**. They use their expertise to match suitable breeding pairs, taking into account factors such as good temperament, health and being *"fit for function."*

2. **Start socialisation right away**. Give a new puppy a couple of days to get used to his new surroundings and then start socialising him – even if this means carrying him places until the vaccination schedule is complete.

    Socialisation does not end at puppyhood. Beagles are social creatures that thrive on sniffing, hearing, seeing, and even licking. While the foundation for good behaviour is laid down during the first few months, good owners reinforce social skills and training throughout a dog's life.

    Beagles love to be at the centre of the action and it is important that they learn when young that they are not also the centre of the universe. Socialisation helps them to learn their place in that universe and to become comfortable with it.

3. **Start training early** - you can't start too soon. Start teaching your puppy to learn his name as well as some simple commands a day or two after you bring him home.

4. **Basic training should cover several areas:** housetraining, chew prevention, puppy biting, simple commands like SIT, COME, STAY and familiarising him with collar and lead. Adopt a gentle but firm approach and keep training sessions short and FUN - start with five minutes a day and build up. Beagles do not respond well to harsh treatment.

    Puppy classes or adult dog obedience classes are a great way to start; be sure to do your homework together afterwards. Spend a few minutes each day reinforcing what you have both learned in class - owners need training as well as dogs!

5. **Reward your dog for good behaviour.** All behaviour training should be based on positive reinforcement. Beagles love rewards and praise, and this trait speeds up the training process. The main aim of training is to build a good understanding between you and your dog.

6. **Ignore bad behaviour**, no matter how hard this may be. If, for example, your dog is chewing his way through your kitchen, shoes, or couch, jumping up or chasing the kids, remove him from the situation and then ignore him. For most dogs even negative attention is some attention.

    Or if he is constantly demanding your attention, ignore him. Remove him or yourself from the room so he learns that you give attention when you want to give it, **not** when he demands it. If your pup is a chewer – and most are - make sure he has plenty of durable toys to keep him occupied.

7. **Take the time to learn what sort of temperament your dog has.** Is he by nature confident or anxious? What was he like as a tiny puppy, did he rush forward or hang back? Does he fight to get upright when on his back or is he happy to lie there? Is he a couch potato or a ball of energy?

Your puppy's temperament will affect his behaviour and how he reacts to the world. A nervous Beagle will certainly not respond well to a loud approach on your part, whereas an energetic, strong-willed one will require more patience and exercise, and a firm hand.

8. **Exercise and stimulation.** A lack of either is another reason for dogs behaving badly. Regular daily exercise, games and toys and organised activities are all ways of stopping your dog from becoming bored or frustrated.

   Pictured looking very alert is Debbie Tantrum's Debles Royal Max, aged three.

9. **Learn to leave your dog.** Just as leaving your dog alone for too long can lead to problems, so can being with him 100% of the time. The dog becomes over-reliant on you and then gets stressed when you leave; this is called *separation anxiety*. When your dog first arrives at your house, start by leaving him for a few minutes every day and gradually build it up so that after a while you can leave him for up to four hours.

10. **Love your Beagle – but don't spoil him,** however difficult that might be. You don't do your dog any favours by giving too many treats, constantly responding to his demands for attention or allowing him to behave as he wants inside the house.

··

Separation Anxiety

It's not just dogs that experience separation anxiety - people do too. About 7% of adults and 4% of children suffer from this disorder. Typical symptoms for humans are:

- 🐾 Distress at being separated from a loved one
- 🐾 Fear of being left alone

Our canine companions aren't much different. When a puppy leaves the litter, his owner becomes his new pack. It's estimated that as many as 10% to 15% of dogs suffer from separation anxiety, which is an exaggerated fear response caused by being apart from their owner. Separation anxiety affects millions of dogs and is on the increase. According to behaviourists, it is the most common form of stress for dogs.

FACT Beagles CAN suffer from it, especially if they have not spent enough time away from their owners when young. Even if yours does not have separation anxiety, being over-reliant on you can lead to other insecurity issues, such as becoming:

- 🐾 Anxious
- 🐾 Over-protective
- 🐾 Too territorial
- 🐾 Too suspicious or aggressive with other people

Separation anxiety can be equally distressing for the owner - I know because one of our dogs suffered from it. He howled whenever we left home without him. He'd also bark if one of us got out of the car - even if other people were still inside

Fortunately, his problem was relatively mild. If we returned after only a short while, he was usually quiet. Although if we silently sneaked back and peeked in through the letterbox, he was never asleep. Instead he'd be waiting by the door looking and listening for our return.

Tell-Tale Signs

Does your Beagle do any of the following?

🐾 Follow you from room to room – even the bathroom - whenever you're home?

🐾 Get anxious or stressed when you're getting ready to leave the house?

🐾 Howl, bark or whine when you leave?

🐾 Chew or destroy things he's not supposed to?

🐾 Dig or scratch at the carpet, doors or windows trying to join you?

🐾 Soil or urinate inside the house, even though he is housetrained? (This only occurs when left alone)

🐾 Exhibit restlessness - such as licking his coat excessively, pacing or circling?

🐾 Greet you ecstatically every time you come home – even if you've only been out to empty the bins?

🐾 Wait by the window or door until you return?

🐾 Dislike spending time alone in the garden or yard?

🐾 Refuse to eat or drink if you leave him?

🐾 Howl or whine when one family member leaves - even when others are still in the room or car?

If so, he may suffer from separation anxiety. Fortunately, in many cases this can be cured.

Causes

Beagles are pack animals and being alone is not a natural state for them. Puppies have to be taught to get used to periods of isolation slowly and in a structured way before they can become comfortable with being alone.

A Beagle puppy will emotionally latch on to his new owner, who has taken the place of his mother and siblings. He will want to follow you everywhere initially and, although you want to shower him with love and attention, it's best to start leaving him, starting with a minute or two, right from the beginning.

In our case I was working from home when we got Max. With hindsight, I should have left him alone more often in those critical first few days, weeks then months.

Adopted dogs may be particularly susceptible to separation anxiety. They may have been abandoned once already and fear it happening again.

One or more of these causes can trigger separation anxiety:

- Not being left alone for short periods when young

- Being left for too long by owners who are out of the house for most of the day

- Anxiety or lack of confidence due to insufficient socialisation, training or both

- Boredom

- Being given TOO MUCH attention

- All of the dog's attention being focussed on one person – usually because that person spends time with him, plays, feeds, trains and exercises him

- Making too much of a fuss when you leave and return to the house

- Mistreatment in the past, a rescue dog may well feel anxious when left alone

FACT ❭ It may be very flattering that your Beagle wants to be with you all the time, but separation anxiety is a form of panic that is distressing for your dog. Socialisation helps a dog to become more confident and self-reliant.

A different scenario is separation anxiety in elderly dogs. As dogs age, their senses, such as scent, hearing and sight, diminish. They often become "clingier" and more anxious when they are separated from their owners - or even out of view.

You may even find that your elderly Beagle reverts to puppyhood and starts to follow you around the house again. In these cases, it is fine to spend more time with your old friend and gently help him through his final years.

So, what can you do if your dog is showing signs of canine separation anxiety? Every dog is different, but here are tried and tested techniques that have worked for some dogs.

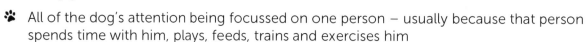

Tips to Combat Separation Anxiety

1. After the first couple of days at home, leave your new puppy or adult dog for short periods, starting with a minute, then two, then gradually increasing the minutes you are out of sight.

2. Use a crate. Crate training helps a dog to become self-reliant.

3. Consider making his night-time bed NOT in your bedroom to get him used to being without you for a few hours a day.

4. Introduce your Beagle to other people, places and animals while young.

5. Get other members of your family to feed, walk and train the dog, so he doesn't become fixated on just one person.

6. Tire your Beagle out before you leave him alone. Take him for a walk, do an activity or play a game before leaving and, if you can, leave him with a view of the outside world, e.g. in a room with a patio door or low window.

7. Keep arrivals and departures low key and don't make a big fuss.

8. Leave him a *"security blanket,"* such as an old piece of clothing that still has your scent on it, a favourite toy, or leave a radio on softly in the room with the dog. Avoid a heavy rock station! If it will be dark when you return, leave a lamp on a timer.

9. Associate your departure with something good. Give him a rubber toy, like a Kong, filled with a tasty treat, or a frozen treat. This may take his mind off your departure. (Some dogs may refuse to touch the treat until you return home).

10. Structure and routine can help to reduce anxiety. Carry out regular activities, such as feeding and exercising, at the same time every day.

11. Dogs read body language very well and may start to fret when they think you are going to leave them. One technique is to mimic your departure routine when you have no intention of leaving. Put your coat on, grab your car keys, go out of the door and return a few seconds later. Do this randomly and regularly and it may help to reduce your dog's stress levels when you do it for real.

12. However lovable your Beagle is, if he is showing early signs of anxiety when separating from you, do not shower him with attention all the time when you are there. He will become too reliant on you.

13. If you have to regularly leave the house for a few hours at a time, try to make an arrangement so the dog is not on his own all day every day during the week. Consider dropping him off with a neighbour or doggie day care if you can afford it.

14. Getting another dog to keep the first one company can help, but can you afford double the food and veterinary bills? We also don't recommend getting two Beagles from the same litter as their strongest bond can be to each other, not you.

15. There are many natural calming remedies available for dogs in spray, tablet or liquid form, such as CBD oil. Another option is to leave him with a Snuggle Puppy, which is warm and has a heartbeat.

Sit-Stay-Down

Another technique for helping to reduce separation anxiety is the *"sit-stay"* or *"down-stay"* exercises using positive reinforcement. The goal is to be able to move briefly out of your dog's sight while he is in the *"stay"* position. Through this, he learns that he can remain calmly and happily in one place while you go about your normal daily life.

You have to progress slowly. Get your dog to sit and stay and then walk away from him for five seconds, then 10, 20, a minute and so on. Reward your dog every time he stays calm. Then move out of sight or out of the room for a few seconds, return and give him a treat if he is calm, gradually lengthen the time you are out of sight.

If you're watching TV snuggled up with your dog and you get up for a snack, say *"Stay"* and leave the room. When you return, praise him quietly. It is a good idea to practise these techniques after exercise or when your dog is a little sleepy (but not exhausted), as he is likely to be more relaxed.

 Canine separation anxiety is not the result of disobedience or lack of training. It's a psychological condition; your dog feels anxious and insecure.

NEVER punish your dog for showing signs of separation anxiety – even if he has chewed your best shoes or dug a hole in your expensive rug. This will only make him more anxious.

NEVER leave your dog unattended in a crate for more than four hours maximum - or if he is frantic to get out, as it can cause physical or mental trauma. If you're thinking of leaving an animal in a crate all day while you are out of the house, get a rabbit or a hamster - not a Beagle.

First Hand Experience

We asked our contributing breeders about their Beagles' typical temperaments and traits. This is what they said:

Sharon Hardisty, Blunderhall Beagles, Lancashire: "Beagles are very intelligent, which can sometimes be confused with naughtiness when they are bored. With training I would say you get back what you put in and if you're prepared to put in the effort they can be well trained.

Pictured is the prizewinning Bugsy (Blunderhall Ray of Hope), aged 12 months.

"They are typically happy, friendly and always on the look-out for food. They love being outdoors and following a scent. They are excellent with children, although I'd be cautious about very young children and a young puppy, as puppies can be boisterous."

Peter Sievwright, Mattily Beagles, Renfrewshire: "My opinion as to why Beagles are so popular is their looks; they are in proportion with short, low-casting hair, so low maintenance. They are also intelligent - so much so that I sometimes think there's a little human inside trying to get out. Somehow they just seem to know what I'm saying. You'd be amazed by some of the conversations I've had with my dogs! They actually respond with expressions and gestures, and vice versa.

"My Beagles can climb, I've had two that can jump fences, one that has climbed out of a window on to a roof, one that opens doors using the door handle, and another that climbs through my cat flap, and they can all squeeze through the tiniest of gaps.

"Beagles can be trained - some with no problems at all and others pick up only a handful of commands. The best way is to start when they are pups and use treat training. I have also found that some Beagles can be walked off a lead with no adverse behaviour. The easiest Beagles I have found to train are tan and whites, or descendants of the tan and white colour group."

Photo: Two of Peter's playful puppies.

"As for barking, some of our dogs bark and some don't. The main issue we've found is diet. If the dog is fed a diet too energetic for its needs and the owner doesn't burn off the dog's energy with exercise, this energy will just fly out of the dog's mouth through excitement in the form of a bark.

"One issue we have come across is dogs barking at other dogs because they want their toys; so we take the toys away so the dogs don't bark out of jealousy. They also bark at people walking by the garden, but overall - with the correct lower energy diet and a close-boarded fence - it is possible to lower the amount of barking."

Peter added: "They are a loveable, determined, loyal and energetic breed and although can be frustrating at times, I wouldn't change them for the world."

Kelly Diamond, Kelcardi Beagles, Fife: "Beagles really do have super temperaments and make excellent family additions. I usually light-heartedly say to people when owning a Beagle they will make you laugh or cry on a regular basis; they are 100% clowns of the dog world and this is one of the reasons I love them so much.

"A Beagle loves nothing more than getting a scent and chasing it, and unfortunately this can get them into some dangerous situations. They are intelligent dogs - they do require more patience than some other breeds, however they are trainable. Just remember you can never switch that nose off or the natural desire to follow a scent, so for that reason off lead work is usually the hardest thing to master."

Debbie Tantrum, Debles Beagles, Shropshire: "Being a scent hound Beagles have many different traits, which are not always the same in each dog. They can smell from afar, their noses twitch at the slightest thing when we are out walking.

"They are solid dogs with a square-shaped head and nose, their ears are long and floppy, chest is deep and their backs are straight with a long tail that likes to swish in your face when they are comfortable on your lap...they are not supposed to be lap dogs, but we disagree!

"Beagles are highly intelligent, and you need to train from as early as six weeks. Our puppies leave us at 10 weeks, and they are trained to sit before they have their food, they have already been on a lead and heel. As long as you do not reward them with too many treats, they will be good - they get incredibly wise to doing things for food! It is not hard work, you just have to be straight and strict.

"Their temperaments are one of a kind, each one of ours is totally different. We have one that will talk to us when she needs a treat, one will rub herself all over you, we have a very naughty one that can get into almost anything, like Houdini. They are all very loveable and lively dogs - they may seem to come across as daft but they are not. They are definitely not a guard dog as they will let people in for their fuss and attention.

"We have had puppies go to homes where people have disabilities, including Autism and Down Syndrome. I work in a hospital and I have also found they are good for healing. I had a lady with very bad dementia, she would not talk or communicate with us, instead she tried to bite and hit us.

When I placed a puppy on her lap she began to sing as it brought back memories of when she was a little girl."

Sarah Porter, Puddlehill Beagles, Norfolk: "Beagles are loving, funny and adorable – they can also be grumpy and sensitive. My Maybel is the most sensitive dog I know – we lost her first-born pup, Beckett, (who we kept from the litter, **pictured,**) very suddenly before she was two years old.

"I think our grief really strengthened our bond – she knows when I'm not right and when I am struggling with day-to-day stuff. She will come and sit behind me on my office chair – her son who lives with a friend is the same! She loves a cuddle and she most definitely knows when I am thinking of her daughter as she just gives me a look that says she knows and she is missing her too, or she will sidle up to me just to be close.

"On the other hand when we get together with her other offspring, she is most definitely the Fun Police – she tells them off, she gets stuck in and rules the roost and puts the 'kids' in their place!

"Beagles are scavengers and will eat anything that smells tasty - with cat poo one of the No.1 delicacies! They also like to eat sticks, stones, leaves etc., so puppy proofing the garden and home should be done before pup comes home. Don't allow pups to be left unsupervised for periods of time as they will find something to chew or destroy if given the opportunity.

"Beagles like to know what's going on and they like to tell you if something is different, but I wouldn't say they are watchdogs; they just let you know when they know that something is different. My girl is my girl and loves a cuddle with me but she wouldn't be protective of me."

"I've never had aggression in my dogs. I would hope that I know my dogs and what might provoke a reaction. For example, my boy will growl if he's asleep and gets startled – let's face it who wouldn't? So if we need to move him, I always place a hand on his body and say his name so he isn't startled.

"As a youngster he would steal items and go and hide with them and resource guard. If it was a tea towel, for example, I would leave him because it became a game and he was getting a reaction from us. If it was something of importance I would swap for a high value item, but on the whole wouldn't leave things out that could be destroyed.

"He also used to resource guard and be fearful about his food bowl. It became an issue about four years ago so I went back to basics and hand-fed him for a few days. Then gave him his bowl back and put my hands in it and then took my hands out, etc and slowly built up again. If approaching him when he has finished his meal, I always say his name so he isn't shocked when I go to take his bowl away.

"In terms of activities: I used to show and will probably get back into it. My eldest Beagle loves scentwork training and will use his nose for ages doing this. He is food-driven, so mantrailing would not be for him. My eldest girl Beagle loves agility training, but we never enter agility competitions unless it's an enclosed ring as she is easily distracted and her nose gets the better of her!"

Georgina Armour-Langham, Robentot Beagles, Leicester: "Beagles are fun, inquisitive, enthusiastic, stubborn and wilful! They have selective hearing, a strong scent drive, they like to escape out of small holes, steal out of the bin and off the table!

"They are very intelligent, although quite tricky to train; be consistent and compassionate. Be firm, always give positive praise and treats to reward, and use a kind voice. They can be harder than you think; don't be fooled by their cute puppy eyes - they will challenge you!"

Lori Norman, Lokavi Beagles, Florida: "They have a voice, long ears; the nose knows all. They are happy, mischievous, sneaky, goofy, and highly entertaining.

"Beagles are also sneaky smart! I think someone who knows the breed will find them easy to train, but hard to convince… they know exactly what you want, but just don't feel like doing it right now. You've got to have a sense of humor to obedience train them. Never confuse their stubbornness with stupidity. They will be testing you at every turn. Once you understand that - just enjoy watching the lengths they go to, to NOT do something."

Photo of the beautiful Genie courtesy of Lori.

"They like to be included in anything going on, they also like to have a job. I had a beautiful boy that was being shown, and was so mentally into anything he was asked to do… he lived for it.

"He hated sitting around, so I found him a job…. He is part of the animal show at Universal in Orlando. Beagles need to be challenged or they get bored, and bored Beagles look for trouble.

"Beagles are very friendly and happy, and social. When people come to visit and want to meet the dogs, I always advise them not to wear light-colored pants. The dogs will jump on them to say hi, and get them dirty."

Darlene Stewart, Aladar Beagles, Alabama: "Oh boy, the main thing is the nose rules. When the nose starts working the ears and eyes don't! A Beagle is definitely a hound and they have been bred for centuries to find the game scent.

"Yell (bark) back to human "Hey I found it!! Come follow me!" That trait means when your sweet laid-back Beagle happens to get on a scent it just triggers that instinct, so don't expect a response to your "Stop! Come Back! Here!" commands. Also that trait makes them want to get to the scent so having a good fence is a must. Mr. Rabbit taking a nap on other side of fence will just be too tempting; under or over a Beagle may go.

"Hounds are pack dogs and do best when in a pack. The pack may be a human pack or other animals. A solitary Beagle left alone during the day may try to dig out if in a yard, tear up furniture if in house. I do not believe a Beagle does well crated all day while at work for eight hours or so at one time.

"Beagles are intelligent but more difficult to train in obedience. Food and their nose rules their world. They do best when training for events like agility, barn hunt, and scent detection. Basic obedience is needed for these activities but the events involve the nose and physical activity for a Beagle. Agility is much like a Beagle running in a field chasing a rabbit, while scent hunt and barn hunt are all about the nose - again!"

Yours Did What...?!

The Beagle is like no other dog. They are handsome, affectionate and quirky. They get into anything, especially if food is involved, escape through anything and run off after the faintest of scents. They drive you mad, sense when you are unhappy, and love you unconditionally.

One breeder has a Beagle who won't go to bed without her favourite toy "Ducky," and another has one who won't go to bed until she has spent quite a long time licking her humans! Here breeders share some of their favourite anecdotes of their beloved offbeat companions:

Georgina: "Lexi is eight and still cheeky with a particular *"woo woo woo"* bark when her lead goes on or when it's 7pm and she gets a chew stick.

"She always manages to climb on the kitchen table to "clean" it, pushing the chairs aside. This unpleasant habit is also followed by drinking my tea as soon as I turn my back. She loves to sleep inside an old sleeping bag underneath two other Beagles. Lexi will also fetch me an egg from under the chicken pen when there has been a random egg laid. She gently retrieves and delivers it to my hand unbroken.

"Breeze is the most placid flop dog, coming to give me kisses and rolling underneath my *"down dog"* whenever I attempt virtual yoga! Despite being calm and gentle she still manages to get into the chicken pen if she smells a crumb, biting and nosing her way under the wire. The chickens don't bother her, she's just after food.

"Hollie is more restless, always prowling around the garden on lookout. She delights in woofing and chasing if a dog goes past the gate. She's the muddiest Beagle, standing out in the rain then bringing lots of dirt inside.

"Lexi and Breeze have a very close bond, allowing each other into the 'puppy bed', even allowing each other to lick and suckle each other's puppies. In fact I have had all three adults sleeping in a raised bed with four puppies tucked in around them. They love being part of a pack."

Sally Kimber, Coachbarn Beagles, Kent: "Mine can tell the time. The pips on Radio 4 at 8am mean its breakfast and the chimes of Big Ben at 6pm mean "dinner," when they fly to the food cupboard and bark. They don't usually bark and certainly not to the doorbell, not to visitors, delivery drivers, postman nor the paper boy, who comes too early for them anyway!

"They also know that if I pick up my glasses and mobile phone from the kitchen – it has to be both - then we're going out. This elicits a rush to the front porch where they sit on the bench for collar and lead to be put on and the treats to be collected.

"I've seen some Beagles mentioned on Facebook that only go to sleep when their head is buried in a blanket or under a pillow and there was the Beagle that peered round the back of the TV when he saw "One Man And His Dog" on the screen!"

Photo: Sally demonstrates the correct way to hold a Beagle puppy, ably assisted by seven-week-old Coachbarn Callum.

Veterinarian Dr Samantha Goldberg, of Molesend Beagles, County Durham, said: "Restive, our first Beagle, ticked all the boxes for naughty Beagle behaviour.

"On one occasion we had a call from the hotel dining room at the end of the road. Restive had climbed a wall and headed into the dining room and was harassing the guests for food!

"On another occasion we were visiting my parents a few months before getting married. We heard a yell from my mother to discover Restive had climbed onto a chair, then on to the top of the freezer top, up to the shelf above and eaten half of the top tier of our wedding cake!

"My mother had made the fruit cake tiers and laced them with brandy. Needless to say despite the dried fruit and brandy, Restive was not ill!"

She also warned against using bonemeal fertiliser – Restive used to dig up the plants and eat that too!

Lori Norman added: "Imagine my shock when I found my 13-inch female Sweetie on TOP of the refrigerator. I had left a piece of dog cookie on top of it and she had smelled it.

"I'd also placed a 12-pack of soda on the floor by the trash can. Sweetie had jumped from the top of the soda cartons on to the top of the trash can, then on to the top of the counter. She went around the counter, over the sink and stove to the countertop microwave. From the top of the microwave she jumped on top of the refrigerator. Now, that is a good nose, thought process, and food motivation!"

"Damn near gave me a heart attack when she jumped down from the top of refrigerator...but luckily she was OK."

Karen Simkin, Simeldaka Beagles, London: "They have a very even temperament, they are such loyal companions and always know when their owner needs a hug.

"My husband David was in hospital for a month in 2015. He was allowed home, but confined to bed. I took our oldest Beagle, Nala (aged 10), upstairs to him - she was always a Daddy's girl. David was propped up in bed with metal framework all over his legs.

"Nala ran in the room, stood still for a moment and then jumped up and down at the side of the bed like a child, making a lot of excitable noises. She then jumped on the bed and both David and her were in a total embrace, kissing each other. Needless to say neither David nor I could control our tears!"

Our photo shows Nala with her beloved David on her 13th birthday

"Throughout the next few weeks she spent so much time on the bed with him, always careful where she lay, but giving comfort. We nicknamed her 'Nurse Nala.' She lived until 13-and-a-half. We talk about her so much, what a character."

8. Basic Training

Raising a young dog is not unlike bringing up a child. Put lots of time in early on to work towards a good mutual understanding and you'll be rewarded with a well-adjusted, sociable member of the family who you can take anywhere.

Some Beagles are more independent and scent-driven than others, and energy levels vary greatly from one Beagle to the next, so training should always be tailored to meet the needs of the individual dog.

A well-trained Beagle doesn't magically appear overnight - it requires lots of time and patience on your part. Beagles are super family dogs and companions, but let yours behave exactly how he or she wants and you could finish up with a stubborn, attention-seeking and overweight adult who rules YOU!

Beagles are highly motivated by rewards, particularly food. But you shouldn't discount the power of praise and playtime.

They are also hounds, and hounds are known for having an independent streak. This is because they have been selectively bred to use their initiative and work independently away from their masters while hunting.

Beagles are not like Border Collies, who hang on your every word, desperate to please you. With training, you have to persuade your Beagle that what YOU want him to do is actually what HE wants to do, because good things will happen.

Beagles like a challenge and a job to keep them occupied. They enjoy games, activities, competitions and, of course, their favourite pastime when not eating: following a scent!

All of these can help to keep Beagles stimulated and improve their interest and receptiveness to training.

Beagles have an amazing ability to focus on one thing - as you will discover when you try to call yours back when they are nose to the ground locked on to a scent — it's almost impossible unless you've spent LOTS of time instilling the Recall. However, this focus can be channelled if you put in the time to make training fun and interesting.

 Bear in mind that Beagles are greedy and affectionate. Give yours a chance to shine; praise and reward him often until the particular training task becomes ingrained.

Shouting, scolding or physical punishment will have the opposite effect. Beagles switch off or otherwise respond poorly to rough or negative training methods. The secret of good training can be summed up in four words:

- 🐾 Consistency
- 🐾 Reward
- 🐾 Praise
- 🐾 Patience

Tip Police and service dogs are trained to a very high level with only a ball for reward. Don't always use treats with your Beagle; praise or play time can be enough. Also, try getting your pup used to a small piece of carrot or apple as a healthy treat.

The Intelligence of Dogs

Psychologist and canine expert Dr Stanley Coren has written a book called *The Intelligence of Dogs* in which he ranks the breeds. He surveyed dog trainers to compile the list and used *Understanding of New Commands* and *Obeying First Command* as his standards of intelligence. He says there are three types of dog intelligence:

* Adaptive Intelligence (learning and problem-solving ability). Specific to the individual dog and is measured by canine IQ tests

* Instinctive Intelligence. Specific to the individual dog and is measured by canine IQ tests

* Working/Obedience Intelligence. This is breed-dependent

He divides dogs into six groups and the brainboxes of the canine world are the 10 breeds ranked in the 'Brightest Dogs' section of his list. It will come as no surprise to anyone who has ever been into the countryside and seen sheep being worked by a farmer and his right-hand man (his dog) to learn that the Border Collie is the most intelligent of all dogs.

Number Two is the Poodle, followed by the German Shepherd, Golden Retriever, Doberman Pinscher, Shetland Sheepdog, Papillon, Rottweiler and Australian Cattle Dog. All dogs in this class:

* Understand New Commands with Fewer than Five Repetitions

* Obey a First Command 95% of the Time or Better

You will be very disappointed to read that Beagles (no distinction between sizes) are ranked 132 out of 138 breeds. They are in the last group:

* Lowest Degree of Working/Obedience Intelligence

* Understanding of new commands: 80 to 100 repetitions or more.

* Obey first command: 25% of the time or worse

The full list can be seen here: https://en.wikipedia.org/wiki/The_Intelligence_of_Dogs

By the author's own admission, the drawback of this rating scale is that it is heavily weighted towards obedience-related behavioural traits often found in working dogs, rather than understanding or creativity found in hunting dogs like the Beagle.

As a result, many hounds and Terriers are ranked low on the list due to their independent or stubborn nature.

This does NOT mean that Beagles are stupid. In fact the opposite it true – they are known for being smart AND creative. It does mean, however, that you've got your work cut out when it comes to training!

Specialist Beagle trainer Kellie Wynn gives a wonderful insight into the Beagle mind and some step-by-step guidance **in Chapter 9. SpecialistTraining.**

Five Golden Rules

1. Training must be reward-based, not punishment based.

2. Keep sessions short or your dog will get bored.

3. Never train when you are in a rush or a bad mood.

4. Training after exercise is fine, but never train when your dog is exhausted.

5. Keep sessions fun

Energetic, stubborn or independent Beagles may try to push the boundaries when they reach adolescence – any time between six months and two years old. They may start behaving badly, and some males may start "marking" or urinating in the house, even when they are housetrained. In all cases, go back to basics and put the time in – sadly, there is no quick fix. You need to be firm with a strong-willed or stubborn dog, but all training should still be carried out using positive techniques.

Tip **Establishing the natural order of things is not something forced on a dog through shouting or violence; it is brought about by mutual consent and good training.**

Dogs are happiest and behave best when they are familiar and comfortable with their place in the household. If you have adopted an older dog, you can still train him, but it will take a little longer to get rid of bad habits and instil good manners. Patience and persistence are the keys here.

Socialisation is a very important aspect of training. A good breeder will have already begun this process with the litter and then it's up to you to keep it going when puppy arrives home. Young pups can absorb a great deal of information, but they are also vulnerable to bad experiences.

They need exposing – in a positive manner - to different people, other animals and situations. If not, they can find them very frightening when they do finally encounter them later.

If they have a lot of good experiences with other people, places, noises, situations and animals before four or five months old, they are less likely to either be timid or nervous or try to establish dominance later. Don't just leave your dog at home in the early days, take him out and about with you, get him used to new people, places and noises. Dogs that miss out on being socialised can pay the price later.

All pups are chewers. If you are not careful, some young pups and adolescents will chew through anything – wires, phone chargers, remote controls, bedding, rugs, etc. Young dogs are not infrequent visitors to veterinary clinics to have *"foreign objects"* removed from their stomachs. Train your young pup only to chew the things you give – so don't give him your old slippers, an old piece of carpet or anything that resembles something you don't want him to chew, he won't know the difference between the old and the new. Buy purpose-made long-lasting chew toys.

A puppy class is one of the best ways of getting a pup used to being socialised and trained. This should be backed up by short sessions of a few minutes of training a day back home. Beagles are great family dogs for anyone prepared to put in a fair bit of time to train one.

Tip Most Beagle puppies, especially those with a lot of working instinct, can be "mouthy." Do not give your young pup too much attention, and choose training times when he is relaxed, perhaps slightly tired, but not exhausted.

If you do need some professional one-on-one help (for you and the dog), choose a Beagle specialist and/or a trainer registered with the Association of Professional Dog Trainers (APDT) or other positive method organisation, as the old Alpha-dominance theories have gone out the window.

17 Training Tips

1. **Start training and socialising straight away**. Like babies, puppies learn quickly and it's this learned behaviour that stays with them through adult life. Start with just a few minutes a day a couple of days after arriving home.

2. **Your voice is a very important training tool.** Your dog has to learn to understand your language and you have to understand him. Commands should be issued in a calm, authoritative voice - not shouted. Praise should be given in a happy, encouraging voice, accompanied by stroking or patting. If your dog has done something wrong, use a stern voice, not a harsh shriek. This applies even if your Beagle is unresponsive at the beginning.

3. **Avoid giving your dog commands you know you can't enforce** or he learns that commands are optional. Give your dog only one command - twice maximum - then gently enforce it. Repeating commands will make him tune out; telling your dog to *"SIT, SIT, SIT, SIT!!!"* is neither efficient nor effective. Say a single *"SIT,"* gently place him in the Sit position and praise him.

4. **Train gently and humanely.** Beagles can be sensitive and do not respond well to being shouted at or hit.

5. **Keep training sessions short and upbeat.** If obedience training is a bit of a bore, pep things up a bit by *"play training"* by using constructive, non-adversarial games.

6. **Do not try to dominate your dog.** Training should be mutual, i.e. your dog should do something because he WANTS to do it and he knows that you want him to do it. Beagles are not interested in dominating you – although they often try and push the boundaries, especially in adolescence.

7. **Begin training at home around the house and garden/yard**. How well your dog responds at home affects his behaviour away from the home. If he doesn't respond well at home, he certainly won't respond any better out and about where there are 101 distractions, e.g. interesting scents, food scraps, other dogs, people, small animals or birds.

8. **Mealtimes are a great time to start training.** Teach Sit and Stay at breakfast and dinner, rather than just putting the dish down and letting him dash over immediately.

9. **Use his name often and in a positive manner** so he gets used to the sound of it. He won't know what it means at first, but it won't take long before he realises you're talking to him.

10. **DON'T use his name when reprimanding, warning or punishing.** He should trust that when he hears his name, good things happen. He should always respond to his name with enthusiasm, never hesitancy or fear. Use words such as *"No," "Ack!"* or *"Bad Boy/Girl"* in a stern (not shouted) voice instead. Some parents prefer not to use "No" with their dog, as they use it so often around the kids that it can confuse the pup!

11. **In the beginning, give your dog attention when YOU want to – not when he wants it.** When you are training, give your puppy lots of positive attention when he is good. But if he starts jumping up, nudging you constantly or barking to demand your attention, ignore him. Wait a while and pat him when you are ready and AFTER he has stopped demanding your attention.

12. **You can give Beagles TOO MUCH attention in the beginning.** This may create a rod for your own back when they grow into needy adults that are over-reliant on you. They may even develop Separation Anxiety, which is stressful for both dog AND owner.

13. **Don't give your dog lots of attention (even negative attention) when he misbehaves.** Beagles love your attention and if yours gets lots when he's naughty, you are inadvertently reinforcing bad behaviour.

14. **Timing is critical.** When your puppy does something right, praise him immediately. If you wait a while, he will have no idea what he has done right. Similarly, when he does something wrong, correct him straight away.

15. **If he has an "accident" in the house, don't shout or rub his nose in it; it will have the opposite effect with a Beagle.** He may start hiding and peeing or pooping behind the couch or other inappropriate places. **If you catch him in the act**, use your *"No!"* or *"Ack!"* sound and immediately carry him out of the house. Then back to basics with housetraining. If you find something but don't catch him in the act, ignore it. If your pup is constantly eliminating indoors, you are not keeping a close enough eye on him.

16. **Start as you mean to go on.** In terms of training, treat your cute little pup as though he were fully-grown. Introduce the rules you want him to live by as an adult.

17. **Make sure that everybody in the household sticks to the same set of rules.** If the kids lift him on to the couch or bed and you forbid it, your dog won't know what is allowed and what isn't.

....

Teaching Basic Commands

The Three Ds

The three Ds – **Distance, Duration** and **Distraction** – are the cornerstone of a good training technique.

Duration is the length of time your dog remains in the command.

Distance is how far you can walk away without your dog breaking the command.

Distraction is the number of external stimuli - such as noise, scents, people, other animals, etc. - your dog can tolerate before breaking the command.

Only increase one of the Three Ds at a time. For example, if your new pup has just learned to sit on command, gradually increase the time by a second or two as you go along. Moving away from the dog or letting the kids or the cat into the room would increase the Distance or Distraction level and make the command too difficult for your pup to hold.

If you are teaching the Stay, gradually increase EITHER the distance OR the time he is in the Stay position; don't increase both at once.

Start off by training your dog in your home before moving into the garden or yard where there are more distractions - even if it is quiet and you are alone, outdoor scents and sights will be a big distraction for a young dog. Once you have mastered the commands in a home environment, progress to the park.

 Implement the Three Ds progressively and slowly, and don't expect too much too soon. Work within your dog's capabilities, move forward one tiny step at a time and set your dog up to consistently SUCCEED, not fail.

Treats

Different treats have different values and using them at the right time will help you to get the best out of your dog:

1. **High Value Food** is human food - usually animal-based - such as sausage, ham, chicken, liver and cheese. All should be cooked if raw and cut into pea-sized treats – you're looking to reward your dog, not feed him! Place the tiny treats in a freezer bag in the freezer, which keeps them fresh, then you can grab a handful when you go out training. There's not much water content and they quickly thaw.

   When training, we want our dog to want more High Value Food. He smells and tastes it on his tongue but it is gone in a flash, leaving him wanting more. *So, all treats should be only as large as a pea - even if you're training a Great Dane!*

2. **Medium Value Food** such as moist pet shop treats or a healthy alternative like sliced apple or carrot.

3. **Low Value Food** such as kibble. Use your dog's own food if you feed dry, or buy a small bag if not.

IMPORTANT: Whenever you are asking your dog **to do something new,** make it worth his while. Offer a High Value treat like liver. Once your dog understands what you are asking, you can move down to Medium Value treat.

When he does it every time use Low Value... reducing the frequency after a while and then only give it every other time... then only occasionally until you have slowly stopped giving any treat when asking for that task.

The aim at this point is to start getting you in control of your dog. And, most importantly, we want your dog to want to be controlled, as control brings good things.

The Sit

Teaching the Sit command to your Beagle is relatively easy. Teaching a young pup to sit still for any length of time is a bit more difficult! If your little protégé is very distracted or high energy, it may be easier to put him on a lead (leash) to hold his attention.

1. **Stand facing each other and hold a treat between your thumb and fingers just an inch or so above his head** and let him sniff it. Don't let your fingers and the treat get much further away or you might have trouble getting him to move his body into a sitting position. In fact, if your dog jumps up when you try to guide him into the Sit, you're probably holding your hand too far away from his nose. If your dog backs up, you can practise with a wall behind him.

2. **As he reaches up to sniff it, move the treat upwards and back over the dog** towards his tail at the same time as saying *"Sit."* Most dogs will track the treat with their eyes and follow it with their noses, causing their noses to point straight up.

3. **As his head moves up toward the treat, his rear end should automatically go down towards the floor.** TaDa! (drum roll!).

4. **The second he sits, say *"Yes!"*** Give him the treat and tell your dog he's a good boy/girl. Stroke and praise him for as long as he stays in the sitting position.

5. **If he jumps up on his back legs** and paws you while you are moving the treat, be patient and start all over again. At this stage, don't expect your bouncy little pupil to sit for more than a nanosecond!

NOTE: For positive reinforcement, use the words *Yes!, Good Boy!* or *Good Girl!*

Another method is to put one hand on his chest and with your other hand, gently push down on his rear end until he is sitting, while saying *"Sit."* Give him a treat and praise; he will eventually associate the position with the word "sit."

Once your dog catches on, leave the treat in your pocket (or have it in your other hand). Repeat, but this time your dog will just follow your empty hand. Say *"Sit"* and bring your empty hand in front of your dog's nose. Move your hand exactly as you did when you held the treat. When your dog sits, say *"Yes!"* and then give him a treat from your other hand or your pocket.

Gradually lessen the amount of movement with your hand. First, say *"Sit"* then hold your hand eight to 10 inches above your dog's face and wait a moment. Most likely, he will sit. If he doesn't, help him by moving your hand back over his head, like you did before, but make a smaller movement this time. Then try again. Your goal is to eventually just say *"Sit"* without having to move or extend your hand at all.

Once your dog reliably sits on cue, you can ask him to sit whenever you meet people (it may not work straight away, but it might help to calm him down a bit). The key is anticipation. Give your dog the cue before he gets too excited to hear you and before he starts jumping up on the person just arrived. Generously reward him the instant he sits.

The Stay

This is a very useful command, but it's not so easy to teach a lively and distracted young Beagle pup - don't ask him to stay for more than a few seconds at the beginning.

This requires concentration from your dog, so pick a time when he's relaxed and well-exercised, or just after a game or mealtimes - but not too exhausted to concentrate.

1. **Tell your dog to sit or lie down,** but instead of giving a treat as soon as he hits the floor, hold off for one second. Then say *"Yes!"* in an enthusiastic voice and give him a treat. If your dog bounces up again instantly, have two treats ready. Feed one right away, before he has time to move; then say *"Yes!"* and feed the second treat.

2. **You need a release word or phrase.** It might be *"Free!"* or *"Here!"* Once you've given the treat, immediately say the word and encourage your dog to get up. Repeat the exercise a few times, gradually waiting a tiny bit longer before releasing the treat. (You can delay the first treat for a moment if your dog bounces up).

3. **A common mistake is to hold the treat high and then give the reward slowly.** As your dog doesn't know the command yet, he sees the treat coming and gets up to meet the food. Instead, bring the treat toward your dog quickly - the best place to deliver it is right between his front paws. If you're working on a Sit-Stay, give the treat at chest height.

4. **When your dog can stay for several seconds, start to add a little distance.** At first, you'll walk backwards, because your dog is more likely to get up to follow you if you turn away from him. Take one single step away, then step back towards your dog and say *"Yes!"* and give the treat. Give him the signal to get up immediately, even if five seconds haven't passed.

5. **Remember DISTANCE, DURATION, DISTRACTION.** Work on one factor at a time. Whenever you make one factor more difficult, ease up on the others then build them back up. So, when you add distance, cut the duration of the stay.

6. Once he's mastered the Stay with you alone, **move the training on so that he learns to do the same with distractions.** Have someone walk into the room, or squeak a toy or bounce a ball once. A rock-solid stay is mostly a matter of working slowly and patiently to start with. Don't go too fast. If he does get up, take a breather and then give him a short refresher, starting at a point easier than whatever you were working on when he cracked.

 If you think he's tired or had enough, leave it for the day and come back later – just finish off on a positive note by giving one very easy command you know he will obey, followed by a reward.

Don't use the Stay command in situations where it is unpleasant for your dog. For instance, avoid telling him to stay as you close the door behind you on your way to work.

Finally, don't use Stay to keep a dog in a scary situation.

Down

There are a number of different ways to teach this command, which here means for the dog to lie down. (If you are teaching this command, then use the *"Off"* command to teach your dog not to jump up). This does not come naturally to a young pup, so it may take a little while to master.

Don't make it a battle of wills and, although you may gently push him down, don't physically force him down against his will. This will be seen as you asserting dominance in an aggressive manner and your Beagle will not like it.

1. Give the Sit command.

2. **When your dog sits, don't give him the treat immediately**, but keep it in your closed hand. Slowly move your hand straight down toward the floor, between his front legs. As your Beagle's nose follows the treat, just like a magnet, his head will bend all the way down to the floor.

1. When the treat is on the floor between your dog's paws, start to move it away from him, like you're drawing a line along the floor. (The entire luring motion forms an L-shape).

2. At the same time say *"Down"* in a firm manner.

3. To continue to follow the treat, your dog will probably ease himself into the Down position. The instant his elbows touch the floor, say *"Yes!"* and immediately let him eat the treat. If your dog doesn't automatically stand up after eating the treat, just move a step or two away to encourage him to move out of the Down position.

Repeat the sequence above several times. Aim for two short sessions of five minutes per day.

If your dog's back end pops up, quickly snatch the treat away. Then immediately say Sit and try again. It may help to let him nibble on the treat as you move it toward the floor. If you've tried to lure your dog into a Down, but he still seems confused or reluctant, try this trick:

1. Sit down on the floor with your legs straight out in front of you. Your dog should be at your side. Keeping your legs together and your feet on the floor, bend your knees to make a 'tent' shape.

2. Hold a treat right in front of your dog's nose. As he licks and sniffs the treat, slowly move it down to the floor and then underneath your legs. Continue to lure him until he has to crouch down to keep following the treat.

3. The instant his belly touches the floor, say *"Yes!"* and let him eat the treat. If your dog seems nervous about following the treat under your legs, make a trail of treats for him to eat along the way.

Some dogs find it easier to follow a treat into the Down from a standing position.

🐾 Hold the treat right in front of your dog's nose, and then slowly move it straight down to the floor, right between his front paws. His nose will follow the treat

🐾 If you let him lick the treat as you continue to hold it still on the floor, your dog will probably plop into the Down position

🐾 The moment he does, say *"Yes!"* and let him eat the treat (some dogs are reluctant to lie on a cold, hard surface. It may be easier to teach yours to lie down on a carpet). The next step is to introduce a hand signal. You'll still reward him with treats, though, so keep them nearby or hidden behind your back.

1. Start with your dog in a Sit.

2. Say *"Down."*

3. **Without** a treat in your fingers, use the same hand motion you did before. As soon as your dog's elbows touch the floor, say *"Yes!"* and immediately get a treat to give him.

   Important: Even though you're not using a treat to lure your dog into position, you must still give a reward when he lies down. You want him to learn that he doesn't have to see a treat to get one.

4. Clap your hands or take a few steps away to encourage him to stand up. Then repeat the sequence from the beginning several times for a week or two. When your dog readily lies down as soon as you say the cue and use your new hand signal, you're ready for the next step.

 To stop bending all the way down to the floor every time, you can gradually shrink the signal to a smaller movement. To make sure your dog continues to understand what you want him to do, progress slowly.

5. Repeat the hand signal, but instead of moving your hand all the way to the floor, move it ALMOST all the way down. Stop when it's an inch or two above the floor. Practise the Down for a day or two, using this slightly smaller hand signal. Then you can make your movement an inch or two smaller, stopping your hand three or four inches above the floor.

6. After practising for another couple of days, shrink the signal again. As you continue to gradually stop your hand signal farther and farther from the floor, you'll bend over less and less. Eventually, you won't have to bend over at all. You'll be able to stand up straight, say *"Down,"* and then just point to the floor.

Your next job is harder: practise your dog's new skill in different situations and locations. Start with calm places, like different rooms in your house or your garden/yard when there's no one around. Then increase the distractions; so, do some sessions at home when family members are moving around, on walks and then at friends' houses, too.

Basic Recall

This basic command is perhaps the most important of all - and definitely one of the hardest with a Beagle. It will require lots and lots of repetition and patience on your part, but you are limiting both your lives if you can't let your Beagle do what he was born to do; run free.

A Beagle who obeys the Recall enjoys freedoms that other dogs cannot. Beagles love to run free, but don't allow yours off-lead beyond fenced areas until he has learned some Recall. If your Beagle has strong hunting instincts, you will have your work cut out, but it is by no means impossible!

Beagle trainer Kellie Wynn has some specific advice for Beagle owners teaching Recall in the next chapter, but here are the basics. Kellie also recommends training to the whistle and fitting your independent-minded pupil with a GPS tracker, see **Chapter 9.**

Tip **Whether you have a puppy or an older dog, the first step is always to establish that coming to you is the BEST thing he can do.**

Any time your dog comes to you - whether you've called him or not - acknowledge that you appreciate it with praise, affection, play or treats. This consistent reinforcement ensures that your dog will continue to "check in" with you frequently.

1. Start off a short distance away from your dog.

2. Say your dog's name followed by the command *"Come!"* in an enthusiastic voice. You'll usually be more successful if you walk or run away from him while you call. Dogs find it hard to resist chasing after a running person, especially their owner.

3. He should run towards you!

4. A young dog will often start running towards you but then get distracted and head off in another direction. Pre-empt this situation by praising your puppy and cheering him on when he starts to come to you and **before** he has a chance to get distracted.

    Your praise will keep him focused so that he'll be more likely to come all the way to you. If he stops or turns away, you can give him feedback by saying *"Oh-oh!"* or *"Hey!"* in a different tone of voice (displeased or unpleasantly surprised). When he looks at you again, smile, call him and praise him as he approaches you.

5. When your puppy comes to you, give him the treat BEFORE he sits down or he may think that the treat was earned for sitting, not coming to you.

6. Another method is to use two people. You hold the treats and let your dog sniff them while the accomplice holds on to the dog by his harness. When you are about 10 or 15 yards away, get your helper to let the dog go, and once he is running towards you, say *"COME!"* loudly and enthusiastically.

    When he reaches you, stop, bend down and make a fuss of him before giving a treat. Do this several times. The next step is to give the Come command just BEFORE you get your helper to release the dog, and by doing this repetitively, the dog begins to associate the command with the action.

NOTE: "Come" or a similar word is better than "Here" if you intend using the "Heel" command, as "Here" and "Heel" sound very similar.

Progress your dog's training in baby steps. If he's learned to come when called in your kitchen, you can't expect him to do it straight away at the park, in the woods or on the beach when surrounded by distractions. When you first use the Recall outdoors, make sure there's no one around to distract your dog.

Tip It's a good idea to consider using a long training lead - or to do the training within a safe, fenced area. Only when your dog has mastered the Recall in a number of locations and in the face of various distractions can you expect him to come to you regularly.

Collar and Lead (Leash) Training

You have to train your dog to get used to a collar and lead, then teach him to walk nicely beside you. This can be challenging with young Beagles, who don't necessarily want to walk at the same pace as you - some puppies might even slump to the ground and refuse to move in the beginning!

All dogs will pull on a lead initially. It's not because they want to show you who's boss, it's simply that they are excited to be out and are forging ahead.

You will need a small collar to start off with. Some puppies don't mind collars, some will try to fight them, while others will lie on the floor. You need to be patient and calm and proceed at a pace comfortable to him; don't fight your dog and don't force the collar on.

1. Start your puppy off with a lightweight collar and give praise or a treat once the collar is on, not after you have taken it off. Gradually increase the length of time you leave the collar on.

 If you leave your dog in a crate, or leave him alone in the house, take off the collar and tags. He is not used to it and it may get caught, causing panic or injury.

2. Put the collar on when there are other things that will occupy him, like when he is going outside to be with you, when you are interacting with him, at mealtimes or when you are doing some basic training. Don't put it on too tight, you want him to forget it's there; **you should be able to get two fingers underneath.**

Some pups may react as if you've hung a two-ton weight around their necks, while others will be more compliant. If yours scratches the collar, get his attention by encouraging him to follow you or play with a toy to forget the irritation.

3. Once your puppy is happy wearing the collar, introduce the lead. Many owners prefer an extending or retractable lead for their Beagle, but consider a fixed-length one to start training him to walk close to you. Begin in the house or garden; don't try to go out and about straight away.

 Think of the lead as a safety device to stop him running off, not something to drag him around with. You want a Beagle that doesn't pull, so don't start by pulling him around.

4. Attach the lead and give him a treat while you put it on. Use the treats (instead of pulling on the lead) to lure him beside you, so that he gets used to walking with the collar and lead on.

You can also make good use of toys to do exactly the same thing - especially if your dog has a favourite. Walk around the house with the lead on and lure him forwards with the toy.

It might feel a bit odd but it's a good way for your pup to develop a positive relationship with the collar and lead with the minimum of fuss. Act as though it's the most natural thing in the world for you to walk around the house with your dog on a lead – and just hope the neighbours aren't watching!

Some dogs react the moment you attach the lead and they feel some tension on it – a bit like when a horse is being broken for the first time. Drop the lead and allow him to run around the house or yard, dragging it behind, but be careful he doesn't get tangled and hurt himself. Try to make him forget about it by playing or starting a short fun training routine with treats. While he is concentrating on the new task, occasionally pick up the lead and call him to you. Do it gently and in an encouraging tone.

5. **Don't yank on the lead.** If it gets tight, just lure him back beside you with a treat or a toy. Remember to keep the hand holding the treat or toy down, so your dog doesn't get the habit of jumping up. If you feel he is getting stressed, try putting treats along the route you'll be taking to turn this into a rewarding game: good times are ahead... and he learns to focus on what's ahead of him with curiosity, not fear.

Darlene Stewart, Chairperson, Health and Genetics Committee, National Beagle Club of America, says: "I agree with starting collar and leash training in the house and yard, but I don't try to lead the puppy. I follow puppy and let him lead me at first. Then I start stopping and calling them to me for a treat.

"As the puppy becomes more comfortable coming to me standing still, I then start backing up as the puppy comes to me, so they learn to keep coming to me even with tension on the leash. This is first step in teaching them to follow me. I am starting to "lead" them."

"I never recommend a standard buckle collar for leash training, I use a **martingale** like this one, **pictured.** They are a good choice in between a choke and regular collar and are more difficult for a Beagle to back out of or escape by slipping it over their heads. You can get them in smaller sizes and adjust them.

"I also use them for adult dogs. If someone does not want to use a choke, then this is what I suggest. Note that it is not to be left on the dog at all times, just when on the leash."

On collars for adult Beagles, she added: "Personally, I do not recommend collars with clips, I always suggest a buckle collar. Dogs get used to the weight and also to you handling it. There have been dogs that have jerked on a clip collar and broken it - and once broken, the dog is loose.

"I also do NOT leave a collar with tags or anything dangling on my Beagles. The tags may catch on many things, including heating vents in floor, nails on boards, tree branches, etc. Keep tags in a file at home, but put a paper copy of tags and tag paperwork in your wallet and in the car. Use a flat buckle collar with ID plate," **pictured.**

Vet Dr Samantha Goldberg, Kennel Club Health Co-ordinator for the UK Beagle Clubs, added: "In the UK it is law to wear a collar with tag on - hardly anyone uses plates, although I agree with Darlene that they are less likely to cause an issue. Our tags are on the D ring but attached by a thick metal ring which will pull open if it gets snagged."

Take collar and lead training slowly. Let him gain confidence in you, the lead and himself. Some dogs sit and decide not to move! If this happens, walk a few steps away, go down on one knee and encourage him to come to you, then walk off again.

Some dogs are perfectly happy to walk alongside you off-lead, but behave differently when they have one on. Others may become more excitable or aggressive on a lead once they gain their confidence when their **Fight-or-Flight** instinct kicks in.

NOTE: A collar is essential for any Beagle who becomes nervous or aggressive in a veterinary clinic. You and the vet will have more control.

Choke Collars

Once relatively common, choke collars are nowadays being used less and less by breeders, owners and trainers, particularly in the UK.

Dr Goldberg says: "Show dogs may be shown in the ring using a light chain or half choke collar with a chain. However, they are taught to walk on a normal collar and lead first and the movement in a show ring is in a controlled environment where they are unlikely to take off and no pulling is used at all.

"Otherwise, in my opinion, choke collars are outdated and there are much better collars which can be used. I use Rogz collars which are secure most of the time for walking my Beagles.

"Beagles are generally not that big; their ideal weight varies according to size, but when they are the correct weight, they range up to a maximum of 17kg (37lb) and so a choke collar for control shouldn't be necessary. Early training means Beagles will generally walk very well on a normal collar and lead. Choke collars can literally choke and cause damage to the throat and trachea."

One thing is certain: choke collars are not for newbies. Breeders, people who show dogs and other canine experts who do use choke collars and slip leads are all experienced dog handlers. If you are considering a choke collar or are worried about your dog slipping his collar while on the lead, we recommend you first try either the **martingale** or the **half choke** (also called **half check**), **pictured.**

Headcollars (Halters)

One option to control an adult dog pulling on the lead is to use a headcollar; the theory being that if you have control of the head, you have control of the dog. When the dog pulls, it turns him, so he stops pulling as he is facing the wrong way. Always make sure a headcollar is fitted properly, it should not restrict breathing nor be too close to the eyes.

Some Beagles really don't like headcollars. One owner said: "When I tried one of the head harnesses on Jubilee, she hated it and would fight it the whole way. Once she just tipped over in the grass like she'd been shot. Wouldn't move, blink or twitch!" Spend time getting your dog used to one – with patience, praise and bribes.

NOTE: A headcollar is NOT for general training, it is for using with adult dogs that pull. As it stays tight whether he pulls or not, you are not teaching your dog anything – although he may pull less.

Use with restraint, as yanking on the headcollar can cause neck or back injuries – particularly if the dog gets to the end of a long extendable lead and is suddenly pulled back. Beagles naturally put their heads to the floor to sniff. If using a headcollar, don't pull his head back every time he does this. Use the headcollar, **pictured,** to control pulling, not sniffing.

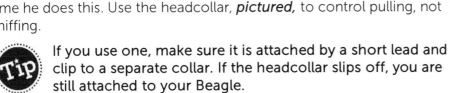

If you use one, make sure it is attached by a short lead and clip to a separate collar. If the headcollar slips off, you are still attached to your Beagle.

Harnesses

Opinions vary as to whether harnesses are a good thing for Beagles. Certainly, many owners and breeders use them, but before deciding, here are some points to consider from Dr Goldberg:

"The question of whether to put a collar or harness on a Beagle is frequently asked by new owners. The question that I see a lot is, "What type of harness shall I buy for my Beagle?" Before making a decision, it is important to understand all the following information:

"Beagles are a hunting breed but not a tracking breed. When out being walked they will follow scents and often pull towards interesting smells. This is natural to them and not a personal thing against their owner! The ideal life for a Beagle is to have controlled exercise and some off-lead time to behave instinctually.

"If your Beagle pulls, changing to a harness will not stop the pulling. You need to train your dog to walk correctly on a lead and it is entirely possible to teach a Beagle not to pull whilst wearing a collar.

"For a Beagle who does pull a lot, a headcollar-type lead such as a Gencol or Gentle Leader can be used. Initially the Beagle may try and rub this off, but with encouragement and rewards for walking properly (a small treat and verbal encouragement), your Beagle will walk well.

"Harnesses were originally developed for working dogs in different roles. Thus tracking dogs, such as Bloodhounds looking for missing people or fallen deer, need freedom to move as they follow a scent. A harness is easier for them to move without being distracted by the handler - but the handler still has an attachment to the dog. You will see videos of people tracking missing people with a long line attached. These dogs are not walking beside a road.

"Dogs such as Siberian Huskies and Alaskan Malamutes pull sleds and harnesses allow them to exert more power and pull more weight, or free a sled caught in ice. Neither of these reasons - freedom to move and to exert more power - make a harness easier to walk your Beagle!

"Many fashion harnesses impede natural movement of the shoulder joints. Reasons given on social media to use a harness include:

- It will stop your dog pulling - false
- It will make your dog behave better - false
- It will stop your dog hurting their neck
- They are safer

"In some VERY SPECIFIC cases, a reduction in pain may be true. For example, using a harness is essential to aid recovery for dogs with Intervertebral Disc Disease (IVDD). Beagles who have had Steroid Responsive Meningitis (SRM) will be more comfortable on a harness during the recovery phase. SRM produces neck and head pain, so this makes sense. However, once recovered they are the same as any other Beagle.

"Harnesses can actually be more detrimental to comfort than a traditional collar. Any harness that is worn should consist of a collar part, nothing around the shoulders and a secure band around the rib cage. Avoid the big heavy harnesses which wrap around the front of the dog as these can prevent the shoulder joint from moving normally.

"When you fit a harness make sure it has a safe collar part which the dog cannot escape from (or attach it to a collar) and that it is tight enough elsewhere to avoid slipping out. Once you have fitted it on your dog, stretch out their forelegs in it and make sure it doesn't impinge on the dog's ability to walk.

"If you need to use one, the ideal type will look like two collars in parallel with a connection between the dogs front legs and one at the top," *(like the one pictured).*

Darlene agrees: "A harness with a front strap that goes directly across the chest interferes with proper shoulder movement and can result in extra pressure on the back and neck.

She adds: "If I am using a harness, I use a step-in harness. I want a harness that has a clip at the top and also the rings for connecting the leash. If the clip was to come undone, the harness would not come off with the leash attached. Harnesses that clip on the side or underneath do not have that safety factor. I also always use a harness with another collar."

 If you've never used a harness before, it's easy to get tangled up while your Beagle is bouncing around, excited at the prospect of a walk. It's a good idea to have a few "dry runs" without the dog!

Lay the harness on the floor and familiarise yourself with it. Learn which bits the legs go through, which parts fit where and how it fits together once the dog is in. If you can train your Beagle to step into the harness, even better...!

Dealing with Common Problems

Puppy Biting and Chewing

Kellie Wynn advises on this in the following chapter. Here we explain why young Beagles nip and chew so much - and what you can do to discourage it.

All puppies spend a great deal of time chewing, playing, and investigating objects; it's natural for them to explore the world with their mouths and needle-sharp teeth. When puppies play with people, they often bite, chew, nip and mouthe on people's hands, limbs and clothing.

Play biting is normal for puppies; they do it all the time with their littermates. They also bite moving targets with their sharp teeth; it's a great game.

FACT ❭ **Most dogs originally bred to work, like the Beagle, are mouthy as pups.**

But when they arrive in your home, they have to be taught that human skin is sensitive and body parts are not suitable biting material. Biting is not acceptable, not even from a puppy, and can be a real problem initially, especially if you have children.

When your puppy bites you or the kids, he is playing and investigating; he is NOT being aggressive. A lively young pup can easily get carried away with energy and excitement.

Puppy biting should be dealt with from the get-go. Every time you have a play session, have a soft toy nearby and when he starts to chew your hand or feet, clench your fingers (or toes!) to make it more difficult and distract him with a soft toy in your other hand.

Keep the game interesting by moving the toy around or rolling it around in front of him. (He may be too young to fetch it back if you throw it). He may continue to chew you, but will eventually realise that the toy is far more interesting and livelier than your boring hand.

If he becomes over-excited and too aggressive with the toy, if he growls a lot, stop playing and walk away. When you walk away, don't say anything or make eye or physical contact with your puppy.

Simply ignore him, this is usually extremely effective and often works within a few days.

If your pup is more persistent and tries to bite your legs as you walk away, thinking this is another fantastic game, stand still and ignore him. If he still persists, say *"No!"* in a very stern voice, then praise him when he lets go. If you have to physically remove him from your trouser leg or shoe, leave him alone in the room for a while and ignore all demands for your attention.

 Try not to put your pup in a crate when he is being naughty, or he will associate the crate with punishment. Remove yourself or the pup from the room instead - or put him in a pen. Wait until he has stopped being naughty before you put him in his crate.

Although you might find it quite cute and funny if your puppy bites your fingers or toes, it should be discouraged at all costs. You don't want biting and nipping to get out of hand; as an adolescent or adult dog, he could inadvertently cause real injury, especially to children.

- Puppies growl and bite more when they are excited. Don't allow things to escalate, so remove your pup from the situation before he gets too excited by putting him in a crate or pen

- Don't put your hand or finger into your pup's mouth to nibble on; this promotes puppy biting

- Limit your children's play time with pup - and always supervise the sessions in the beginning. Teach them to gently play with and stroke your puppy, not to wind him up

- Don't let the kids (or adults) run around the house with the puppy chasing – this is an open invitation to nip at the ankles

- If your puppy does bite, remove him from the situation and people – never smack him

 Beagles are very affectionate and another tried and tested method is to make a sharp cry of "OUCH!" when your pup bites your hand – even when it doesn't hurt.

This has worked very well for us. Most pups will jump back in amazement, surprised to have hurt you. Divert your attention from your puppy to your hand. He will probably try to get your attention or lick you as a way of saying sorry. Praise him for stopping biting and continue with the game. If he bites you again, repeat the process. A sensitive dog should stop biting you.

You may also think about keeping special toys you use to play with your puppy separate from other toys he chews alone.

That way he can associate certain toys with having fun with you and may work harder to please you. Beagles are playful and you can use this to your advantage by teaching your dog how to play nicely with you and the toy, and then by using play time as a reward for good behaviour.

As well as biting, puppies also chew, it is a normal part of the teething process. Some adolescent and adult dogs chew because they are bored - usually due to lack of exercise and/or mental stimulation. If puppy chewing is a problem, it is because

your pup is chewing something you don't want him to.

So, the trick is to keep him, his mouth and sharp little teeth occupied with something he CAN chew on, such as a durable toy – see **Chapter 4. Bringing Puppy Home** for more information.

You might also consider freezing peanut butter and/or a liquid inside a Kong toy. Put the Kong into a mug, plug the small end with peanut butter and fill it with gravy before putting it into the freezer. (Check it doesn't contain the sweetener xylitol as this is harmful to dogs). Don't leave the Kong and your Beagle on your precious Oriental rug! This will keep your pup occupied for quite a long time.

It is also worth giving the dog a frozen Kong or Lickimat when you leave the house if he suffers from Separation Anxiety. There are lots of doggie recipes for Kongs and other treats online.

Excessive Barking

Beagles are hounds and there's no getting away from the fact that they are vocal - with a howl or whine that cuts right through you! They were bred to hunt and their bay (a howling bark with their nose in the air) alerts others that they are on the scent. If you want a dog that hardly barks, consider a Bulldog or a Greyhound.

You DO want your Beagle to bark. He will alert you to approaching strangers before you hear a thing - even if he immediately becomes their new best friend, especially if they have food!

The trick is to get him to bark at the right times and then to stop, as incessant barking will drive you and your neighbours nuts.

Dogs, especially youngsters, sometimes behave in ways you might not want them to until they learn that this type of unwanted behaviour doesn't earn any rewards.

Young Beagles can become overly-fond of the sound of their own voices - until they learn that when they stop their indiscriminate barking, good things happen, such as treats, praise, a game.

The problem often develops during adolescence when a dog becomes more confident.

 Also, puppies teethe until about seven or eight months of age, so make sure yours has hardy chews, and perhaps a bone with supervision, to keep him occupied and gnawing. Give these when he's quiet, not when he is barking.

Is your dog getting enough exercise and mental stimulation? Barking can be a way of letting off steam. Or he may be lonely, bored, attention-seeking, possessive or over-protective.

Sometimes it is the Beagle's alert system going into overdrive. Is he barking at people he can see through the window or coming to the door? You want an alert bark, but not a constant bark.

Your behaviour can also encourage excessive barking. If your dog barks his head off and you give him a treat to quieten down, he associates his barking with getting a nice treat.

Tone of voice is very important. Do not use a high-pitched or semi-hysterical STOP!! or NO!! Use low, firm commands.

One method is to set up a situation where you know he is going to bark, such as somebody arriving at your house, and put him on a lead beforehand. When he has barked several times, give a short, sharp tug on the lead and the **"Quiet"** command - spoken, not shouted. Reward him when he **stops** barking, not before.

If he's barking to get your attention, ignore him. If that doesn't work, leave the room and don't allow him to follow, so you deprive him of your attention.

Do this as well if his barking and attention-seeking turns to nipping. Tell him to **"Stop"** in a firm voice, or use the **"ACK!"** sound, remove your hand or leg and, if necessary, leave the room.

FACT As humans, we use our voice in many different ways: to express happiness or anger, to scold, to shout a warning, and so on. Dogs are the same; different barks and whines give out different messages.

LISTEN to your dog and try and get an understanding of Beagle language. Learn to recognise the difference between an alert bark, an excited bark, a demanding bark, a fearful, high-pitched bark, an aggressive bark or a plain *"I'm barking 'coz I can bark"* bark!

Speak and Shush!

The Speak and Shush technique teaches your dog or puppy to bark and be quiet on command. When your dog barks at an arrival at your house, gently praise him after the first few barks. If he persists, tell him **"Quiet."**

Get a friend to stand outside your front door and say **"Speak"** or **"Alert."** This is the cue for your accomplice to knock on the door or ring the bell – don't worry if you both feel like idiots, it will be worth the embarrassment!

When your dog barks, say **"Speak"** and praise him profusely. After a few good barks, say **"Shush"** or **"Quiet"** and then dangle a tasty treat in front of his nose. If he is food-motivated, he will stop barking as soon as he sniffs the treat, because it is **physically impossible for a dog to sniff and woof at the same time.**

Praise your dog again as he sniffs quietly and give him the treat. Repeat this routine a few times a day and your Beagle will quickly learn to bark whenever the doorbell rings and you ask him to **"Speak."** Eventually your dog will bark AFTER your request but BEFORE the doorbell rings, meaning he has learned to bark on command.

Even better, he will learn to anticipate the likelihood of getting a treat following your **"Shush"** request and will also be quiet on command.

With Speak and Shush training, progressively increase the length of required shush time before offering a treat - at first just a couple of seconds, then three, five, 10, 20, and so on.

By alternating instructions to speak and shush, the dog is praised and rewarded for barking on request and also for stopping barking on request.

In the unlikely event that you have a Beagle who is silent when somebody approaches the house, you can use the following method to get him to bark on the command of **"Speak."**

This is also a useful command to teach if you walk your dog alone, especially at night; the Beagle's loud baying will help keep you safe:

1. Have some treats at the ready, waiting for that rare bark.

2. Wait until he barks - for whatever reason - then say **"Speak"** or whatever word you want to use.

3. Praise him and give a treat. At this stage, he won't know why he is receiving the treat.

4. Keep praising him every time he barks and give a treat.

5. After you've done this for several days, hold a treat in your hand in front of his face and say **"Speak."**

6. Your dog will probably still not know what to do, but will eventually get so frustrated at not getting the treat that he will bark.

7. At which point, praise him and give the treat.

We trained a quiet dog to do this in a week and then, like clockwork, he barked enthusiastically every time anybody came to the door or whenever we gave him the "Speak" command, knowing he would get a treat for stopping.

....

Personal Experience

Georgina Armour-Langham, of Robentot Beagles, Leicester, says: "Treats are the main motivation; some love toys. Always exchange something they steal for food – but don't try and take food out of their mouths.

"I have three girls, they sleep all tucked up in the same bed and are good companions together. *(Pictured left to right: Breeze, Lexi and Holly).*

"They are friendly and affectionate, but don't expect them to do anything without a treat! Use treats as part of their daily food so they don't become overweight.

"I homed Holly as she was resource guarding socks and tea towels. A year on and she still has the behaviour. We have learned not to take anything off her, but expect her to leave it for a treat and we can then go and pick it up. We give lots of praise for leaving, and use **"Mine"** as a command. We've seen quite an improvement with positive training.

"Think ahead, if they like socks and tea towels, don't give them access to them; use stair gates to restrict access. Kellie Wynn, the Beagle behaviour lady on Facebook, offers some great advice and has a group all new owners should follow.

"Toilet training can be tricky, always praise with treats when they go out, little and often, and use bells at the back door. Don't let them beg - put them outside or in bed when you eat, and don't feed them at table! Scatter food occasionally so they can sniff it out.

"Don't reward negative behaviour like barking to come in, and if you pick them up, they will learn to jump up. If your Beagle is barking too much, use a *"Quiet"* word and signal and reward them as soon as they are quiet. Don't do anything while they are barking: patiently wait until quiet then reward and praise.

"Crate train your puppy for time-out and encourage 16 hours sleep a day. Use a long line and whistle training with a GPS for when they get a scent. Socialise in the park with a ball for recall practice and treat. Get them used to being tethered to experience different noises, people and environments to encourage a chilled-out relaxed Beagle."

Darlene Stewart, Aladar Beagles, Alabama: "Training time should be a happy experience for you and your Beagle. Beagles can sometimes be stubborn and get bored with training unless you make it FUN. Positive reinforcement, praise, and FOOD are the major motivators for a Beagle. While working or training your Beagle, talk in happy cheerful tones and if you feel yourself getting aggravated, take a break. Keep the sessions short and try to always end on a positive note."

Taylor (Ch AlaDars Just Idolize'N) is pictured enjoying the snow with his favourite toy.

"Training your puppy should start as soon as you get home. Look for habits that your puppy already does and reinforce them. For example: puppy always comes to you and sits. When a dog does this and this is what you want them to do, always praise with *"Good Boy/Girl."*

"A treat at this time would also help to strengthen the signal that sit is a GOOD thing. Start saying *"Sit"* as your Beagle approaches you and when he sits give him a reward/praise. Soon the puppy will relate the word sit with "I've been good." This type of behavioral training can be used with any habit you want to train your Beagle to do on command. Remember -KEEP IT FUN!"

Lori Norman, Lokavi Beagles, Florida: "Beagles are motivated by two things: food and fun. I always keep dog treats in my right pocket and all of my dogs know it. If they get out all I have to do is call them and put my hand in my right pocket; it gets their immediate attention. Other dogs may prefer to be rewarded with a game of some type, like throwing a ball, or squeaking a toy which becomes more fun than leaving.

"When training any dog, the key to success is consistency and confidence. The bond you create with your Beagle is going to be the reason he even wants to listen. If the bond (trust) is strong, he will want to hang out with you, otherwise it will be a struggle. The sharpness of an obedience routine is directly correlated to the food or fun connected with the end result. That is where consistency comes in, the reward must be reliable.

"Correction is as important as reward. Just as they should be rewarded when obedient, they should be corrected when not. Be consistent, don't repeat yourself or they'll know they don't have to do it until the last time you say it. Give them a command once, if they do nothing then show them what to do, reward them, then repeat. When they do it correctly make a big deal over it so they know they did well."

Peter Sievwright, Mattily Beagles, Renfrewshire, Scotland: "When training you will need to assign words to every task and command that you want your dog to do. Some of the ones that we use are.: Good Boy/Good Girl. Sit, Come, Stand, Out, Down, Leave, Go Get, Bring It Back, Drop, No, Walk on, Walkies, Go for a Wee, etc. You can use any word you want for any task you want to train your dog to do. Some of the essential things to train your dog are: sit, recall, no, leave, walk on and to pee on command.

"To get your dog to pee on demand, do this: When your dog is actually going to the toilet use your chosen word and reward your dog for the act with treat, praise and Good Boy/Girl and as your puppy grows, they should encourage them to pee on command.

"This is especially useful when you let them out last thing at night or when the weather is bad and you don't want to go out in the pouring rain for ages waiting for the dog to go to the toilet!"

This pup is trying to make up his mind whether he wants to go or not! Photo courtesy of Peter.

Sarah Porter, Puddlehill Beagles, Norfolk: "When training a Beagle you need consistency and nerves of steel! A few of my puppy owners are successful with allowing their pups off the lead. They have been consistent with their training, etc. My dogs will come back but when they feel like it – my nerves can't take it so I would rather not take the risk even if I have extra tasty hotdog sausages etc. I do, however, think Beagles are keen to please."

Debbie Tantrum, Debles Beagles, Shropshire: "We make training fun, and enjoyable; it does not take them long at all to learn new tricks, and Recall. We tell all our new owners to let them off the lead as soon as possible as the puppy will not stray too far whilst they are young; this then helps when they are older. We use balls and other toys, and have lots of photos of lovely Beagles running on the beach - we also advise people not to believe everything you read!"

Kelly Diamond, Kelcardi Beagles, Fife, Scotland: "Beagles are intelligent dogs, but they do require more patience that some other breeds. However, they are trainable - but just remember you can never switch that nose off or the natural desire to follow a scent. For those reasons off-lead work is usually the hardest thing to master."

Butter wouldn't melt in their mouths! Photo of these five little innocents courtesy of Sarah and Ben Porter, Puddlehill Beagles.

9. Specialist Training

After 18 years in the police force, the job had taken its toll on Detective Sergeant Kellie Wynn and she was diagnosed with cumulative post-traumatic stress disorder (PTSD). Knowing a dog would help her relax and get her out of the house – she was starting to become agoraphobic - she adopted a two-year-old Beagle.

However, the free-spirited Daisy was unaware of her remit to help Kellie chill, and what followed was "a baptism of fire!" Daisy chewed everything – she had chewed her way through her previous owner's sofa – she was hyperactive, excitable on the lead and had no Recall. Yet this mischievous dog with the huge heart changed Kellie's life forever.

Over the next two years she devoted her time to finding the best way to train Daisy before resigning from the police force, taking qualifications and becoming a professional dog trainer. Known as "The Beagle Lady," Kellie trains only Beagles and has helped countless owners and Beagles have a better understanding of each other.

She says: "I don't want anyone to think they can't train their Beagle; they can." Here Kellie tells her story in her own words and shares some of her methods to get the best out of your Beagle.

....

Background

I knew I needed help with Daisy, but I really struggled to find a dog trainer who would take me seriously and who understood Daisy and her breed. I was recommended to one trainer who was amazing at his job, but he was a Spaniel guy and when I arrived with my Beagle, I could see the blood drain from his face!

He said: "You have a Beagle. She is selfish, stubborn and won't ever listen to you. And whatever you do, don't ever let her off-lead if you ever want to see her again."

I left that session, got in my car and cried my eyes out - with Daisy licking my face. How dare he tell me my dog was selfish? She was my baby, and I knew back then just how smart she was. I tried other trainers, but Daisy either didn't want to train - she wanted to scent and explore - or the style of training was with toys, and Beagles are rarely motivated by toys.

Photo of Kellie and Daisy.

I am not one to give up and in the police you become adept at problem solving. I watched hours of YouTube, read every book I could get my hands on and tried everything out on Daisy. Some things worked and some didn't, and I knew something was missing.

As a police officer I was skilled with human body language and how to change my behaviour and language depending on who I was interacting with. I realised I needed to do the same with dogs. I studied dog behaviour and psychology and took practical training and online training courses. My original intention was to use my knowledge and experience to train Daisy, but I realised I could help other Beagle owners to successfully train their dogs in a positive way.

All my training is tailored to Beagles because they are motivated and genetically programmed so differently to say a Labrador or Spaniel. Recall is now one of my specialisms; it's not really about the Beagle, it's about our mindset, which I help my clients to learn.

I use the techniques myself; we adopted Billy when he was four years old. He has a wealth of medical issues and some serious behavioural issues and is currently a work in progress! My mission is to help Beagle owners have the most loving and happy life with their Beagle. I hope you find the following training and information helpful with yours.

The Importance of Sleep

All the books and online literature will tell you that Beagles make awesome family pets - and they DO! But there isn't much about what to expect from the outset with puppies and adolescents. I'm going to give you an insight into how a Beagle puppy thinks and how to manage some of the common topics owners contact me about.

I want to start with sleep because it is **THE most important aspect of owning a Beagle puppy**. Not many owners know or realise that a Beagle puppy actually needs 18-20 hours' sleep per day. And anything less can lead to problems developing.

For the first 12 weeks a Beagle pup can only manage 30-60 minutes awake before needing to nap. After 12 weeks they can manage 60-90 minutes.

But they don't always know to nap! They are unlike puppies of other breeds who will take themselves off to sleep. Once Beagle puppies hit around 10-12 weeks, they start powering on through, making us believe they aren't tired when they are.

But as they get more and more tired and overstimulated, their behaviour changes to "zoomies" (hyperactivity), over-nipping and inappropriate chewing. People assume that their pup isn't tired because of the behaviour and will play with them or take them for a walk in a bid to tire them out.

 **This is actually counterproductive as it makes a Beagle puppy's behaviour worse, and overstimulates their brain.**

When they exhibit zoomies or over-nipping in the evening, this is an indication that it is their bedtime. Sometimes called "The Witching Hour" in the Beagle world, I call it "Bedtime!" Toddlers are a nightmare when over-tired in the evening, so we put them to bed and it is the same with Beagle puppies. They need lots of overnight sleep.

This means you'll need a strict wake-and-sleep routine. Because if you don't, you could end up with an over-nippy puppy who is chewing everything. Use a timer set for one hour and then assess whether your pup needs to nap or can go another 30 minutes.

And to get your puppy to sleep, I cannot recommend a crate more strongly. Please try to see it as a cot or crib; a place where we can keep our puppy safe and encourage a long nap. This means that, once your puppy has got used to the crate, you have to close the door no matter how upset your pup appears to be. Babies and toddlers regularly cry when put in the cot for a nap. We ignore their protests and then they finally go off to sleep; again it's the same with a Beagle puppy. Sit by the crate if needs be until they go off to sleep, but don't engage. You are there to reassure your pup so he feels safe to sleep.

A nap is no less than an hour. They have a 20-minute sleep cycle. They will wake up after 20 minutes and have you believe they're done, so ignore the whining and barking. Encourage them to go back to sleep. Bedtime is between 5pm and 7pm to 7.30pm, depending on the time of year.

One of the biggest *"no, nos"* is to walk them outside before bed, especially if it's dark, thinking it will tire them out. In reality it overstimulates them, then they are really wired and don't want to go to bed.

 Get sleep right and you'll have a much calmer Beagle, one who then goes on to be a calm adult dog. Keep a sleep schedule until your pup is 18 months old, when they start to nap and sleep themselves.

An Awake Beagle Puppy

When Beagle puppies wake up their brain is saying, *"Go find a playmate and learn how to hunt."* Their first choice is always another dog, but if there isn't one then they will choose a human. This human tends to be the one that played the most with them in the first couple of weeks of being home or children as they are smaller, run a lot and squeal when played with!

This is when I get calls from Beagle parents. Their Beagle is nipping them hard, biting ankles, trying to bite their face and growling or snarling when they play. Most people interpret this as aggression. It isn't, I promise. We have hunting dogs; dogs who initially learn to hunt through play.

 The things they are doing with you, they would do with another dog. They nip to initiate play. They bite ankles as they would their prey. They try to bite your face like they would with another dog, which we call *"bitey face."* They growl and snarl because they are a hunting breed.

However, if their play is really over the top, then you can pretty much guarantee that they are overstimulated or over-tired. Either way, they need a nap. And if you can't get them to stop playing or disengage from your clothes, they need a nap.

In each awake period, a Beagle puppy wants to exercise, scent and chew. I recommend in this order. So, play or a walk first after a nap. They will get their scenting on the walk but if you have played with them rather than a walk, then scenting work is needed. And just before their nap they need to chew on a long-lasting food chew. This acts like a dummy or pacifier, which starts to make them sleepy and ready for their nap.

Walking

I very much buy into the **five minutes of exercise per one month of life** until around 10-12 months. This rule is in place to protect your Beagles' ligaments and joints, but in the Beagle world it is also because of the amount of scenting they do on a walk.

Ten minutes of scenting is the equivalent of one hour cardio. It is also the scenting that can overstimulate and make them hyper.

If they try to bite you or the lead, they're overstimulated. If, when you get home, they are nipping you or doing zoomies, they are overstimulated. If they can't nap after a walk, they are overstimulated...It's time to reduce the walk time!

It may seem that the opposite should be true; that they need more exercise if they are hyper. But this is the trap many owners fall into. More exercise and more scenting only makes a Beagle MORE hyper, not less. Beagles are different from most other breeds in this respect.

For example, a 16-week puppy can walk 20 minutes, twice a day. But if they are overstimulated reduce it to 10 to 15 minutes. Gradually increasing again as they get used to being outside and walking.

The optimum walking time for Beagle puppies is between 11am and 4pm. Early morning walks and late evening walks can really overstimulate them and not encourage napping or bedtime.

Common Behavioural Issues

Nipping and Chewing

Often, the biggest problem Beagle parents have is nipping and chewing; nipping being the worst of the two. It's important that we never use our hands or allow our body to be used for play. You might be able to do this with other breeds, but not a Beagle. They will believe it's acceptable and as they get older the nipping hurts.

REDIRECT, REDIRECT, REDIRECT!

Big toys. Bigger the better. As soon as puppy uses you as a toy, redirect to the right toy. If they won't redirect and are nipping you, then their energy level has risen too high and they can't make the right decisions. They will need to be helped to calm down through some basic training: Sit, Lie, Lie Down, Wait, etc. But if this doesn't work, then it's nap time.

Nipping is normal. But it does need to be trained out of Beagles because otherwise they will take this into adulthood. They are a nippy breed, again down to their hunting instincts. It's important that you limit the nipping because otherwise you are giving your pup a positive response.

That's why I highly recommend puppy pens - at least 100cm tall. If you feel that the over-nipping isn't because they are tired because they've only been up 10 minutes, then placing them in pen with toys, scent work and chews is the best way forward.

Beagles also love to chew. All their life. But Beagle puppies have four to five hours of chewing time in them which, in the beginning, practically covers the time they are awake!

Before 16 weeks you are limited to what you can give them, but once 16 weeks passes and they have the majority of their adult teeth, you can give them some great chews such as hooves or trachea filled with pâté, or pigs' trotters. Yep, gross but necessary for a hunting dog!

Whining and Barking

Beagle puppies will pull on your heart strings. They will have you believe they don't like their crates by whing and barking when you put them in. They will whine and bark if you leave a room. They will bark and whine to get something. As humans we feel we have to do something if our puppy is whining or barking, like we would with a crying baby or child.

STOP!!

Your Beagle puppy is smart. They will try behaviour to see if it gets them what they want. They will go through a repertoire of behaviours to get you to do what THEY want you to do. If you give in, then they store that information away in their brain and try again next time. After some repetitions of the same behaviour which works for them, they then do it all the time.

Don't give in to the whining and demand barking, no matter how long it goes on for. Give the neighbours a bottle of wine and earplugs and ask them to bear with you as you train your Beagle!

It can take days of training. But each day it will get easier.

....

Resource Guarding

Dogs think that whatever they have found or stolen is now their property. So, when they appropriate something - whether it was found on the floor, you dropped something or they got up on the counter and stole the beef joint - they aren't thinking about this as right or wrong. To them this is fair game.

Then when you try to take back what they have, World War III can erupt! We want our item back

because we feel cheated and disappointed that our Beagle has stolen our sandwich or our favourite sweater. If they loved and respected us, they wouldn't do that, right? Wrong!

Your Beagle does love you but there is something genetically programmed into them to seize an opportunity and guard it with their life - even if that means they might bite you in the process.

In their minds you should have known better. However, if you approach your Beagle with some chicken or other favourite treat, they may swap the stolen item.

They have to perceive that what you are offering is higher in value then what they currently have.

But before we really get into the best way to handle resource guarding, I want to highlight what resource guarding isn't:

1. **It is not aggression.** Yes, I know, sometimes you can end up with a bite, but that still doesn't mean you have an aggressive dog. You have a dog who is predisposed to guard things from humans. This does not mean that your Beagle will now be aggressive towards you all the time. Once you know how to manage, minimise and handle resource guarding, these outbursts will be a thing of the past.

2. **Your Beagle is not trying to be dominant over you.** No matter what you've heard about how this is your Beagle trying to dominate you and doesn't respect you, it's a load of twaddle! Yes, this was a belief that many people and trainers believed until fairly recently, but the dominance theory has been debunked - by the chap who came out with it in the first place.

3. **You do not need to show them who is boss.** In fact, if you try to pin your Beagle down, get them to submit or use force to remove an item (all methods that were recommended in the past), I can pretty much guarantee you will make the situation a lot worse and over time your Beagle will be a serious resource guarder who no longer trusts you and feels let down by you.

But it's not all doom and gloom. I have a resource guarder. Billy was terrible when he first came to us. But with a different approach to what I suspect was happening in his previous home, his aggressive-looking outbursts are now practically non-existent. We still have the odd hiccup, but I'll explain more in a second.

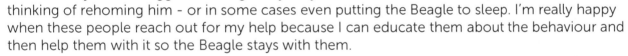

To prevent resource guarding getting out of hand, doing work with your puppy from Day 1 is crucial. Even if at this stage your puppy isn't showing any signs of growling or biting when you take something away from him or remove things from their mouth.

Resource guarding tends to start to present as they get older and, in a lot of cases, when they are in adolescence. They become more confident in themselves and also they decide any subtle signals they may have given off to tell you to leave them and their stuff alone no longer work and they become more obvious with growling, snarling and biting.

This is when I'm contacted by the Beagle owner who believes they have an aggressive dog. They may be thinking of rehoming him - or in some cases even putting the Beagle to sleep. I'm really happy when these people reach out for my help because I can educate them about the behaviour and then help them with it so the Beagle stays with them.

Resource Guarding Training for Puppies and Adults

Start with a little bit of hand feeding along with letting them eat from the bowl. Put your hands in the feed bowl and get them to take it from your hands. This does two things:

1. Your Beagle learns that you don't take food away and in fact you help him to eat.

2. Hands are positive. We want to make hands positive so they don't feel they need to bite them.

When they have a particularly high value treat such as a bone, pig's ear or long-lasting chew, sit with them and have another one exactly the same. Offer the exact same treat and swap it for the one they have. Again, this teaches them that you aren't there to take their treat, in fact you want to give them another in exchange. You can also try to swap the treat with something awesome like a Lickimat with dog food on, pâté or dog-friendly peanut butter.

We want them to know that we are willing to offer them something else for the thing they have.

If they growl or snap if you approach their food bowl, start by dropping something high value near them or into the bowl as you pass: chicken, ham, cheese, etc. This teaches them that you are not a threat to their food and in fact you are a positive because you give them more food.

Or you can split their meal into three bowls. Once they finish the first bowl, swap it for another bowl of food and same with the third one. This teaches them that you are the giver of plenty. You will take their bowl away only when they are done and give them more!

What if your puppy or Beagle steals items that they are not allowed or are dangerous for them? We still need to pick our battles. If they are stealing the item in a bid to get you to chase them, then this is part of the game. Then when we try to get the item off them, it turns into resource guarding.

If your Beagle is stealing items to get you to chase them...STOP!

Are they doing anything with the item? If they are just guarding it and not destroying it, then ignore them.

Eventually they will get bored because you aren't doing anything and they'll wander off, giving you the opportunity to get your item. You'll find that over time your Beagle will steal less because you are not playing the game.

If they take the item and chew it, then the best way to work with this is to swap or distract. Swapping the item for a high reward treat is not bribery. You are saying to your Beagle, "Hey, can I have that item and you can have this piece of chicken?" It's a fair exchange and both of you gain something in the interaction.

You obviously need to be careful they are not stealing to get a treat every time. This is where distraction can work as well. Squeaky toys, making something in the other room seem exciting, getting the lead out of the cupboard, anything you know your Beagle will like. You can then reward them with praise or give them the squeaky toy for being such a good puppy or a walk around the block.

I also recommend that you try to train your puppy to come to you if you do need to swap for a treat. We do this in our house with Billy. The treats are kept in a cupboard. I will shout: *"Billy, what've I got?"* He will either come running with the item or leave it behind.

I then shut the hall door so he can't then go back after his item if he's left it and give him a treat. And sometimes, now he's got so used to this, I'll just give him praise. If he brings the item with him, I throw the treat down the hallway, so he chases it and then I retrieve my item.

And what if the item is dangerous and if swallowed is harmful? I still do not recommend putting your hands anywhere near their mouth. I have seen injuries to people who have forced things out of their Beagle's mouth.

If you have tried everything - swapping and distracting - and it isn't working, then we deal with the consequences afterwards. Billy once got hold of chewing gum that my daughter accidently left out. I couldn't get it from him. I had to watch him eat it and then call my vet. We went straight down, and he was given an injection to make him sick and bring up the chewing gum.

I would rather pay £100 to my vet than risk injuring myself by trying to get it off Billy. Also, there is the psychological damage this can do to your relationship. People lose trust in and become scared of their Beagle. Whereas if they hadn't attempted to take the item, this wouldn't have happened.

And my last bit of guidance that I have also used with Billy is leave things around the house they CAN steal and destroy.

Billy loves socks. Billy has his own stash of socks he's allowed to steal and because we're not worried about them getting destroyed, we can ignore him. He now steals fewer things because it's not giving him the response he's looking for.

NOTE: Don't leave socks lying around if you believe your Beagle will swallow them!

What if the item they have stolen is food related?

Food-related items can be actual food, food wrappers or anything your Beagle perceives to be food, which was chewing gum in the previous example. Billy also guarded a box of paracetamol before that.

When it is food they have stolen, this will intensify the reaction; aggression and biting become worse. Billy has a snarling noise he makes if it is food-related, but only growls or barks if it's an item like a sock.

No. 1 Rule is we still don't try to forcibly remove it from them or out of their mouths. I can pretty much guarantee you'll end up being bitten.

The other thing you'll probably find is you can't swap for other food. Why would they? They already have food, so your bit of food isn't of any interest to them. They can rarely be distracted as food is THE biggest prize of all to a Beagle. So what can you do?

Again, you have to let them have it and deal with the consequences after. Yes, it might make them sick or they get a runny bum or you may have to go to the vet to get them to be sick. I know some people feel uncomfortable about this, like they are rewarding their Beagle for stealing, or that their Beagle will do it again because they got to keep and eat the stolen item. I'm afraid dogs don't think like that!

FACT ➤ **Dogs - and Beagles in particular - are opportunists.**

Make sure your Beagle doesn't have access to food, neither of mine is allowed in the kitchen. If this isn't possible in your house, put any food away or completely out of reach. Never leave food out and then leave the room, because Beagles are skilled at jumping and climbing to get food.

If they get hold of a food wrapper or packaging, again just let them have it. Most just rip it apart and if they do swallow anything, in the majority of cases they will either poop it out or vomit it back up. And in my experience, this tends to be at 3am when you are in a nice deep sleep!!

What to do with children and a resource guarder? How you handle this depends on the age of the children. If your child is at an age where they can't be told or don't understand that they need to go get Mummy or Daddy if the Beagle steals anything, then you are going to have to manage this very carefully.

This means that they can't be left together. An adult needs to supervise at all times. This is because children who are crawling or too young to understand how to be around a dog will take things off a dog without thinking.

Get a stairgate so your child and Beagle have space from each other. If your Beagle likes to steal your child's toys and things, then again Beagle will need to be in another room. A stairgate tends to work better than a door - they can still see you with a stairgate.

At one point when we first adopted Daisy, she was a destroyer of everything, so we had five stairgates in our house! But it worked and she also learnt to accept boundaries.

If you have an older child, sit them down and explain the situation. They are not allowed to take anything from the Beagle no matter how important it is to them. Get Mum or Dad to help.

For the first 12 months of Billy living with us, I would hear those immortal words five to 10 times a day from my daughter, screaming at the top of her voice: *"MUM!! Billy's got something he shouldn't have!"*

Then as the resource guarding gets easier to manage and it can be done safely, you can teach your child how to do it. I supervised my daughter swapping items with Billy for a few weeks until I was satisfied that nothing would go horribly wrong. Now she swaps or distracts Billy like a pro!

No one wants a Beagle that resource guards. But it is actually far more common than people think. And due to the fact that historically we've been told this is aggression or dominance, we can panic when our Beagle displays this behaviour.

Billy is my first dog with resource guarding problems when it comes to humans. When I adopted him, I was the only person who could swap with or distract him. My husband and daughter would call me to handle it. Now, 18 months later, Bill hardly steals anything and if he does, we tend to ignore him unless it's my daughter's favourite teddy. Both hubby and my daughter now know how to safely manage Billy's guarding.

Billy is still a loving, gorgeous, silly Beagle, but he will always be a resource guarder and if you have a resource guarder it is important to learn how to manage and accept that this is part of your dog. Dealt with correctly, calmly and with confidence, you will minimise their reaction and also the guarding episodes.

And each time they do guard something, you learn. We know that my daughter has to keep her bedroom door shut all the time or Bill will go in there and steal her teddies. I know that if I drop a chocolate biscuit covered in foil on the floor, I let Billy eat it knowing it was just one chocolate biscuit and he'll poop the foil out!

I'm going to leave you with a great game you can play with your Beagle to teach them to *"Drop, drop,"* where we make dropping things positive. It will help you with most things. Bill will drop at lot of things now, but there are times when the prize is too high value and swapping has to happen.

I prefer to use the phrase *"Drop, drop"* because you can say it positively. Try it, say *"Drop, drop"* in a light and happy way. Then say: *"Drop it"* or *"Leave it"* - they sound negative, don't they?

I want you to get a flirt pole, I really like this telescopic one from eBay, **pictured.** The string is really thick, and the fluffy thing works well with a Beagle's prey drive.

You are going to play with your Beagle. Make sure the fluffy bit is moving along the floor and your dog is chasing it. Two to three circles from you and then let your Beagle win the prize. This is also great for cardio and they will have lots of fun. When they catch the toy on the end, you are going to swap immediately!

Have a bunch of high-reward treats ready for this, cheese, chicken, hot dog sausage, etc. Waft the treat under their nose or show it to them and, as they are dropping the toy from their mouth, you say: *"Drop, drop."* When they drop the toy, give them the treat and at the same time place your foot over the toy.

Make sure you are wearing some tough shoes because they may take the treat and then try to get the toy from under your foot. Just let them try to get the item and all you have to do is ignore them. They have to figure out for themselves that they can't get the toy back from under your foot.

They will eventually disengage and then you can play the game again. Pups' can manage about 10 minutes of this game and adults around 15-20 minutes. They will be lovely and tired out after this as well as learning to drop things.

The great thing about putting your foot over the item is that you're also teaching them that anything under your foot can't ever be retrieved. I can now put my foot over stolen items in the house with bare feet when Billy steals something and he doesn't try to get a hold of it. But that took weeks of *"Drop, drop"* training to get to that point, so please use shoes to start with!

And have fun yourself - our Beagles love us to play with them. This game helps develop a great bond and they learn that dropping things is a positive.

Flirt poles are also great for children and Beagles to play together at arm's length. But if your Beagle starts to divert from the flirt pole to you, then they have become overstimulated and you'll need to stop the game and either pop your Beagle in the crate for a nap or use your treats to swap the game to basic training like Sit, Lie Down and Wait. This will help bring their energy down.

Recall, or Getting your Dog to Come Back to You

Many Beagle parents are worried about letting theirs off lead. You'll either have been told by others or dog trainers not to ever let your Beagle off-lead or you have read things online where Beagles get lost because of being off-lead. I am a massive fan of *#getBeaglesofflead* (I made up this hashtag!).

It is so important for their mental health. Beagles were born to have autonomy and make their own decisions while off-lead. They hunted, we followed. They caught or cornered the prey and then used that beautiful howl to tell us where to find them.

Being on the lead means they may become frustrated and reactive, which is another behaviour I work with daily.

I know that in some countries the law states you can't let your dog off-lead, so try to utilise dog parks and hire areas to give your Beagle the freedom they crave. In the UK, we are allowed to have our dogs off the lead in most places outdoors as long as they are under control and have recall.

But, what about a Beagle? Well, for starters they don't and won't ever have the same recall as a Labrador or Spaniel. Both of these breeds are people pleasers and will learn recall pretty quickly. They also can be trained to walk by their owner's side while off-lead.

Beagles are not people pleasers. They weren't bred to walk by your side and when in *"job zone,"* recall doesn't work. Job zone is scenting, tracking or chasing. When my Billy sniffs a bush, no recall under the sun works until he's finished!

Tracking is where they pick up a scent and want to follow it to get to the potential prize at the end. When they are tracking and you try recall, I can almost hear them thinking: *"Why on earth are they calling me. Can't they see I'm working?"* It is only when they are finished that recall works.

Chasing is where they have seen an animal and their prey drive kicks in. My Daisy loves to chase squirrels. There is absolutely no point in me recalling her at this point. Only when that squirrel has run up a tree will she recall.

The key to Beagle recall is our mindset. When I teach Beagle recall, I spend more time educating the Beagle parent and getting them ready for when their Beagle is in *job zone.*

The best time to start Beagle training is before your pup is five or six months old. They are like toddlers, they want to explore but really don't want you out of their sight. Then when they hit adolescence at around five or six months, we have to manage the recall until they are 18 months old, which is when they become an adult.

During adolescence they are typical teenagers and are feeling braver. They don't need us as much and they have little to no impulse control, so if they see a dog, they're gone!

Adolescent Recall involves letting them off the lead when there are no distractions and putting them on the lead when there are. It's usually during this period of time that Beagle parents put their Beagles back on-lead forever. They think that their Beagle will behave recklessly for the rest of its life.

This is just not the case. Adolescence is the hardest time for recall in a Beagle's life. Management is key until they are an adult.

Both my Beagles are off-lead every day. Daisy is the hunter and she regularly is out of my sight in a bush or the next field, but recalls when she's finished doing her job. Billy hasn't got a hunting bone in his body and is rarely out of my sight.

Both my Beagles and all Beagles that come to me for recall training, are whistle-trained. This is the most effective tool for training them. They can hear it more than our voices and if they do go off chasing something, they use the sound to track back to us.

 And get a GPS tracker linked to your mobile phone; they were made for Beagles. They have helped so many owners have peace of mind and tracked Beagles who have gone a little too far. I use Tracktive, *pictured,* but there are several options available.

There is nothing better than watching a Beagle off lead doing what they were bred to do. It makes me so happy to watch Daisy. Each time I see a Beagle off-lead, I punch the air in happiness.

Adolescence

This can be a tough time for Beagle owners. You have a teenager in your house whose hormones are going crazy, and their brain is telling them to learn to hunt. They have a bit more confidence and they want to do things their way both inside and outside your house.

They will be reluctant when it comes to naps. They still need them, but will have you believe they don't need them - they do! Still at least 16 hours of sleep a day. You will need to power on through and ignore their barking and whining. They will stop doing things like coming in from the garden when you ask, and back-chatting you, which is growling and trying to nip you if they don't want to be moved or you try to stop them digging up your garden!

Recall is difficult as they want to investigate everything and if they see another dog, it's game on! They want to play with that dog to learn how to hunt. They may chew more, and their toileting can go backwards. Weeing in the house again and on things like sofas and your bed. It's all just a phase.

You need be a strong and assertive parent to your Beagle, as you would with a human teenager. If you don't follow through with your requests to come in from the garden or get off the sofa, you'll have a troublesome adult Beagle.

This isn't about being dominant. This is about using a lead in the garden to get them in and using a house lead to get them off the sofa. Rewarding them when they are in the house and off the sofa. Praise is enough in this case.

Just know that this isn't your Beagle forever. People panic that their Beagle is going to behave like a wayward teenager for the rest of its life. That's just not the case and they settle in adulthood, but still with the quirky aspects like stealing socks, which is Billy's favourite game even at six years old.

Being a Beagle parent is about knowing and understanding the life stages - puppyhood and adolescence being the most challenging – putting in the time and then reaping the training rewards when they are become adults.

I cannot recommend training your Beagle puppy **from the very beginning** strongly enough. You wouldn't just wing it with a new-born baby. That's why we have midwives, books and people to talk to who have had a baby before.

It's the same with Beagle puppyhood. You can get help and guidance from books like this one, speaking to other Beagle parents - either in person or online - or getting help from a trainer who understands Beagles.

So without further ado, I bid you farewell for now and wish you lots of fun and happiness with your Beagle.

....

Copyright 2021 Kellie Wynn and The Canine Handbooks

Kellie offers 1-1 training in person and via Zoom. She also has online courses on bringing up a Beagle puppy, working your way through adolescence, lead etiquette, lead reactivity and recall.

*She can be contacted via her website at: www.thebeaglelady.com
or at "The Beagle Lady" on Facebook: www.facebook.com/groups/304903677065175*

10. Exercise and Socialising

One thing all dogs have in common — including every Beagle ever born - is that they need daily exercise. Even if you have a large garden or back yard where your dog can run free, there are still lots of benefits to getting out and about.

Beagles love going for walks, but are happy to lounge around at home as well. Don't think that because they are happy to snuggle up on the sofa, they don't need regular exercise — THEY DO.

Daily exercise helps to keep your Beagle happy and healthy. It:

- Strengthens respiratory and circulatory systems
- Helps get oxygen to tissue cells
- Helps keep a healthy heart
- Wards off obesity
- Keeps muscles toned and joints flexible
- Aids digestion
- Releases endorphins that trigger positive feelings
- Helps to keep dogs mentally stimulated and socialised

FACT Beagles were bred as working hunters. One thing that surprises many new owners is their level of "drive," which requires physical and mental activity to stop them becoming bored or mischievous.

If you have the time and interest, an excellent way of keeping your Beagle's mind and body exercised is to take part in a canine activity or competition.

....

How Much Exercise?

The amount of exercise each adult Beagle needs varies tremendously from one dog to the next. Some Beagles are quite laid back and need "less exercise than people think." However, it's fair to say that most Beagles require **more** time and energy than people think!

The amount of exercise your Beagle needs depends on various factors, including:

- Temperament
- Natural energy levels
- Bloodline
- Your living conditions
- Whether your dog is kept with other dogs
- What she gets used to

Beagles are known for being very playful and enjoy toys and games. Some of your dog's natural temperament and energy level will depend on the bloodline - ask the breeder how much exercise he or she recommends.

 A minimum of an hour a day spread over at least two walks will keep your adult Beagle fit and stimulated. Those with strong hounding instincts will take a lot more exercise, even all-day hikes, once they have built up to it.

Owning more than one dog - or having friends with dogs - is a great way for Beagles to get more exercise. A couple of dogs running around together will get far more exercise than one on her own.

A garden or yard with a secure, close-boarded fence at least five or six feet high is a **must** for a Beagle.

But it should not be seen as a replacement for daily exercise away from the home, where a dog can experience new places, scents, other people and dogs. If you live in an apartment, you may have no outside space, so it is especially important to commit to and make time for daily walks.

Your Beagle will enjoy going for walks on the lead (leash), but will enjoy life much more when she is allowed to run free, following a scent or chasing a ball. If your dog is happy just to amble along beside you, think about playing some games to raise her heartbeat, build muscle and get her fit.

Beagles have no road sense! You must make sure it's safe, away from traffic and other hazards, before letting her off the lead - and only after she has learned the Recall. Some American breeders recommend only letting your Beagle run free in securely fenced areas, although in the UK and Europe, most owners prefer to let their dogs off the lead on walks.

 Beagles are instinctive dogs ruled by their noses - and when their noses latch on to a scent, their ears stop working! The Recall is the most important command you can teach your dog - and even then, we recommend fitting a GPS collar when you let yours run free. NOTE: A scenting game or activity can be just as tiring as a walk for a Beagle.

Never underestimate a Beagle's hunting instinct and keep them on a lead near livestock and wild animals if you are hiking in the countryside. If you want to hike or take part in canine competitions with your dog, build up time and distance gradually. Always exercise within your dog's limits - on both land and water.

Whether your Beagle enjoys swimming varies from one individual to the next. If your dog is to be around water regularly, introduce them to the water in a positive manner; NEVER throw them in or entice them out of their depth. Although most Beagles that want to swim can swim, a doggie life vest is an option that gives you peace of mind if your dog spends a lot of time on or near water - and in an emergency you can use a boat hook to keep your Beagle out of danger using the vest's substantial ring.

Remember that swimming is a very strenuous activity for a canine, so keep any swim sessions SHORT. Don't repeatedly throw a ball or toy into water; your Beagle will not know when to stop and may get into difficulties.

If your dog does enjoy swimming, it is an excellent way to exercise; many veterinary clinics now use water tanks not only for remedial and IVDD therapy, but also for canine recreation.

Mental Stimulation

Without mental challenges, dogs can become bored, destructive, attention-seeking and/or depressed. Beagles are playful and love a game or challenge. If this "drive" is not channelled in a positive manner, it can turn to naughtiness.

If you return home to find your favourite cushions shredded or the contents of the kitchen bin strewn around the floor, ask yourself: *"Is she getting enough exercise/mental stimulation?"* and *"Am I leaving her alone for too long?"* Have toys and chews, and factor in regular play time with your Beagle – even gentle play time for old dogs.

 A washable *Snuffle Mat, pictured,* is an interesting toy as it can help to satisfy a Beagle's hunting instinct and reduce boredom. (It also helps fussy eaters, but that doesn't usually apply to Beagles!). Hide a treat, toy or food in there and let your Beagle work out how to get it. NOTE: Always use under supervision.

Most Beagles are chasers; they love running after birds, other dogs, squirrels, and especially a ball or toy – some even get obsessed with them. You can make *Fetch* more challenging by hiding the ball or toy and training your dog to find it.

 Sticks can splinter in a dog's mouth or stomach, and jumping up for a Frisbee can cause back damage. Balls should be big enough not to choke your dog.

A Beagle at the heart of the family getting regular exercise and mental challenges is a happy dog and an affectionate snuggle bug second to none.

NOTE: Both dognapping and dog attacks are on the increase - even in dog parks and public parks. Keep a close eye on your dog and, if you are at all worried, avoid popular dog walking areas and find other places where your dog can exercise safely. The UK police are advising owners not to walk their dogs at the same time and places each day, but to vary your routine.

Routine

Establish an exercise regime early in your dog's life. If possible, get your dog used to a walk or walks at similar times every day and gradually build that up as the puppy reaches adulthood. Start out with a regime you know you can continue with, as your dog will come to expect it and will not be happy if the walks suddenly stop.

If you haven't enough time to give your Beagle the exercise she needs, consider employing a daily dog walker, if you can afford it, or take her to doggie day care once or twice a week. As well as the exercise, she will love the interaction with other dogs.

Beagles are curious and love investigating new scents and places, which is why you need to plug every little gap in your fence – they will be off given half a chance!

Older dogs still need exercise to keep their body, joints and systems functioning properly. They need a less strenuous regime – they are usually happier with shorter walks, but still enough to keep them physically and mentally active. Again, every dog is different; some are willing and able to keep on running to the end of their lives, others slow right down.

If your old or sick dog is struggling, she will show you she's not up to it by stopping and looking at you or sitting/lying down and refusing to move. If she's healthy and does this, she is just being lazy!

Regular exercise can add months or even years to a dog's life.

It's quite common for Beagles to love snow – even though some of them hate rain! Be aware that snow and ice can clump on paws, ears, legs and tummy. Salt or de-icing products on roads and pathways contain chemicals that can be poisonous to dogs and cause irritation – particularly if she tries to lick it off. If your dog gets iced up, bathe paws and other affected areas in lukewarm - NOT HOT - water.

Exercising Puppies

There are strict guidelines for puppies. It's important not to over-exercise young pups as, until a puppy's growth plates close, they're soft and vulnerable to injury.

Too much impact can cause permanent damage. So, playing Fetch or Frisbee for hours on end with your young Beagle is definitely not a good plan, nor is allowing a pup to freely run up and down stairs in your home. You'll end up with an injured dog and a pile of vet's bills.

Just like babies, puppies have different temperaments and energy levels; some need more exercise than others. Start slowly and build it up. The worst combination is over-exercise and overweight.

Don't take your pup out of the yard or garden until the all-clear after the vaccinations - unless you carry her around to start the socialisation process. Begin with daily short walks (literally just a few minutes) on the lead.

Get yours used to being outside the home environment and experiencing new situations as soon as possible. The general guideline for exercise is:

Five minutes of on-lead exercise every day per month of age

So, a total of 15 minutes per day when three months (13 weeks) old

30 minutes per day when six months (26 weeks) old, etc.

This applies until around one year to 18 months old, when most of their growing has finished. Slowly increase the time as she gets used to being exercised and this will gradually build up muscles and stamina.

It is OK for your young pup to have free run of your garden or yard, provided it has a soft surface such as grass. This does not count in the five minutes per month rule.

If the yard is stone or concrete, limit the time your dog runs around on it, as the hard surface will impact joints. It is also fine for your pup to run freely around the house to burn off energy - although not up and down stairs or jumping on and off furniture.

A pup will take things at her own pace and stop to sniff or rest. If you have other dogs, restrict the time pup is allowed to play with them, as she won't know when she's had enough. When older, your dog can go out for much longer walks.

One breeder added: "For the first 18 months whilst the puppy's bones are soft and developing, it's best not to over-exert and put strain on the joints. Daily gentle walking is great, just not constant fast and hard running/chasing in the puppy stage, as too much is a big strain."

And when your little pup has grown into a beautiful adult Beagle with a skeleton capable of carrying her through a long and healthy life, it will have been worth all the effort:

A long, healthy life is best started slowly

Beagle Exercise Tips

- Don't over-exercise puppies

- Don't allow them to run up and down stairs or jump on and off furniture

- Aim for two walks away from the house every day

- Vary your exercise route – it will be more interesting for both of you

- Triple check the fencing around your garden or yard to prevent The Great Escape

- Do not throw a ball or toy repeatedly if your dog shows signs of over-exertion. Beagles have no sense of their own limitations. Stop the activity after a while - no matter how much she begs you to throw it again

- The same goes for swimming; ensure any exercise is within your dog's capabilities – look out for heavy panting

- Don't strenuously exercise your dog straight after or within an hour of a meal as this can cause Bloat, which mainly affects deep-chested dogs. Canine Bloat is extremely serious, if not fatal. See **Chapter 6. Feeding a Beagle** for details

- Beagles have "drive" and need play time as well as walk time to keep their creative minds engaged – and they love interaction with their owners

- In hot weather, exercise your dog early morning or in the evening

- Exercise old dogs more gently - especially in cold weather when it is harder to get their bodies moving. Have a cool-down period after exercise to reduce stiffness and soreness; it helps to remove lactic acids - our 13-year-old loves a body rub

❧ Make sure your dog has constant access to fresh water. Dogs can only sweat a tiny amount through the pads of their paws, they need to drink water to cool down

Admittedly, when it is raining, freezing cold or scorching hot, the last thing you may want to do is to venture outdoors with your dog. And some Beagles may not be too keen on going out in the rain either!

But make the effort; the lows are more than compensated for by the highs. Don't let your dog dictate if she doesn't want to go out, it will only make her lazier, fatter and less sociable with others.

Exercise helps you bond with your dog, keep fit, see different places and meet new companions - both canine and human. In short, it enhances both your lives.

Socialisation

Your adult dog's character will depend largely on two things: inherited temperament and environment, or **NATURE AND NURTURE**. And one absolutely essential aspect of nurture for all dogs, but especially Beagles, is socialisation.

FACT ▶ Scientists now realise the importance that socialisation plays in a dog's life. There is a fairly small window regarded as the optimum time for socialisation - and this is up to the age of four to five months.

Socialisation means *"learning to be part of society,"* or *"integration."* This means helping dogs become comfortable within a human society by getting them used to different people, environments, traffic, sights, noises, smells, animals, other dogs, etc.

It actually begins from the moment the puppy is born, and the importance of picking a good breeder cannot be over-emphasised.

Not only will he or she breed for good temperament and health, but the dam (puppy's mother) will be well-balanced, friendly and unstressed, and the pup will learn a lot in this positive environment.

Learning When Young Is Easiest

Most young animals, including dogs, are naturally able to get used to their everyday environment until they reach a certain age. When they reach this age, they become much more suspicious of things they haven't yet experienced. This is why it often takes longer to train an older dog.

When you think about it, humans are not so different. Babies and children have a tremendous capacity to learn, we call this early period our *"formative years."* As we age, we can still learn, but not at the speed we absorbed things when very young. Also, as we get older, we are often less receptive to new ideas or new ways of doing things.

This age-specific natural development allows a puppy to get comfortable with the normal sights, sounds, people and animals that will be a part of her life. It ensures that she doesn't spend her life jumping in fright, barking or growling at every blowing leaf.

The suspicion that dogs develop later also ensures that they react with a healthy dose of caution to new things that could really be dangerous - Mother Nature is clever!

It is essential that your dog's introductions to new things are all **positive**. Negative experiences lead to a dog becoming fearful and untrusting.

Your dog may already have a wonderful temperament, but she still needs socialising to avoid her thinking that the world is tiny and it revolves around her. Beagles can be very demanding – don't let yours become an attention-seeker.

 Good socialisation gives confidence and helps puppies – whether bold or timid – to learn their place in society. The ultimate goal is to have a happy, well-adjusted Beagle you can take anywhere - and one that doesn't spend her entire life barking at anything and everything.

Ever seen a therapy dog in action and noticed how incredibly well-adjusted to life they are? This is no coincidence. These dogs have been extensively socialised and are ready and able to deal in a calm manner with whatever situation they encounter. They are relaxed and comfortable in their own skin - just like you want your dog to be.

 Spend as much time as you can socialising your dog when young. It's just as important as training. Start as soon as you bring your puppy home. Regular socialisation should continue until your dog is around 18 months of age.

After that, don't just forget about it; socialisation isn't only for puppies, it should continue throughout life. As with any skill, if it is not practised, your dog will become less proficient at interacting with other people, animals, noises and new situations.

Developing the Well-Rounded Adult

Dogs that have not been properly integrated are more likely to react with fear or aggression to unfamiliar people, animals and experiences. Beagles who are relaxed around strangers, dogs, cats and other animals, honking horns, cyclists, joggers, veterinary examinations, traffic, crowds and noise are easier to live with than dogs who find these situations challenging or frightening. And if you are planning on taking part in canine competitions, get yours socialised and used to the buzz of these events early on.

 Well-socialised dogs live more relaxed, peaceful and happy lives than dogs that are constantly stressed by their environment.

Socialisation isn't an *"all or nothing"* project. You can socialise a puppy a bit, a lot, or a whole lot. The wider the range of positive experiences you expose her to (positively) when young, the better. Socialisation should never be forced, but approached systematically and in a manner that builds confidence and curious interaction.

If your pup finds a new experience frightening, take a step back, introduce her to the scary situation much more gradually, and make a big effort to do something she loves during the situation or right afterwards.

For example, if your puppy seems to be frightened by noise and vehicles at a busy road, a good method would be to go to a quiet road, sit with the dog away from - but within sight of - the traffic. Every time she looks towards the traffic say *"YES!"* and reward her with a treat.

If she is still stressed, you need to move further away. When your dog takes the food in a calm manner, she is becoming more relaxed and getting used to traffic sounds, so you can edge a bit nearer - but still just for short periods until she becomes totally relaxed. Keep each session short and **POSITIVE**.

Meeting Other Dogs

When you take your gorgeous and vulnerable little pup out with other dogs for the first few times, you are bound to be a bit apprehensive. To begin with, introduce your puppy to just one other dog – one that you know to be friendly, rather than taking her straight to the park where there are lots of dogs of all sizes racing around, which might frighten the life out of your timid little darling.

On the other hand, your pup might be full of confidence right from the off, but you still need to approach things slowly. If your puppy is too cocksure, she may get a warning bite from an older dog, which could make her more anxious when approaching new dogs in the future.

Tip Always make initial introductions on neutral ground, so as not to trigger territorial behaviour. You want your Beagle to approach other dogs with friendliness, not fear.

From the first meeting, help both dogs experience good things when they're in each other's presence. Let them sniff each other briefly, which is normal canine greeting behaviour. As they do, talk to them in a happy, friendly tone of voice; never use a threatening tone.

Don't allow them to sniff each other for too long as this may escalate to an aggressive response. After a short time, get the attention of both dogs and give each a treat in return for obeying a simple command, e.g. *"Sit"* or *"Stay."* Continue with the *"happy talk,"* and rewards.

Learn to spot the difference between normal rough and tumble play and interaction that may develop into fear or aggression. Here are some signs of fear to look out for when your dog interacts with other canines:

- Running away or freezing on the spot
- Licking the lips or lips pulled back
- Trembling or panting, which can be a sign of stress or pain
- Frantic/nervous behaviour, e.g. excessive sniffing, drinking or playing frenetically with a toy
- A lowered body stance or crouching
- Lying on her back with paws in the air – this is submissive, as is submissive urination
- Lowering of the head or turning the head away, when you may see the whites of the eyes as the dog tries to keep eyes on the perceived threat
- Growling and/or hair raised on her back (raised hackles)
- Tail lifted in the air or ears high on the head

Some of these responses are normal. A pup may well crouch on the ground or roll on to her back to show other dogs she's not a threat. If the situation looks like escalating, calmly distract the dogs or remove your puppy – don't shout or shriek. Dogs will pick up on your fear.

Another sign to look out for is *eyeballing.* In the canine world, staring a dog in the eyes is a challenge and may cause an aggressive response.

NOTE: whereas we might look someone in the eye when we are first introduced, it is normal for dogs to sniff the scent glands in another dog's bottom!

 Your puppy has to learn to interact with other dogs. Don't be too quick to pick her up; she will sense your anxiety, lose confidence and become less independent. The same is true when walking on a lead – don't be nervous every time you seen another dog – your Beagle will pick up on it and may react by barking, lunging or snapping.

Always follow up a socialisation experience with praise, petting, a fun game or a special treat. One positive sign from a dog is the *"play bow" pictured,* when she goes down on to her front elbows but keeps her backside up in the air.

This is a sign that she's feeling friendly towards the other dog and wants to play. Relaxed ear and body position and wagging tail are other positive signs.

Although Beagles are not normally aggressive dogs, aggression is often grounded in fear, and a dog that mixes easily is less likely to be combative. Similarly, without frequent and new experiences, other Beagles can become timid and anxious.

Take your new dog everywhere you can. You want her to feel relaxed and calm in any situation, even noisy and crowded ones. Take treats with you and praise her when she reacts calmly to new situations.

Once settled into your home, introduce her to your friends and teach her not to jump up. If you have young children, it is not only the dog that needs socialising! Youngsters also need training on how to act around dogs, so both parties learn to respect the other.

An excellent way of getting your new puppy to meet other dogs in a safe environment is at a puppy class. We highly recommend this for all puppies. Ask around locally if any classes are being run. Some vets and dog trainers run classes for very junior pups who have had all their vaccinations. These help pups get used to other dogs of a similar age.

What the Breeders Say

Lori Norman, Lokavi Beagles, USA: "Socialisation and training are extremely important! The goal is to have a puppy that is confident and happy. To build this confidence, pups must learn that they can handle themselves in any situation.

They need to have various forms of interaction to learn that they are OK. Just as with children, they have to interact with peers and travel through a variety of situations; puppies that are sheltered will be fearful because they are overwhelmed with life outside of their bubble.

"Training and discipline are important to dogs in the same way they are important to children. Remember, dogs need to feel loved, validated, and safe. Training provides those guide rails. It is very important that they learn what is appropriate and what is not. We can never expect a dog to learn these things just by talking to other dogs.... We must be clear and concise with what we expect."

This graceful mover strutting her stuff in the showring is Ch Macushla Lokavi's Moon Shadow owned by Lori and Jennifer Hayes.

"Like children, dogs don't like to "have" to do things they don't want to do, but it is how we keep them safe and happy and it is what they trust us to do. Undisciplined children grow up with a plethora of issues, just as dogs do. No dog knows the rules until you teach them.

"I had a call from a puppy owner who had a five-month-old puppy, they were upset because the puppy chewed up their new leather chair. My first question was: "Why did the puppy have unsupervised access to the chair?" She said they had run to the grocery store.

"I told her: "Don't blame the dog! You left him where he could do that." If you aren't watching him, how is he to know? When you aren't there, he should be confined somewhere safe. That isn't the puppy's fault, it is clearly the fault of the owner. You may be surprised at that, but it is the owner's responsibility to teach their puppy right and wrong. The easiest way to avoid the wrong behavior is to confine the puppy when you aren't watching."

Lori added: "My dogs are out a good part of the day. I like for them to run, corner, turn, and build core muscles - additionally, a tired Beagle is always a nice thing!

"I am third generation showing dogs (my mother and grandfather before me), and I have done quite a bit of obedience work with Beagles over the years. I am getting too old to run in Agility, but I do have pups that do Agility with their owners. I love Performance work as it gives them a job."

Sharon Hardisty, Blunderhall Beagles, UK: "Socialisation and training are essential to make a well-adjusted adult dog who is a pleasure to own and can be taken anywhere.

"Both the Kennel Club and Dogs Trust recommend the Puppy Socialisation Plan as an effective plan for breeders and new owners to prepare their puppies as best they can for life as family pets. It is simple to complete, and can be tailored to suit you and your lifestyle."

Pictured is Sharon's Shiloh (Blunderhall in Lockdown), aged six months.

"It is critical that this is done from birth up to 16 weeks of age, otherwise important learning and development phases have passed. The Plan covers everything from getting used to household noises, to getting out and about and meeting new people and other dogs.

"Therefore, you need to plan and incorporate some extremely important life lessons during the early stages of your puppy's development, so that you end up with a well-balanced and sociable dog. You can find The Puppy Socialisation Plan at www.thepuppyplan.com

"As for exercising, I have an area large enough for my Beagles to exercise freely every day. I usually walk them each day, with longer walks at weekends. They are meant to *"go all day"* so it shouldn't come as a surprise if owners have done their homework! I also take part in conformation showing with mine."

Karen Simkin, Simeldaka Beagles: "Socialisation is very important as it builds confidence from an early age. As for exercise, we have four Beagles and they get lots of play time together in the garden. They are walked for an hour a day divided into two walks, but if we meet up with others, we have a longer walk, and sometimes go out for the day."

Pictured relaxing at home on the chaise longue are father and son Wilbur and Haidar (Eardley Will Power at Simeldaka and Simeldaka Senglea Squire). Photo courtesy of Karen.

"Please explain to puppy buyers how important it is to slowly build up the exercise time and NOT to over-exercise a pup."

Sarah Porter: "Beagles are very sociable, so they need to learn how to act around other dogs and people. Socialisation and training should continue throughout the dog's life.

"As for exercise, I probably go against the norm here as my Beagles really don't need that much exercise. Yes, mine can go out and trek for a few hours but equally two 20-minute walks or a 40-minute to an hour walk once a day is sufficient. The more you do with them the more they need.

"I mix their walks up by going to enclosed fields for an hour or two and then the next day just going out for a quick walk round. I think the mixing up of walks, rather than the same old walks for the same duration, is probably better in some instances."

Peter Sievwright, Mattily Beagles: "Socialisation is important. The last thing you want is every time your pup meets another dog is them to bark and attack it - sooner or later you will be rushing your pet to the vet just because he didn't like the look of another dog four times his size."

"My dogs are exercised for a minimum of two-and-a-half hours a day, slightly shorter in really bad weather and slightly longer in nicer weather.

"I believe the amount of exercise depends on the food that is fed and the age of the dog; the younger the adult dog, the more exercise needed to keep them fit and healthy. The older the dog, the less exercise your dog will need. But again all this depends on the weather, Beagles are fair weather dogs and don't like wet, cold weather they prefer over cast and sunshine to exercise and play in. They love to play fetch and chase balls and other toys and run about burning off energy."

Kelly Diamond, Kelcardi Beagles: "I actually think people think Beagles need a lot more exercise than they do. My dogs have free running time in a fenced paddock for around three hours per day; this is split up into regular intervals.

"We advise one to two hours minimum of exercise per day, but as adults these dogs will take as much as you will give them. Mental stimulation for me is the key, and playing with other dogs does tire them out physically and mentally."

Georgina Armour-Langham, Robentot Beagles: "I exercise mine for different times and lengths; sometimes play is just as good. I don't like my dogs to demand to be walked, rather as I choose. I have done some ringcraft - and agility is fun - they were good at it.

"Socialisation is very important to let them experience different sights and sounds. For example, ours come camping and are expected to be chilled in all circumstances. I take them to the allotment (community garden) where they are expected to lie in the vegetable beds, tethered, to watch the world go by."

Debbie Tantrum, Debles Beagles: "As soon as the new owners and puppy get home, they can meet up with other dogs, animals and other people. They need to socialise and start training from Day 1.

"This is a must as the pups leave us having been used to other dogs and then go to new surroundings. It can be a shock for them as they may be on their own. By then our puppies have had both their first and second sets of vaccinations, so there is no waiting time; they are free to socialise and start puppy classes. Training is needed for puppy to learn and you need to show puppy who is leader.

"You will never outwalk a Beagle! These dogs have stamina that can last a whole day. Our dogs are walked in the morning for around three miles, and on an evening for four miles, depending on the weather. They are free to roam outside in the back yard all day - we have a dog flap on the door. They are never penned up, they will never give up! They do like to sunbathe in the sun and love exercising in the snow."

11. Beagle Health

The Beagle is generally regarded as a healthy breed with a relatively long lifespan of 12 to 15 years - even more if you're very lucky. However, health should always be an important factor when choosing and raising a dog.

Firstly, select a puppy from a breeder who produces Beagles sound in both body and temperament – and this involves health screening - and secondly, play your role in helping to keep your dog healthy throughout his or her life.

NOTE: This chapter is intended to be used as an encyclopaedia to help you to identify potential health issues and act promptly in the best interests of your dog. Please don't read it thinking your Beagle will get lots of these ailments – he or she WON'T!

....

It is becoming increasingly evident that genetics can have a huge influence on a person's health and even life expectancy, with a great deal of time and money currently being devoted to genetic research.

A human is more likely to suffer from a hereditary illness if the gene or genes for that disorder is passed on from parents or grandparents. That person is said to have a *"predisposition"* to the ailment if the gene is in the family's bloodline. Well, the same is true of dogs.

There is not a single breed without the potential for some genetic weakness. For example, many Cavalier King Charles Spaniels have heart problems and 25% of all West Highland White Terriers have a hereditary itchy skin disease.

A Cavvie or a Westie from unscreened parents will be more likely to suffer from these disorders than one from health-tested parents.

The 2015 UK scientific study *The Challenges of Pedigree Dog Health: Approaches to Combating Inherited Disease* states:

"The development of (such) pedigree dog breeds can be both a blessing and a curse: desirable features are rigidly retained, but sometimes, undesirable disease-causing genes can be inadvertently fixed within the breed."

In other words, bad genes can be inherited along with good ones.

To read the full study, type the title into Google and click on Table 1 at the bottom to view individual breed statistics.

The good news is that there is plenty you can do to help your Beagle live a long and healthy life.

....

Health Certificates for Puppy Buyers

Anyone thinking of getting a Beagle puppy today can reduce the chance of their dog having a genetic disease by choosing a puppy from healthy bloodlines.

If you're actively searching for a puppy, you might be considering a breeder based on the look or colour of her dogs or their success in the show ring, but consider the health of the puppy's parents and ancestors as well. Could they have passed on unhealthy genes along with the good genes for all those features you are attracted to?

 Check what tests the parents have passed and ask to see original certificates where relevant - a good breeder will be happy to provide them. A puppy is considered hereditary clear if BOTH parents have tested Clear. These are the main tests for hereditary illnesses:

UK:

* MLS (Musladin-Leuke Syndrome)
* Lafora (a form of epilepsy)

These first two tests are compulsory for Kennel Club Assured Breeders. The next is strongly recommended:

* NCCD (Neonatal Cerebellar Cortical Degeneration, a disease of the brain)

These next two are also inheritable diseases for Beagles:

* IGS (Imerslun-Gräsbeck Syndrome or Cobalamin Malabsorption, a gut disorder)
* FVIID (Factor VII Deficiency, a blood clotting disorder)

Although it may look complicated, it's not. All of these five tests can be carried out using a single swab and a CombiBreed test.

USA:

The National Beagle Club of America recommends the following health screening tests for all breeding Beagles. Dogs meeting these requirements qualify for Canine Health Information Center (CHIC) certification. OFA (The Orthopedic Foundation for Animals) says: "For potential puppy buyers, CHIC certification is a good indicator the breeder responsibly factors good health into their selection criteria.

"The breed-specific list below represents the basic health screening recommendations. It is not all-encompassing. There may be other health screening tests appropriate for this breed. And, there may be other health concerns for which there is no commonly accepted screening protocol available."

* Hip Dysplasia
* Eye Examination
* MLS
* Cardiac Evaluation
* Autoimmune Thyroiditis
* Lafora (optional)
* FVIID (optional)
* Patellar Luxation (optional)

❧ NCCD (optional)

Darlene Stewart, Chairperson, Health and Genetics Committee, National Beagle Club of America said: "A good breeder should always provide a contract and health guarantee and take back, if needed, any puppy bred by them for the life of that dog.

"The major health problems currently in Beagles are epilepsy, autoimmune conditions, cancer and back issues. One common preventable health problem is overweight Beagles. Their eyes plead for food and we weak humans give in to those eyes. This is very bad health-wise, a Beagle needs to be kept at a reasonable weight."

Tip A pedigree certificate from the Kennel Club or AKC does NOT mean that that puppy or its parents have passed any health tests. The only thing a pedigree certificate guarantees is that the puppy's parents can be traced back several generations and that the ancestors were purebred Beagles.

As well as asking to see health certificates, prospective buyers should always find out exactly what health guarantees, if any, the breeder is offering with the puppy.

FACT ❯ If a puppy is sold as "Vet Checked," it does not mean that the parents have been health screened. It means that a vet has given the puppy a brief physical and visual examination, worming and vaccinations are up to date, and the pup appears to be in good health on the day of the examination.

If you have already got your dog, don't worry! There is plenty of advice in this book on how to take excellent care of your Beagle. Taking extra care with a puppy, feeding a quality food, monitoring your dog's weight, regular grooming and check-overs, plenty of exercise and socialisation will all help to keep him in tiptop condition. Good owners can certainly help to extend the life of their Beagle.

....

Beagle Insurance

Insurance is another point to consider for a new puppy or adult dog. All puppies from reputable breeders in the UK come with four weeks' or 30 days' insurance that can be extended before it expires. USA breeders may or may not provide insurance, if not, ask if they can recommend a plan. If you are getting an older dog, get insurance BEFORE any health issues develop, or you may find any pre-existing conditions are excluded.

If you can afford it, take out life cover. This may be more expensive, but will cover your dog throughout his or her lifetime - including for chronic (recurring and/or long term) ailments, such as joint, heart or eye problems, ear infections, epilepsy and cancer.

Insuring a healthy puppy or adult dog is the only sure-fire way to ensure vets' bills are covered before anything unforeseen happens - and you'd be a rare owner if you didn't use your policy at least once during your dog's lifetime.

Costs in the UK range from around £15 a month for Accident Only to around £30-£50 per month for Lifetime Cover, depending on where you live, how much excess you are willing to pay and the total in pounds covered per year.

I ran a few examples for US pet insurance on a three-month-old Beagle pup with a deductible of $100-$200 and came back with quotes from $24 to $50, depending on location, the excess and amount of coverage per year in dollars. With advances in veterinary science, there is so much more vets can do to help an ailing dog - but at a price. Surgical procedures can rack up bills of thousands of pounds or dollars. According to www.PetInsuranceQuotes.com these are some of the most common ailments affecting Beagles, and typical treatment costs:

> Hip Dysplasia $4,000 to $6,000 per hip, Cherry Eye $500 to $1,000 per eye, Cancer $5,000 to $20,000, Curvature of the Spine $6,000 to $15,000, Dental Problems $250 to $1,500, Intervertebral Disc Disease $3,000 to $9,000, Luxating Patella $1,500 to $3,000, Hypothyroidism Varies, Epilepsy $200 to $15,000, Glaucoma $2,000 to $3,000 ($1.3 = approximately £1 at the time of writing).

Of course, if you make a claim, your monthly premium will increase, but if you have a decent insurance policy BEFORE a recurring health problem starts, your dog should continue to be covered if the ailment returns. You have to decide whether insurance is worth the money. On the plus side, you'll have:

1. Peace of mind financially if your beloved Beagle falls ill, and

2. You know exactly how much hard cash to part with each month, so no nasty surprises.

Three Health Tips

1. **Buy a well-bred puppy -** Good Beagle breeders select their stock based on:

   - General health and the DNA test of the parents

   - Conformation (physical structure)

   - Temperament

Although well-bred puppies are not cheap, believe it or not, committed Beagle breeders are not in it for the money, often incurring high bills for health screening, stud fees, veterinary costs, specialised food, etc. Their main concern is to produce healthy, handsome puppies with good temperaments and instincts that are *"fit for function"* – whether from working or show lines.

2. **Get pet insurance as soon as you get your dog -** Don't wait until your dog has a health issue and needs to see a vet. Most insurers will exclude all pre-existing conditions on their policies. Check the small print to make sure that all conditions are covered and that if the problem is recurring, it will continue to be covered year after year. When working out costs of a dog, factor in annual or monthly pet insurance fees and trips to a vet for check-ups, annual vaccinations, etc.

3. **Find a good vet -** Ask around, rather than just going to the first one you find. A vet that knows your dog from his or her puppy vaccinations and then right through their life is more likely to understand your dog and diagnose quickly and correctly when something is wrong. If you visit a big veterinary practice, ask for the vet by name when you make an appointment.

We all want our dogs to be healthy - so how can you tell if yours is? Well, here are some positive things to look for in a healthy Beagle:

Health Indicators

1. **Movement –** Beagles can be prone to back problems. A healthy dog will have a fluid, pain-free gait. Look out for warning signs of stiffness, wobbliness, shivering, a reluctance to move, an arched back or the head hung low.

2. **Eyes -** A Beagle's eyes should be clear with an intelligent, alert expression and no sign of tears.

   These are dark with dark rims. Paleness around the eyeball (conjunctiva) could be a sign of underlying problems. A red swelling in the corner of one or both eyes could be cherry eye, and a cloudy eye could be a sign of cataracts. Sometimes the dog's third eyelid (nictating membrane) is visible at the inside corner - this is normal. There should be no thick, green or yellow discharge from the eyes.

3. **Nose –** A dog's nose is an indicator of health. Regardless of colour, the nose should be free from clear, watery secretions. Any yellow, green or foul-smelling discharge is not normal - in younger dogs this can be a sign of canine distemper.

   Beagle nose colour is associated with the genetic colour. Tri-colours have black or dark noses, while bi-colours may have lighter-coloured noses. A pink *"snow nose"* can appear in winter due to a lack of Vitamin D, but usually returns to black during summer. Some dogs' noses turn pinkish with age, due to them producing less pigment and is not a cause for concern. If you want your dog to have a black nose, supplements such as seaweed tablets can help.

4. **Ears –** If you are choosing a puppy, gently clap your hands behind the pup (not so loud as to frighten him) to see if he reacts. If not, this may be a sign of deafness (more so in puppies with white on the head or ears). Floppy ears are more susceptible to infections than pricked-up ears. Make sure the ears look clean and smell nice.

5. **Mouth –** Beagle gums should be black or pink or a mixture. Paleness or whiteness can be a sign of anaemia, Bloat or lack of oxygen due to heart or breathing problems (this is harder to see with black gums). Blue gums or tongue are a sign that your dog is not breathing properly. Red, inflamed gums can be a sign of gingivitis or other tooth disease.

   Young dogs have sparkling white teeth, whereas older dogs have darker teeth, but they should not have any hard white, yellow, green or brown bits. Your dog's breath should smell OK.

6. **Coat and Skin** – These are easy-to-monitor indicators of a healthy dog. A healthy, clean Beagle coat is smooth and silky with a sheen. Any dandruff, bald spots, a dull, lifeless, discoloured or oily coat, or one that loses excessive hair, can all be signs that something is amiss. Skin should be smooth without redness or rashes. If a dog is scratching, licking or biting a lot, he may have a condition that needs addressing.

   Open sores, scales, scabs, red patches or growths can be a sign of a skin issue or allergy. Signs of fleas, ticks and other external parasites should be treated immediately; check for small black or dark red specks, which may be fleas or flea poo, on the coat or bedding.

7. **Weight –** Your Beagle's stomach should be above the bottom of his rib cage when standing, and you should be able to feel his ribs beneath his coat without too much effort and see a visible waistline. If the stomach is level or hangs below, your dog is overweight - or may have a pot belly, which can also be a symptom of other conditions.

8. **Temperature** – The normal temperature of a dog is 101°F to 102.5°F. (A human's is 98.6°F). Excited or exercising dogs may run a slightly higher temperature. Anything above 103°F or below 100°F should be checked out. The exceptions are female dogs about to give birth that will often have a temperature of 99°F. If you take your dog's temperature, make sure he is relaxed and *always* use a purpose-made canine thermometer.

9. **Stools** - Poo, poop, business, faeces - call it what you will - it's the stuff that comes out of the less appealing end of your Beagle on a daily basis! It should be mostly firm and brown, not runny, with no signs of blood or worms. Watery stools or a dog not eliminating regularly are both signs of an upset stomach or other ailments. If it continues for a couple of days, consult your vet.

 If puppies have diarrhoea they need checking out much quicker as they can quickly dehydrate.

10. **Energy** – Beagles are energetic, alert dogs. Yours should have good amounts of energy with fluid and pain-free movements. Lack of energy or lethargy could be a sign of an underlying problem.

11. **Smell** – Beagles love running about outdoors and can have a doggie smell. But if yours has a musty, 'off' or generally unpleasant smell, it could be a sign of a yeast infection. There can be a number of causes; the ears may require attention, it could be a food allergy, anal sac issue (usually accompanied by 'scooting'). Whatever the cause, you need to get to the root of the problem quickly before it develops into something more serious.

12. **Attitude** – A generally positive attitude is a sign of good health. Beagles are engaged and involved, so symptoms of illness may include one or all of the following: a general lack of interest in his or her surroundings, tail not wagging, lethargy, not eating food and sleeping a lot (more than normal). The important thing is to look out for any behaviour that is out of the ordinary for YOUR Beagle.

There are many different symptoms that can indicate your canine companion isn't feeling great. If you don't yet know your dog, his habits, temperament and behaviour patterns, then spend some time getting acquainted with them.

What are his normal character and temperament? Lively or calm, playful or serious, a joker or an introvert, bold or nervous, happy to be left alone or loves to be with people? How often does he empty his bowels, does he ever vomit? (Dogs will often eat grass to make themselves sick, this is perfectly normal and a natural way of cleansing the digestive system).

You may not think your Beagle can talk, but he most certainly can!

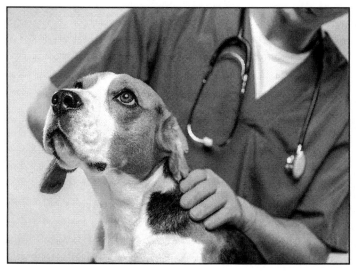

If you really know your dog, his character and habits, then he CAN tell you when he's not well. He does this by changing his patterns. Some symptoms are physical, some emotional and others are behavioural. It's important to be able to recognise these changes, as early treatment can be the key to keeping a simple problem from snowballing into something more serious.

If you think your dog is unwell, it is useful to keep an accurate and detailed account of his symptoms to give to the vet, perhaps even take a video of him on your mobile phone. This will help the vet to correctly diagnose and effectively treat your dog.

Four Vital Signs of Illness

1. **Heart Rate** - You can feel your Beagle's heartbeat by placing your hand on his lower ribcage – just behind the elbow. Don't be alarmed if the heartbeat seems irregular compared to that of a human; it often is in dogs. Your dog will probably love the attention, so it should be quite easy to check his heartbeat. Just lay him on his side and bend his left front leg at the elbow, bring the elbow in to his chest and place your fingers on this area and count the beats. The larger the dog, the slower the heartbeat.

   - ❧ Big dogs have a normal resting heart rate of 70 to 120 beats per minute
   - ❧ With medium-sized dogs its 80 to 120 beats per minute
   - ❧ Small dogs have a normal rate of 90 to 140 beats per minute
   - ❧ A young puppy has a heartbeat of around 220 beats per minute
   - ❧ An older dog has a slower heartbeat

2. **Temperature** - A new-born puppy has a temperature of 94-97°F. This reaches the normal adult body temperature of around 101°F at four weeks old. A vet takes a dog's temperature reading via the rectum. If you do this, only do it with a special digital rectal thermometer (not glass), get someone to hold the dog and be very careful. Ear thermometers *(pictured)* are now widely available for home use.

   NOTE: Exercise or excitement can cause temperature to rise by 2°F to 3°F when your dog is actually in good health, so wait until he is relaxed before taking his temperature. If it is above or below the norms and the dog seems under par, give your vet a call.

3. **Respiratory Rate** - Another symptom of illness is a change in breathing patterns. This varies a lot depending on the size and weight of the dog. An adult dog will have a respiratory rate of 15-25 breaths per minute when resting. You can easily check this by counting your dog's breaths for a minute with a stopwatch handy. Don't do this if he is panting; it doesn't count.

4. **Behaviour Changes** - Classic symptoms of illness are any inexplicable behaviour changes. If there has NOT been a change in the household atmosphere, such as another new pet, a new baby, moving home, the absence of a family member or the loss of another dog, then the following symptoms may well be a sign that all is not well:

   - Depression or lethargy
   - Anxiety and/or shivering, which can be a sign of pain
   - Falling or stumbling
   - Loss of appetite
   - Walking in circles
   - Being more vocal - grunting, whining or whimpering
   - Aggression
   - Tiredness - sleeping more than normal or not wanting to exercise
   - Abnormal posture

If any of them appear for the first time or worse than usual, you need to keep him under close watch for a few hours or even days. Quite often he will return to normal of his own accord. Like humans, dogs have off-days too.

If he is showing any of the above symptoms, then don't over-exercise him, and avoid stressful situations and hot or cold places. Make sure he has access to clean water. Keep a record and it may be useful to take a fresh stool sample to your vet.

If your dog does need professional medical attention, most vets will want to know:

WHEN the symptoms first appeared in your dog

WHETHER they are getting better or worse, and

HOW FREQUENT the symptoms are - intermittent, continuous or increasing?

....

Hereditary Diseases

There are DNA tests for all the main hereditary diseases affecting Beagles. The way to eliminate the disease is NOT to mate two dogs with the faulty gene. If a Carrier or Affected dog is mated with a Clear dog, the puppies will NOT have MLS - although some will be Carriers. If you are buying a puppy, always ask to see the parents' health test certificates.

Many inherited diseases are *"Autosomal Recessive,"* below are all possible outcomes. They are the same for all autosomal recessive genetic diseases. (Carriers carry the faulty gene(s) but do not show signs of the disease):

PARENT CLEAR + PARENT CLEAR = pups clear

PARENT CLEAR + PARENT CARRIER = 50% will be carriers, 50% will be clear

PARENT CLEAR + PARENT AFFECTED = 100% will be carriers

PARENT CARRIER + PARENT CLEAR = 50% will be carriers, 50% will be clear

PARENT CARRIER + PARENT CARRIER = 25% clear, 25% affected and 50% carriers

PARENT CARRIER + PARENT AFFECTED = 50% affected and 50% carriers

PARENT AFFECTED + PARENT CLEAR = 100% will be carriers

PARENT AFFECTED + PARENT CARRIER = 50% affected and 50% carriers

PARENT AFFECTED + PARENT AFFECTED = 100% affected

MLS (Musladin-Leuke Syndrome)

MLS (previously known as Chinese Beagle Syndrome) is a recessive genetic disorder that affects the development and structure of connective tissue. It involves multiple body systems, including bone, heart, skin and muscle. It is similar to "Stiff Skin Syndrome" in humans.

Affected Beagles have several defects which start to show at around four weeks of age: short outer toes on the front (and sometimes all four) feet, high set, creased ears with extra cartilage on a flat skull, slant, narrowed eyes and very thick, tight skin with little scruff.

Such pups have a very stiff gait, but not all affected pups show all the signs. The short toes make them walk like a ballerina on their middle toes. They have a very good gregarious temperament, although many have been reported to develop seizures.

MLS sufferers have a thick inelastic skin and thick fibrous muscles with little flex. This leads to the stiff gait and also the hard abdominal wall. Tails are often carried in a straight, stiff fashion and some Beagles also have noticeable kinks in their tails.

MLS can be seen very early - two to four weeks and it gets worse until the dog is about one year old, when it stabilises. Unless there are associated congenital or genetic problems, Beagles with MLS will have a normal life span. There are varying degrees of severity, and some Beagles that look totally normal have been proved to be carriers.

Some of the poor affected Beagles develop early onset osteoarthritis, and the ones with severely shortened toes often wear their nails right down to the quick; some need boots when out walking. If you are buying a puppy, always ask to see the parents' certificate for MLS.

Lafora

Lafora or Lafora Disease (LD) is an aggressive inherited form of epilepsy that affects several breeds including Beagles, Basset Hounds and Miniature Wirehaired Beagles. A genetic defect prevents the dog from efficiently processing starch into sugar, causing insoluble starch platelets to gradually build up in the central nervous system.

Typical symptoms, which appear at five years of age or older, are a sudden jerking or shaking of the head, which can be triggered by bright lights (even the TV) or sudden

noises or movements, especially near the dog's head. Also, seizures and high-pitched barking or whining.

The disease is progressive, and eventually, wobbliness (ataxia), blindness and dementia can develop, when the dog may have to be put to sleep. Although Lafora is incurable, medication, a special diet free from starch and sugars, doggie sunglasses and keeping the dog away from flashing/bright lights may slow down the disease.

The faulty gene is recessive, so both parents must have a copy to pass it on to their puppies. There is no cure, but genetic testing has made great strides. For example, in just five years, the proportion of Miniature Wirehaired Beagle litters bred with a risk of Lafora-affected puppies has been reduced from 55% to under 5%.

If you are buying a Beagle, ask to see the Lafora screening certificate for the parents. If you live in the USA, visit www.beaglelafora.com for a voluntary database of Beagles screened for Lafora.

....

Factor VII Deficiency

FVIID is a genetic mild bleeding disorder. Statistics from various labs that offer the genetic test for the disease indicate that well over 50% of Beagles are either Affected or Carriers. Affected Beagles have been noted in the United States, Canada, Europe and Australia, in both show and field bloodlines.

Factor VII is an essential protein needed for normal blood clotting. However, many affected dogs with the deficiency have no symptoms at all. Symptoms, when they occur are:

- ❧ Bruising easily
- ❧ Frequent nosebleeds
- ❧ Prolonged bleeding after surgery or injury

In rare cases, the bleeding may be severe. Due to the mild nature of this disorder, affected dogs may not be identified until surgery is performed or an injury occurs, when the dog may bleed excessively. Vets performing surgery on affected dogs may want to ensure ready access to blood banked for transfusions.

Most dogs with Factor VII Deficiency will have a normal lifespan despite increased blood clotting times. Again, puppy buyers should ask whether the parents have been tested for this disease - or whether there is any history of FVIID in their bloodlines.

....

NCCD (Neonatal Cerebellar Cortical Degeneration)

Also called "Drunken Puppy Syndrome " or "Tumbling Puppy Syndrome," this has been identified as a hereditary neurological disease among European Beagles and a small number of UK Beagles; it is present right from birth. An affected puppy is slower to walk than his littermates, he is very unsteady on his feet and often circles to the same side or falls to the same side. He may also tilt his head and have odd side-to-side eye movements.

By the age of 10-12 weeks the odd behaviours of circling, falling and being off balance are "just how this puppy moves." The puppy is uncoordinated, like a drunk person, staggering and falling. The symptoms soon peak and rarely worsen beyond this stage.

Sometimes with maturity the puppy can walk straight, but when trying to move at a fast pace such as a trot, the uncoordinated side motions return. Going up or down stairs is a challenge.

For a puppy to be born with the disease, both parents have to have the faulty gene (it is autosomal recessive). While the condition is relatively rare, health screening for NCCD is compulsory for all breeding stock of UK Kennel Club Assured Beagle Breeders.

IGS (Imerslun-Gräsbeck Syndrome)

IGS is a genetic disorder found in Beagles and Border Collies where the dog can't absorb Vitamin B12 through the gut. It has been recognised as an issue that should be tested for in the UK and Europe, and has also been found in Australia, but testing is not currently necessary in the USA.

Vitamin B12, also known as cobalamin, is important in dogs for many reasons, including producing red blood cells and developing and maintaining the nervous system. Without adequate B12, dogs rapidly develop anaemia and have poor weight gain and growth.

Initial symptoms are often vague: poor appetite, apparent stomach pain and rather poor looking puppies. They also start to show neurological signs as the nerve structure does not develop correctly.

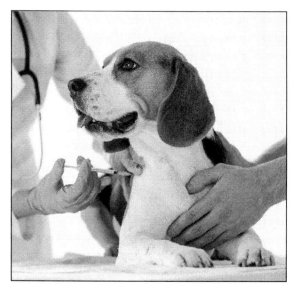

Unless a vet checks B12 levels, it's hard to pinpoint what is going on, and many affected puppies have initially been thought to have a faulty liver or stomach/intestinal issue until B12 levels are checked – when they can be as low as 1%.

All of this happens within a few weeks of birth and, sadly, without supplementation such dogs will eventually die. Once diagnosed, the treatment is weekly injections of B12 for life. Although, once the condition is stable, some dogs only need treatment many weeks apart. Normally puppies improve rapidly and, if treated early enough, they may return to normal.

There is an oral medication called Cobalaplex which does have some gut absorption, even with IGS-affected cases, and can be useful.

UK veterinarian Dr Samantha Goldberg added: "There is a DNA test available to check the status of any Beagles used for breeding. The test is available in several different labs around the world. So far, the condition has been reported from three different continents so may be present in many different countries although not always recognized by vets and owners."

··

Joints

Hip Dysplasia

Hip Dysplasia, or *Canine Hip Dysplasia (CHD),* is the most common inherited orthopaedic problem in dogs of all breeds. The hips are the uppermost joints on the rear legs of a dog, either side of the tail, and *"Dysplasia"* means *"abnormal development."* Dogs with this condition develop painful degenerative arthritis of the hip joints.

The hip is a ball and socket joint. Hip dysplasia is caused when the head of the femur, or thigh bone, fits loosely into a shallow and poorly developed socket in the pelvis. The joint carrying the weight of the dog becomes loose and unstable, muscle growth slows and degenerative joint disease often follows.

Symptoms often start to show at five to 18 months of age. Occasionally, an affected dog will have no symptoms at all, while others may experience anything from mild discomfort to extreme pain.

Diagnosis is made by X-ray, and an early diagnosis gives a vet the best chance to tackle HD, minimising the chance of arthritis. Symptoms are:

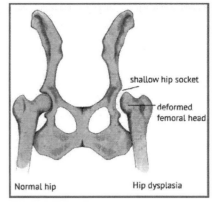

- Hind leg lameness, particularly after exercise
- Difficulty or stiffness when getting up, climbing stairs or walking uphill
- A reluctance to jump, exercise or climb stairs
- A "bunny hop" gait or waddling gait
- A painful reaction to stretching the hind legs, resulting in a short stride
- Side-to-side swaying of the croup (area above the tail)
- Wastage of the thigh muscles

While hip dysplasia is usually inherited, other factors can trigger or worsen it, including:

- Too much exercise, especially while the dog is still growing
- Obesity
- Extended periods without exercise

Prevention and Treatment

There is a system called **hip scoring,** run by the BVA and Kennel Club in the UK and PennHIP or OFA in the USA. A UK dog's hips are X-rayed at a minimum age of 12 months; in the US, dogs must be 24 months old before they can receive their final hip certification.

In the UK, the X-rays are submitted to a specialist panel at the BVA who assess nine features of each hip, giving each feature a score. **The lower the score, the better the hips,** so the range can be from **0** CLEAR to **106** BADLY DYSPLASTIC. A hip certificate shows the individual score for each hip.

It is far better if the dog has evenly matched hips, rather than a low score for one and a high score for the other. Listed here are the American ratings, with the UK ratings in brackets:

Excellent (0-4, with neither hip higher than 3)

Good (5-10, with neither hip higher than 6)

Fair (11-18)

Borderline (19-25)

Mild (26-35)

Moderate (36-50)

Severe (51-106)

This section of UK BVA certificate, pictured, shows a hip score of 10, which is good.

There is no 100% guarantee that a puppy from low scoring parents will not develop hip

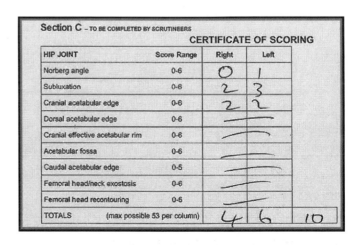

HIP JOINT	Score Range	Right	Left	
Norberg angle	0-6	0	1	
Subluxation	0-6	2	3	
Cranial acetabular edge	0-6	2	2	
Dorsal acetabular edge	0-6			
Cranial effective acetabular rim	0-6			
Acetabular fossa	0-6			
Caudal acetabular edge	0-5			
Femoral head/neck exostosis	0-6			
Femoral head recontouring	0-6			
TOTALS (max possible 53 per column)		4	6	10

Section C – TO BE COMPLETED BY SCRUTINEERS — CERTIFICATE OF SCORING dysplasia, as the condition is caused by a combination of genes, rather than just one. However, the chances are significantly reduced with good hip scores. In the USA the Beagle is ranked 53 out of 195 breeds, with nearly one in five having some form of dysplasia. The figures are similar for the UK.

Treatment is geared towards preventing the hip joint getting worse. Vets usually recommend restricting exercise, **keeping body weight down** and managing pain with analgesics and anti-inflammatory drugs.

Various medical and surgical treatments are now available to ease discomfort and restore some mobility. They depend on factors such as age, how bad the problem is and, sadly, sometimes how much money you can afford. Cortisone can be injected directly into the affected hip to provide almost immediate relief for a tender, swollen joint. In severe cases, surgery may be an option.

IVDD (Intervertebral Disc Disease)

IVDD is the specific name given to a variety of back problems, such as slipped, ruptured, herniated or bulging disk(s), and it's the most common spinal disease in dogs. Like Dachshunds, Pekinese and some other breeds, Beagles are *"chondrodystrophic;"* they have been bred down from larger dogs and have short, curved limbs in relation to their bodies. These factors make the breed genetically prone to back problems.

Recent research has identified the gene responsible for this predisposition to IVDD in Beagles, it is called CDDY and is widespread in the Beagle population. Disc disease is a process that affects many Beagles, usually occurring from three years onwards.

In Beagles it generally occurs in the neck (cervical) vertebrae, but may also occur in the chest (thoracic) or lower back (lumbar) vertebrae.

Intervertebral disks are cushions between each vertebra and under the spinal cord. They allow the spine to flex and they help to spread pressure placed on the spinal column. They have two parts, a firm, rubbery outer portion and a soft, jelly-like inner portion - visualise a vitamin E capsule!

When the IVDD occurs, the disks begin to dehydrate. This causes the outer portion to become brittle and the inner portion to become dried out and mineralised. The disks lose their flexibility and are not able to withstand the movement of the spine.

When they can no longer flex, they can begin to protrude from between the vertebrae, and in severe cases a disk can even rupture or burst, spilling out the inner portion.

Because the disk's outer covering is thinnest at the top of the disk, the protrusion or rupture usually occurs in that area. Unfortunately, the spinal cord is directly above the top of the disk and can be injured.

There is currently no DNA test to prevent IVDD. However, there is an X-ray scheme to test for calcification (thickening and hardening of the disks) in dogs aged 24 to 48 months.

FACT ❯ The Dachshund Breed Council's DachsLife 2018 health survey found that only 13% of unneutered/unspayed dogs over the age of three developed IVDD, compared with 26% of dogs neutered or spayed at 7-12 months old, and 25% of dogs done at 13-18 months.

Symptoms vary according to severity:

- Stiffness of the neck, limbs or back
- Reluctance to go up or down a step
- Hanging head when standing
- Reluctance to lift or lower the head
- Arched back
- Knuckling (paws upside down)
- Swollen or hard abdomen
- Wobbliness, stumbling, unusual gait – often mainly affecting the hind legs
- Yelping, either unprovoked or when touched - a sign of pain
- Trembling, panting or licking the lips
- Dragging the rear leg(s)
- In very extreme cases: paralysis, loss of bladder control and inability to feel pain

Choosing a puppy from bloodlines with no history of back problems is a good place to start. But if you've already got yours, there's still lots you can do to help keep your Beagle free from back pain:

1. VERY IMPORTANT: Don't let your Beagle get overweight - it puts strain on the spine.

2. Don't let your puppy run up and down stairs or jump on and off furniture.

3. Don't over-exercise puppies.

4. Don't play vigorous games with a young Beagle - avoid Tug-o-War, Frisbee, etc.

5. Avoid any activity where your dog's spine may twist, *pictured.*

6. Mixing with other dogs is fine, but avoid roughhousing with bigger or boisterous dogs.

7. Hiking and long walks (for healthy <u>adult</u> Beagles) help to strengthen muscles around the spine. General activity and events such as Agility, Tracking etc. should be encouraged.

8. Learn how to handle a Beagle puppy properly - and teach the kids how to do it.

Many people pick up a Beagle incorrectly under the rib cage, which puts pressure on the middle of the back. The correct way to pick up a Beagle is to support the back by reaching under the chest and running your arm from front to back under the dog. Pick up the dog with your lower arm supporting the entire length of back.

Follow the advice above and the likelihood is that your Beagle will remain untroubled by IVDD.

Diagnosis and Treatment

If your dog is showing any of the above signs, get him down to the vet immediately. It's important to get the right diagnosis straight away as a delay may cause a more serious rupturing of the disk(s). Ask if your vet has experience of canine spinal issues; IVDD is sometimes misdiagnosed as arthritis, muscle pain or a gastro problem.

IVDD cannot be diagnosed with normal X-rays or a blood test. A special type of X-ray called a **myelogram** can detect spinal cord problems, but an MRI or CT scan is better. Extensive diagnostic tests and treatment are expensive - another reason to have good pet insurance in place.

If IVDD is confirmed, the vet will give a grading. Grade 1 is the least serious, when a dog is walking normally, but feels some pain. Grade 5 is the most serious, when paralysis and urinary incontinence are evident. Even then, there is a 50%-60% chance that the dog will walk normally again after surgery. With Grades 1 and 2, this can be as high as 95%.

If surgery is decided as the best option, the procedure is often carried out by a veterinary neurologist, rather than a general veterinary surgeon. Recovery varies according to severity; the dog can start walking again within anything from one to 12 weeks, although full recovery may take the best part of a year in extreme cases. The owner plays a large part in the dog's return to normal or near-normal, as several weeks of crate rest, carefully-monitored exercise, a healthy diet and bucketloads of patience are all essential.

For all but the most severe cases, there are *"conservative (non-surgical) treatments"* to consider. These may involve painkillers and anti-inflammatories (NSAIDS), crate rest, rehabilitation exercises, massage, acupuncture, hydrotherapy, physiotherapy and even the use of mobility devices.

Tips for Crate Rest

This can be a challenging time for the owner as well as a Beagle. Here are a few tips:

- Crate-train your puppy, so if a problem arises later in life, he will be used to a crate
- Place the crate near the family, don't leave him isolated
- A recovering dog needs a calm environment
- Use a Vetbed or folded blanket for him to lie on

- When you open the crate door, get down to your dog's level and be ready to put on a lead – don't let him dash out
- Take your dog outside on a lead to eliminate, don't allow him to freely wander
- If your dog is likely to be mainly in two places, consider getting a second crate
- DAP (Dog Appeasing Pheromone) diffusers, melatonin, hemp oil and other natural products help some dogs to stay calm and relaxed
- Some dogs do well with part of their crate covered with a sheet
- A Kong or puzzle toy may help to stave off boredom, or a drive in the car
- Finally - **DON'T stop the crate rest too early** – it's a mistake many owners make when they see their dog improving. Stick to what the vet says

Eyes

Cherry Eye

This can develop in dogs of all breeds, particularly young dogs. Humans have two eyelids, but dogs have a third eyelid, called a *nictating membrane.* This is a thin, opaque tissue with a tear gland that rests in the inner corner of the eye.

It provides extra protection for the eye and spreads tears over the eyeball. Usually it is retracted and therefore you can't see it, although you may notice it when your dog is relaxed and falling asleep.

Cherry Eye, *pictured,* is a collapse of the gland of the third eyelid, thought to be due to a weakness of the fibrous tissue that attaches the gland to the surrounding eye. The gland falls down, exposing it to dry air, irritants and bacteria, when it can become infected and begin to swell.

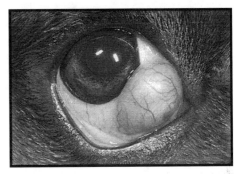

There is sometimes a mucous discharge and if the dog rubs or scratches it, he can further damage the gland and even possibly create an ulcer on the surface of the eye. Although it looks sore, it is not generally painful.

Mild cases are treated with a steroid ointment to try and get the gland back to its normal position, and antibiotics to prevent infection. If that doesn't work, surgery to reposition the gland should be considered. A simple stitch or two can tack the gland down into the conjunctiva.

Cataracts

Cataracts can affect any breed, although they are not common in Beagles.

The lens is transparent and its function is to focus rays of light to form an image on the retina. A cataract occurs when the lens becomes cloudy. Less light enters the eye, images become blurry and the dog's sight diminishes as the cataract becomes larger.

Age-related or *late onset cataracts* can develop in any breed any time after the age of eight years and usually have less impact on a dog's vision that those seen in younger dogs.

If the cataract is small, it won't disturb the dog's vision too much, but owners must monitor cataracts because the thicker and denser they become, the more likely they will lead to blindness or glaucoma. Diabetes is a known trigger for cataracts, and overweight dogs are more susceptible to diabetes than dogs of a healthy weight.

Depending on the cause, severity and type of cataract, surgery is an option for some dogs; the lens is removed and replaced with a plastic substitute. It costs around £2,500-£3,500 per eye (around $2,700-$4,000 in the US), but if the dog is a suitable candidate, it is successful in 90% of cases. In less severe cases, dogs can live a perfectly normal life with daily eye drops and vigilance on the part of the owner.

Tip Beware of miracle cures! If you do try drops, look for some containing the effective ingredient N-Acetyl Carnosine, or NAC.

As well as a cloudy eye, other signs are the dog bumping into things, especially in dimly-lit situations, squinting or pawing at the eye, eye redness, an inflamed eye socket, or a bulging eye. If you suspect your Beagle has cataracts, get him to the vet for an examination as soon as possible. Early intervention can prevent complications developing.

Dry Eye (Keratoconjunctivitis sicca)

Keratoconjunctivitis sicca is the technical term for **Dry Eye,** which is caused by not enough tears being produced. With insufficient tears, a dog's eyes can become irritated and the conjunctiva appears red. It's estimated that as many as one in five dogs can suffer from Dry Eye at one time or another in their lives.

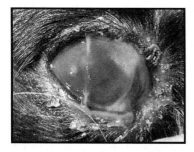

Beagles are more likely than some other breeds to suffer from Cherry Eye and Dry Eye.

Dry Eye causes a dog to blink a lot, the eye or eyes typically develop a thick, yellow discharge, **pictured,** and the cornea develops a film. Infections are common as tears also have anti-bacterial and cleansing properties, and inadequate lubrication allows dust, pollen and other debris to accumulate. The nerves of these glands may also become damaged.

Dry eye is often associated with skin disorders, it may be due to increased rubbing and secondary infection in the eyes or it may be part of the immune disorder. It may also be caused by injuries to the tear glands, eye infections, disease such as distemper or reactions to drugs.

Left untreated, the dog will suffer painful and chronic eye infections, and repeated irritation of the cornea results in severe scarring, and ulcers may develop which can lead to blindness. Early treatment is essential to save the cornea and usually involves drugs: cyclosporine, ophthalmic ointment or drops. In some cases, another eye preparation – Tacrolimus - is also used and may be effective when cyclosporine is not. Sometimes artificial tear solutions are also prescribed.

Treating Dry Eye involves commitment from the owner. Gently cleaning the eyes several times a day with a warm, wet cloth helps a dog feel better and may also help stimulate tear production.

In very severe and rare cases, an operation can be performed to transplant a salivary duct into the upper eyelid, causing saliva to drain into and lubricate the eye.

Distichiasis

This occurs when eyelashes grow from an abnormal spot on the eyelid. (**Trichiasis** is ingrowing eyelashes and **Ectopic Cilia** are single or multiple hairs that grow through the inside of the eyelid - **cilia** are eyelashes).

With distichiasis, an eyelash or eyelashes abnormally grow on the inner surface or the very edge of the eyelid, and both upper and lower eyelids can be affected. The affected eye becomes red, inflamed, and may have a discharge.

The dog typically squints or blinks a lot, just like a human with a hair or other foreign matter in the eye. The dog can make matters worse by rubbing the eye against furniture, other objects or the carpet. In severe cases, the cornea can become ulcerated and it looks blue.

Often, very mild cases require no action, mild cases may require lubricating eye drops and in more severe cases, surgery may be the best option to remove the offending eyelashes and prevent them from regrowing. Left untreated, distichiasis can cause corneal ulcers and infection which can ultimately lead to blindness or loss of the eye.

Entropion

Some Beagles are susceptible to Entropion, particularly heavy-headed puppies with excess wrinkle on the head.

It occurs when the edge of the lower eyelid rolls inward, causing the dog's fur to rub the surface of the eyeball, or cornea. In rare cases the upper lid can also be affected, and one or both eyes may be involved. This painful condition is thought to be hereditary and is more commonly found in dog breeds with a wrinkled face, such as the Bulldog.

The affected dog scratches at his painful eye with his paws and this can lead to further injury. If your Beagle suffers from it, he will usually show signs at or before his first birthday. You will notice that his eyes are red and inflamed and they will produce tears. He will probably squint.

The tears typically start off clear and can progress to a thick yellow or green mucus. If left untreated, entropion causes corneal ulcers and you might also notice a milky-white colour develop. This is caused by increased fluid which affects the clarity of the cornea. For your poor dog, the irritation is constant. Imagine how painful and uncomfortable it would be if you had permanent hairs touching your eyes. It makes my eyes water just thinking about it.

FACT ❯❯ It's important to get your dog to the vet as soon as you suspect Entropion before your dog scratches his cornea and worsens the problem.

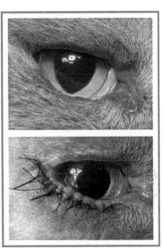

A vet will make the diagnosis after a painless and relatively simple inspection of your dog's eyes. He or she will first have to rule out other issues, such as allergies. In mild cases, the vet may successfully prescribe eye drops, ointment or other medication. However, the most common treatment for more severe cases is a fairly straightforward surgical procedure to pin back the lower eyelid, *pictured.*

In young Beagles, some vets may delay surgery and treat the condition with medication until the dog's face is fully formed to avoid having to repeat the procedure later.

Tip Any eye condition can be worsened by irritants and injury. Remove or fence off low, spiky plants in your garden or yard. And although your Beagle may look like the Snoopy version of Easy Rider when he sticks his head out of the open car window with his ears flapping in the wind, bear in mind that dust, insects and dirt particles can hit and damage those beautiful eyes.

NOTE: There is also a type of hereditary PRA (Progressive Retinal Atrophy) in Beagles called CRD4 (cone Rod dystrophy 4). Although the gene is present, it is not active in Beagles, so currently there is no cause for concern.

Epilepsy

Epilepsy means repeated seizures (also called fits or convulsions) due to abnormal electrical activity in the brain. Epilepsy affects around four or five dogs in every 100 across the dog population as whole.

Epilepsy can be classified as *structural,* when an underlying cause can be identified in the brain, or *idiopathic,* when the cause is unknown. The type of epilepsy affecting most dogs of all breeds is *idiopathic epilepsy.* (Lafora is a specific genetic epileptic disorder covered earlier in this chapter).

In some cases, the gap between seizures is relatively constant, in others it can be very irregular with several occurring over a short period of time, but with long intervals between *"clusters."*

Affected dogs behave normally between seizures. If they occur because of a problem somewhere else in the body, such as heart disease (which stops oxygen reaching the brain), this is not epilepsy.

Seizures are not uncommon; however, many dogs only ever have one. If your dog has had more than one, it may be that he is epileptic. Anyone who has witnessed their dog having a seizure knows how frightening it can be. The good news is that, just as with people, there are medications to control epilepsy in dogs, allowing them to live happy lives with normal lifespans.

Symptoms

Some dogs seem to know when they are about to have a seizure and may behave in a certain way. You will come to recognise these signs as meaning that an episode is likely. Often dogs just seek out their owner's company and come to sit beside them. There are two main types of seizure:

- **Petit Mal**, also called a Focal or Partial Seizure, which is the lesser of the two as it only affects one half of the brain.

   This may involve facial twitching, staring into space with a fixed glaze and/or upward eye movement, walking as if drunk, snapping at imaginary flies, and/or running or hiding for no reason. Sometimes this is accompanied by urination. The dog is conscious throughout

- **Grand Mal,** or Generalised Seizure, affects both hemispheres of the brain and is more often what we think of when we talk about a seizure. Most dogs become stiff, fall onto their side and make running movements with their legs. Sometimes they will cry out and may lose control of their bowels, bladder or both

FACT > With Grand Mal the dog is unconscious once the seizure starts – he cannot hear or respond to you. While it is distressing to watch, the dog is not in any pain - even if howling.

It's not uncommon for an episode to begin as Petit Mal, but progress into Grand Mal. Sometimes, the progression is pretty clear - there may be twitching or jerking of one body part that gradually increases in intensity and progresses to include the entire body – other times the progression happens very fast.

 Most seizures last between one and three minutes - it is worth making a note of the time the seizure starts and ends – or record it on your phone because it often seems to go on for a lot longer than it actually does.

If you are not sure whether or not your dog has had a seizure, look on YouTube, where there are many videos of dogs having epileptic seizures.

Dogs behave in different ways afterwards. Some just get up and carry on with what they were doing, while others appear dazed and confused for up to 24 hours afterwards. Most commonly, dogs will be disorientated for only 10 to 15 minutes before returning to their old self.

FACT > Most seizures occur while the dog is relaxed and resting quietly, often in the evening or at night; it rarely happens during exercise. In a few dogs, seizures can be triggered by particular events or stress.

They often have a set pattern of behaviour that they follow - for example going for a drink of water or asking to go outside to the toilet. If your dog has had more than one seizure, you may well start to notice a pattern of behaviour that is typically repeated.

The most important thing is to **STAY CALM**. Remember that your dog is unconscious during the seizure and is not in pain or distressed. It is probably more distressing for you than for him. Make sure that he is not in a position to injure himself, for example by falling down the stairs, but otherwise do not try to interfere with him.

NEVER try to put your hand inside his mouth during a seizure or you are very likely to get bitten.

It is very rare for dogs to injure themselves during a seizure. Occasionally, they may bite their tongue and there may seem to be a lot of blood, but it's unlikely to be serious; your dog will not swallow his tongue.

If it goes on for a very long time (more than 10 minutes), his body temperature will rise, which can cause damage to the liver, kidneys or brain. In very extreme cases, some dogs may be left in a coma after severe seizures. Repeated seizures can cause cumulative brain damage, which can result in early senility (with loss of learned behaviour and housetraining, or behavioural changes).

When Should I Contact the Vet?

Generally, if your dog has a seizure lasting more than five minutes or is having them regularly, you should contact your vet. When your dog starts fitting, make a note of the time. If he comes out of it

within five minutes, allow him time to recover quietly before contacting your vet. It is far better for him to recover quietly at home rather than be bundled into the car right away.

If your dog does not come out of the seizure within five minutes, or has repeated seizures close together, contact your vet immediately, as he or she will want to see your dog as soon as possible. Call the vet before setting off to make sure there is someone who can help when you arrive.

Tip If you can, record your dog's seizure on your mobile phone; it will help your vet.

The vet may need to run a range of tests to ensure that there is no other cause of the seizures. These may include blood tests, X-rays or an MRI scan of your dog's brain. If no other cause can be found, then a diagnosis of epilepsy may be made. If your Beagle already has epilepsy, remember these key points:

- 🐾 Don't change or stop any medication without consulting your vet
- 🐾 See your vet at least once a year for follow-up visits
- 🐾 Be sceptical of *"magic cure"* treatments

Treatment

As yet, it is not possible to cure epilepsy, so medication is used to control seizures – in some cases even a well-controlled epileptic may have occasional fits. There are many drugs available including Levetiracetam (brand names: Keppra, Elepsia, Spritam), Phenobarbital and Potassium Bromide; some may have side effects. There are also a number of holistic remedies advertised, but we have no experience of them or any idea if any are effective.

FACT Purina NeuroCare dog food, *pictured,* is reportedly helping to reduce seizure activity or severity in many affected dogs. Other factors useful in some cases are: avoiding dog food containing preservatives, adding vitamins, minerals and/or enzymes to the diet and ensuring drinking water is free of fluoride.

Each epileptic dog is an individual and a treatment plan will be designed specifically for yours, based on the severity and frequency of seizures and how he responds to different medications. Many epileptic dogs require a combination of one or more types of drug for best results.

Keep a record of events in your dog's life, note down dates and times of episodes and record when you have given medication. Each time you visit your vet, take this diary along with you so he or she can see how your dog has been since his last check-up. If seizures are becoming more frequent, it may be necessary to change the medication.

 Owners of epileptic dogs need patience and vigilance. Treatment success often depends on owners keeping a close eye on the dog and reporting any physical or behavioural changes to the vet.

It is also important that medication is given at the same time each day, as he becomes dependent on the levels of drug in his blood to control seizures. If a single dose of treatment is missed, blood levels can drop, which may be enough to trigger a seizure.

It is not common for epileptic dogs to stop having seizures altogether. However, provided your dog is checked regularly by your vet, *there is a good chance that he will live a full and happy life; most epileptic dogs have far more good days than bad ones.*

LIVE *WITH* EPILEPSY NOT *FOR* EPILEPSY.

Hypothyroidism

Beagles can suffer from a number of auto-immune diseases, including Hypothyroidism, SRM, allergies and Puppy Strangles. Hypothyroidism is a common hormonal disorder in dogs and is due to an under-active thyroid gland.

The gland (located on either side of the windpipe in the dog's throat) does not produce enough of the hormone thyroid, which controls the speed of the metabolism. Dogs with very low thyroid levels have a slow metabolic rate.

It usually happens in middle-aged dogs of both sexes aged four to eight and in medium to large breeds, including some Beagles. The symptoms are often non-specific and quite gradual in onset, and they may vary depending on breed and age. They are:

* High blood cholesterol
* Lethargy
* Hair Loss
* Weight gain or obesity
* Dull, dry coat or excessive shedding
* Hyperpigmentation or darkening of the skin, seen in 25% of cases
* Intolerance to cold, seen in 15% of dogs with the condition

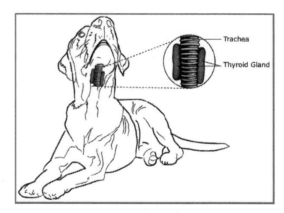

Although hypothyroidism is a type of auto-immune disease and cannot be prevented, symptoms can usually be easily diagnosed and treated. Most forms of hypothyroidism are diagnosed with a simple blood test, and most affected dogs can be well-managed on thyroid hormone replacement therapy tablets.

The dog is placed on a daily dose of a synthetic thyroid hormone called thyroxine (levothyroxine, **pictured**). He is usually given a standard dose for his weight and then blood samples are periodically taken to check his response and the dose is adjusted accordingly.

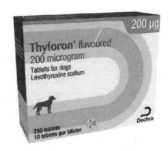

Depending upon the dog's preferences and needs, the medication can be given in different forms; a solid tablet, or a liquid or gel that can be rubbed into the dog's ears. Treatment is lifelong. In some less common situations, surgery may be required to remove part or all of the thyroid gland.

Happily, once the diagnosis has been made and treatment has started, the majority of symptoms disappear.

By the way, Hyperthyroidism (as opposed to hypothyroidism) is caused by the thyroid gland producing too much thyroid hormone. It doesn't affect dogs, but it does affect cats. A common symptom is the cat being ravenously hungry, but losing weight.

NOTE: Beagles are also thought to be one of the breeds with an increased chance of being affected by autoimmune disorders. Under normal circumstances the dog's immune system recognises tissues and cells that are part of itself, and the immune system only produces antibodies against foreign cells.

However, sometimes the immune system produces antibodies which attack the dog's own body tissues. These are called *"autoantibodies"* and the result is called an autoimmune disease. The reasons are as yet not fully understood.

Autoimmune diseases can result in a wide range of symptoms and a range of treatments, depending on the exact cause. According to Provet Healthcare: "The prognosis is always guarded, with only fair to poor chances of long-term survival without treatment. However some dogs respond well to therapy."

SRM (Steroid Responsive Meningitis)

This is a syndrome that occurs in many breeds and is again a disease affecting the immune system. It was first call Beagle Pain Syndrome (BPS) due to the fact it was found in a colony of research beagles in the late 1980s.

Symptoms vary and are often misdiagnosed as Lyme disease, cervical or spinal injury, or massive bacterial infection.

Typical symptoms, which can appear very quickly, are:

- Neck pain or stiffness
- Shaking
- Hunched back
- Fever
- Lack of appetite
- Muscle spasms, especially in front legs and neck
- Lethargy, and unwillingness to move
- A hesitancy to bark and opening of the jaw seems to be painful

SRM is most often being seen around six to eight months of age for the first time, although it has been seen as young as 10 weeks and in dogs of over two years. The cause is unknown; it is known to be an immune response, but the trigger has not been identified.

The immune response results in an intense inflammation of the blood vessels supplying the neurological system particularly the meninges (lining around the brain) and the cervical spinal cord (neck). The body is "attacking" its own cells and treatment revolves around suppressing the immune system.

Diagnosis is most commonly based on symptoms and a spinal tap, when samples of fluid are taken under a general anaesthetic. MRI scans are also proving very useful in assessing the severity of the condition, and C reactive protein levels are also used to diagnose and monitor therapy.

Treatment has usually involved steroids along with a short course of antibiotics. However, there is a new and very effective treatment called cytarabine. More commonly used in chemotherapy, this is given as an injection - initially intravenously, but can be given under the skin at a later stage. Side effects are rare and it produces a quicker response with fewer relapses than steroids alone.

The outlook for an affected dog depends on his or her response to treatment, but the majority can be cured with early detection and aggressive treatment. In the past many dogs have relapsed after initially successful treatment with steroids, but early signs are that cytarabine reduces the chances of this happening.

Dr Samantha Goldberg, Kennel Club Health Co-ordinator for the UK Beagle Clubs, is currently compiling a database of affected Beagles.

Puppy Strangles

This is an immune disorder that occasionally develops in puppies usually between the ages of three weeks and six months when the muzzle, eyelids and face suddenly swell. The cause is uncertain, but there may be a genetic link. The normal treatment is a course of steroids, with antibiotics if the skin has become infected, and the puppy is usually back to normal within a couple of weeks.

....

Diabetes

Diabetes can affect dogs of all breeds, sizes and both genders - and overweight dogs are particularly susceptible. There are two types:

Diabetes insipidus (DI) is caused by a lack of vasopressin (ADH), a hormone that controls the kidneys' absorption of water. It gets its name from the fact that the urine of these patients is dilute enough to be tasteless or *insipid.*

Although relatively rare, symptoms are excessive drinking and the production of enormous volumes of extremely dilute urine. Some dogs may produce so much urine that they become incontinent. Despite drinking large volumes of water, the dog can become dehydrated from urinating so much.

Once other causes have been ruled out, diagnosis is made by a complete blood count and there is also something called a water deprivation test which involves restricting the dog's water intake and then measuring the concentration of urine.

There are two types of DI, and they are treated either with synthetic ADH applied as eye drops or by injection or with diuretic tablets and a low-salt diet. Diabetes insipidus cannot be cured, but it can usually be successfully controlled.

Diabetes mellitus occurs when the dog's body does not produce enough insulin and therefore cannot successfully process sugars. This is the type overweight dogs get. Dogs, like us, get their energy by converting the food they eat into sugars, mainly glucose. This travels in the bloodstream and then, using a protein called *insulin,* cells remove some of the glucose from the blood to use for energy.

Most diabetic dogs have Type 1 diabetes; their pancreas does not produce any insulin. Without it, the cells can't use the glucose that is in the bloodstream, so they *"starve"* while the glucose level in the blood rises.

Diabetes mellitus (sugar diabetes) is the most common form and affects mostly middle-aged and older dogs. Both males and females can develop it, although unspayed females have a slightly higher risk. Vets take blood and urine samples in order to diagnose diabetes. Early treatment helps to prevent further complications developing.

FACT The condition is treatable and need not shorten a dog's lifespan or interfere greatly with quality of life. Due to advances in veterinary science, diabetic dogs undergoing treatment now have the same life expectancy as non-diabetic dogs of the same age and gender.

Symptoms of Diabetes Mellitus:

- Extreme thirst
- Excessive urination
- Weight loss
- Increased appetite
- Coat in poor condition
- Lethargy
- Vision problems due to cataracts

If left untreated, diabetes can lead to cataracts or other ailments.

Treatment and Exercise

It is EXTREMELY IMPORTANT that Beagles are not allowed to get overweight, as obesity is a major trigger for diabetes.

FACT Many cases of canine diabetes can be successfully treated with a combination of a diet low in sugar, fat and carbs (a raw diet is worth considering), alongside a moderate and consistent exercise routine and medication. More severe cases may require insulin injections.

In the newly-diagnosed dog, insulin therapy begins at home after a vet has explained how to prepare and inject insulin. Normally, after a week of treatment, you return to the vet for a series of blood sugar tests over a 12 to 14-hour period to see when the blood glucose peaks and troughs.

Adjustments are made to the dosage and timing of the injections. You may also be asked to collect urine samples using a test strip of paper that indicates the glucose levels.

Tip If your dog is already having insulin injections, beware of a "miracle cure" offered on the internet. It does not exist. There is no diet or vitamin supplement that can reduce a dog's dependence on insulin injections, because vitamins and minerals cannot do what insulin does in the dog's body.

If you think that your dog needs a supplement, discuss it with your vet first to make sure that it does not interfere with any other medication.

Exercise burns up blood glucose the same way that insulin does. If your dog is on insulin, any active exercise on top of the insulin might cause him to have a severe low blood glucose episode, called *"hypoglycaemia."*

Keep your dog on a reasonably consistent exercise routine. Your usual insulin dose will take that amount of exercise into account. If you plan to take your dog out for some demanding exercise, such as running around with other dogs, you may need to reduce his usual insulin dose.

Tips

- 🐾 Specially-formulated diabetes dog food is available from most vets

- 🐾 Feed the same type and amount of food at the same times every day

- 🐾 Most vets recommend twice-a-day feeding for diabetic pets (it's OK if your dog prefers to eat more often)

- 🐾 Help your dog to achieve the best possible blood glucose control by NOT feeding table scraps or treats between meals

- 🐾 Watch for signs that your dog is starting to drink more water than usual. Call the vet if you see this happening, as it may mean that the insulin dose needs adjusting

Food raises blood glucose - Insulin and exercise lower blood glucose - Keep them in balance

For more information visit **www.caninediabetes.org**

....

Cushing's Disease

This complex ailment, also known as *hyperadrenocorticism,* is caused when a dog produces too much Cortisol hormone. It develops over a period of time, which is why it is more often seen in middle-aged or senior dogs. Beagles are more susceptible than some other breeds.

Cortisol is released by the adrenal gland near the kidneys. Normally it is produced during times of stress to prepare the body for strenuous activity. Think of an adrenaline rush. While this hormone is essential for the effective functioning of cells and organs, too much of it can be dangerous.

The disease can be difficult to diagnose, as the most common symptoms are similar to those for old age. A dog may display one or more:

- 🐾 A ravenous appetite

- 🐾 Drinking excessive amounts of water

- 🐾 Urinating frequently or urinary incontinence

- 🐾 Hair loss or recurring skin issues

- 🐾 Pot belly

- 🐾 Thin skin

- 🐾 Muscle wastage

- 🐾 Insomnia

- 🐾 Lack of energy, general lethargy

- 🐾 Panting a lot

Cushing's disease cannot be cured, but it can be successfully managed and controlled with medication, giving the dog a longer, happier life. Some dogs with mild symptoms do not require treatment, but should be closely monitored for signs of them worsening.

Lysodren (mitotane) or Vetoryl (trilostane) are usually prescribed by vets to treat the most common pituitary-dependent Cushing's disease. Both can have a number of side effects – so your dog needs monitoring - and the dog remains on the medication for life.

The Heart

Just as with humans, heart problems are not uncommon among the population in general. The heart is a mechanical pump. It receives blood in one half and forces it through the lungs, then the other half pumps the blood through the entire body.

Two of the most common forms of heart failure in dogs are Degenerative Valvular Disease (DVD) and Dilated Cardiomyopathy (DCM), also known as an enlarged heart.

Beagles are not prone to heart problems, but one specific disease known to affect the breed is Pulmonic Stenosis, a narrowing in the region of the pulmonary valve. Virtually all affected dogs will have a heart murmur. Often, but not always, the loudness of the murmur is an indication of the severity of the disease.

Beagles only mildly affected may never develop any symptoms and may live a normal lifespan. However, in severe cases, a dog may show signs of exercise intolerance, collapsing, irregular heartbeat or heart failure.

In people, heart disease usually involves the arteries that supply blood to the heart muscle becoming hardened over time, causing the heart muscles to receive less blood than they need. Starved of oxygen, the result is often a heart attack.

FACT Although heart disease is quite common, hardening of the arteries (arteriosclerosis) and heart attacks are very rare in dogs. More usually, heart failure occurs, which means that the muscles *"give out"* after months or even years of heart disease.

This is usually caused by one chamber or side of the heart being required to do more than it is physically able to do. It may be that excessive force is required to pump the blood through an area, causing the muscles to eventually fail.

Symptoms of a heart condition:

- Tiredness
- Decreased activity levels
- Restlessness, pacing around instead of settling down to sleep
- Intermittent coughing - especially during exertion or excitement. This tends to occur at night, sometimes about two hours after the dog goes to bed or when he wakes up in the morning. This coughing is an attempt to clear the lungs

As the condition worsens, other symptoms may appear:

- 🐾 Lack of appetite
- 🐾 Rapid breathing
- 🐾 Abdominal swelling (due to fluid)
- 🐾 Noticeable loss of weight
- 🐾 Fainting (syncope)
- 🐾 Paleness

A vet will carry out tests that may include listening to the heart, chest X-rays, blood tests, electrocardiogram (a record of your dog's heartbeat) or an echocardiogram. If the heart problem is due to an enlarged heart or valve disease, the condition cannot be reversed.

Treatment focuses on managing exercise and various medications, which may change over time as the condition progresses. The vet may also prescribe a special low salt diet, as sodium determines the amount of water in the blood.

 Pay attention to your Beagle's oral health, as dental problems can increase the risk of heart disease. There is evidence that fatty acids and other supplements may be beneficial for a heart condition; discuss this with your vet.

Heart Murmurs

Heart murmurs are not uncommon in dogs – particularly older ones - and are one of the first signs that something may be amiss. One of our dogs was diagnosed with a Grade 2 murmur several years ago and, of course, your heart sinks when the vet gives you the terrible news.

But once the shock is over, it's important to realise that there are several different severities of the condition and, at its mildest, it is no great cause for concern. Our dog lived an active, healthy life and died at the age of 13.

Literally, a heart murmur is a specific sound heard through a stethoscope, which results from the blood flowing faster than normal within the heart itself or in one of the two major arteries. Instead of the normal *"lubb dupp"* noise, an additional sound can be heard that can vary from a mild *"pshhh"* to a loud *"whoosh."* The different grades are:

- 🐾 **Grade 1 -** barely audible
- 🐾 **Grade 2 -** soft, but easily heard with a stethoscope
- 🐾 **Grade 3 -** intermediate loudness; most murmurs that are related to the mechanics of blood circulation are at least Grade 3
- 🐾 **Grade 4 -** loud murmur that radiates widely, often including opposite side of chest
- 🐾 **Grade 5 and Grade 6 -** very loud, audible with the stethoscope barely touching the chest; the vibration is strong enough to be felt through the dog's chest wall

Murmurs are caused by a number of factors; it may be a problem with the heart valves or could be due to some other condition, such as hyperthyroidism, anaemia or heartworm.

In puppies, there are two major types of heart murmurs, often detected by a vet at the first or second vaccination visit. The most common type is called an innocent *"flow murmur."* This type of murmur is soft - typically Grade 2 or less - and is not caused by underlying heart disease. An innocent flow murmur typically disappears by four to five months of age.

However, if a puppy has a loud murmur - Grade 3 or louder - or if it is still easily heard with a stethoscope after four or five months of age, it's more likely that the pup has an underlying heart problem.

The thought of a puppy having congenital heart disease is worrying, but it is important to remember that the disease will not affect all puppies' life expectancy or quality of life.

Canine Cancer

This is the biggest single killer and will claim the lives of one in four dogs, regardless of breed. It is the cause of nearly half the deaths of all dogs aged 10 years and older, according to the American Veterinary Medical Association. Beagles live longer than many other breeds and may be therefore more prone to cancer in their golden years.

One type of cancer that can affect Beagles *Hemangiosarcoma,* a malignant cancer in the blood vessel walls, most commonly found in the spleen or heart. Symptoms include:

- Pale gums
- Disorientation, tiredness or collapse
- Rapid breathing
- Extreme thirst
- Lack of appetite

Unfortunately, affected Beagles can die from internal bleeding or the cancer spreading to other parts of the body. In some cases, however, if the cancer is in the spleen and discovered early, the spleen may be removed before the malignant cells spread to other organs.

Symptoms of other types of cancer include:

- Swellings anywhere on the body or around the anus
- Sores that don't heal
- Weight loss
- Lameness, which may be a sign of bone cancer, with or without a visible lump
- Laboured breathing
- Changes in exercise or stamina level
- Change in bowel or bladder habits
- Increased drinking or urination
- Bad breath, which can be a sign of oral cancer
- Poor appetite, difficulty swallowing or excessive drooling
- Vomiting

 **FACT** ⟩ There is evidence that the risk of testicular, uterine and mammary cancers decreases with neutering and spaying. See Chapter 14. The Facts of Life for more detailed information.

Treatment and Reducing the Risk

Just because your dog has a skin growth doesn't mean that it's serious. Many older dogs develop fatty lumps, or lipomas, which are often harmless, but it's still advisable to have the first one checked. Your vet will make a diagnosis following an X-ray, scan, blood test, biopsy or combination of these.

If your dog is diagnosed with cancer, there is hope. Advances in veterinary medicine and technology offer various treatment options, including chemotherapy, radiation and surgery. Unlike with humans, a dog's hair does not fall out with chemotherapy.

We had a happy ending. We had a four-year-old dog develop a lump like a black grape on his anus. We took him down to the vet within a day or so of first noticing it and got the dreaded diagnosis of T-cell lymphoma, a particularly aggressive form of cancer.

The vet removed the lump a couple of days later and the dog went on to live into his teens.

 Every time you groom your dog, get into the habit of checking his body for lumps and lift his top lip to check for signs of paleness or whiteness in the gums. As with any illness, early detection often leads to a better outcome.

We have all become aware of the risk factors for human cancer - stopping smoking, protecting ourselves from over-exposure to strong sunlight and eating a healthy, balanced diet all help to reduce cancer rates.

We know to keep a close eye on ourselves, go for regular health checks and report any lumps to our doctors as soon as they appear.

The same is true with your dog.

The outcome depends on the type of cancer, treatment used and, importantly, how early the tumour is found. The sooner treatment begins, the greater the chances of success. While it is impossible to completely prevent cancer, the following points can help to reduce the risk:

- Feed a healthy diet with few or no preservatives
- Don't let your Beagle get overweight
- Consider dietary supplements, such as antioxidants, Vitamins, A, C, E, beta carotene, lycopene or selenium, or coconut oil – check compatibility with any other treatments
- Give pure, filtered or bottled water (fluoride-free) for drinking
- Give your dog regular daily exercise
- Keep your dog away from chemicals, pesticides, cleaning products, etc. around the garden and home
- Avoid passive smoking

- 🐾 Consider natural flea remedies (check they are working) and avoid unnecessary vaccinations
- 🐾 Check your dog regularly for lumps and any other physical or behavioural changes
- 🐾 If you are buying a puppy, ask whether there is any history of cancer among the ancestors

Canine cancer research is currently being conducted all over the world, and medical advances are producing a steady flow of new tests and treatments to improve survival rates and cancer care.

....

Beagle Tail

Beagle Tail, also called Limber Tail or Limp Tail, occurs in other breeds as well. It most commonly occurs after a Beagle has been bathed or been swimming and results in a tail which hangs down after the first few inches. The tail is painful and the Beagle is unable to lift it properly.

NOTE: It should not confused with a tail which is dropped due to nervousness or a tail which is limp and has no tone (commonly associated with a tail which has been trapped in something).

Beagle Tail is associated with the dog having shaken to rid himself of water and the tail is concussed. It doesn't have to actually hit something as it is a form of whiplash. The condition can take hours or days to resolve.

Even with pain relief in the form of anti-inflammatory drugs, the bruising in the tail nerves needs time to settle, and patience is required.

The best way to avoid this is not to let your Beagle shake himself too violently after being in water, so consider draping a towel along his back and tail.

It is also important to towel your dog as dry as you can, and monitor him for a short while to reduce shaking. Also, wet dogs shouldn't be crated, as they are still likely to shake themselves.

Reverse Sneezing

Some Beagles may display a condition known as backwards or **reverse sneezing** - the medical name is a **pharyngeal gag reflex.** It's called a reverse sneeze, because it sounds like the dog is pulling air into his nose, whereas in a normal sneeze, the air is pushed out through the nose.

An affected Beagle will make rapid and long intakes of breath, stand still and stretch his head forwards. He'll make a loud snorting sound, a bit like a goose honking, which may make you think he has something stuck in his nose.

The most common cause is irritation of the soft palate, which results in a spasm. This narrows the airway and makes it temporarily more difficult for the dog to take in air. Factors that may trigger reverse sneezing include excitement, eating or drinking, exercise, physical irritation of the throat - such as from pulling on a lead - respiratory tract mites, allergies, irritating chemicals like perfumes or household cleaners, viral infections or foreign bodies caught in the throat.

Episodes usually only last a few seconds, but can be longer. Some owners claim that a spasm can be shortened by making the dog swallow by briefly placing your hands over the nostrils. Another technique is to massage your dog's throat to try and get rid of the irritant.

While it may seem alarming, infrequent cases of reverse sneezing are not normally a problem. It is not a harmful condition, there are no ill after-effects, and treatment is unnecessary. Usually the dog is completely normal before and after the episode.

With huge thanks to Dr Samantha Goldberg, Kennel Club Health Co-ordinator for the UK Beagle Clubs, and Darlene Stewart, chairperson, Health and Genetics Committee, National Beagle Club of America, for their invaluable contributions to this chapter.

Two excellent sources of further information on Beagle health are: www.beaglehealth.info and www.aladarbeagles.com/toc.html

Disclaimer: The author is not a vet. This chapter is intended to give owners an outline of some of the main health issues and symptoms that may affect their Beagles. If you have any concerns regarding your dog's health, our advice is always the same: consult a veterinarian.

12. Beagle Skin & Allergies

Visit any busy veterinary clinic these days – especially in spring and summer – and you'll see itchy dogs. Skin conditions, allergies and intolerances are on the increase in the canine world as well as the human one. While the Beagle is generally regarded as a healthy breed, some dogs can be susceptible to skin issues.

How many children did you hear of having asthma or a peanut allergy when you were at school? Not too many, I'll bet. Yet allergies and adverse reactions are now relatively common – and it's the same with dogs. The reasons are not clear; it could be connected to genetics, diet, environment, over-vaccination – or a combination. As yet, there is no clear scientific evidence to back this up.

The skin is a complicated topic and a whole book could be written on this subject alone. While many dogs have no problems at all, some suffer from sensitive, itchy, dry or oily skin, hot spots, bald spots, yeast infections or other skin disorders, causing them to scratch, bite or lick themselves excessively. Symptoms vary from mild itchiness to a chronic reaction.

Canine Skin

The skin is the dog's largest organ. It acts as the protective barrier between your dog's internal organs and the outside world; it also regulates temperature and provides the sense of touch. Surprisingly, a dog's skin is actually thinner than ours, and it is made up of three layers:

1. **Epidermis** or outer layer, the one that bears the brunt of your dog's contact with the outside world.

2. **Dermis** is the extremely tough layer mostly made up of collagen, a strong and fibrous protein. This is where blood vessels deliver nutrients and oxygen to the skin, and it also acts as your dog's thermostat by allowing her body to release or retain heat, depending on the outside temperature and your dog's activity level.

3. **Hypodermis** is a dense layer of fatty tissue that allows your dog's skin to move independently from the muscle layers below it, as well as providing insulation and support for the skin.

FACT ❯ Human allergies often trigger a reaction within the respiratory system, causing us to wheeze or sneeze, whereas allergies or hypersensitivities in a dog often cause a reaction in her **SKIN**.

🐾 Skin can be affected from the **INSIDE** by things that your dog eats or drinks

🐾 Skin can be affected from the **OUTSIDE** by fleas, parasites, or inhaled and contact allergies triggered by grass, pollen, man-made chemicals, dust, mould, etc.

Most Beagles can run through fields, digging holes and rolling around in the grass with no after-effects at all. Others may spend more time indoors and have an excellent diet, but still experience itching, hot spots, bald patches or recurring ear infections. Some can eat anything and everything with no issues at all, while owners of others spend a lot of time trying to find the magic bullet – the ideal food for their dog's sensitive stomach.

It's by no means possible to cover all of the issues and causes in this chapter. The aim here is to give a broad outline of some of the more common ailments and how to deal with them. We have also included remedies tried with some success by ourselves (we had a dog with skin issues) and other owners of affected dogs, as well as advice from a holistic specialist.

This information is not intended to take the place of professional help; always contact your vet if your dog appears physically unwell or uncomfortable. This is particularly true with skin conditions:

Tip SEEK TREATMENT AS SOON AS POSSIBLE. **If you can find the cause(s) early, you reduce the chances of it taking hold and causing secondary issues and infections.**

Whatever the cause, before a vet can make a diagnosis, you'll have to give details of your dog's diet, exercise regime, habits, medical history and local environment. The vet will then carry out a physical examination, possibly followed by further tests, before a course of treatment can be prescribed. One of the difficulties with skin ailments is that the exact cause is often difficult to diagnose, as the symptoms are similar to other issues.

If environmental allergies are involved, specific and expensive tests are available. You'll have to take your vet's advice on this, as the tests are not always conclusive. And if the answer is pollen, it can be difficult – if not downright impossible - to keep your Beagle away from the triggers. You can't keep a Beagle permanently indoors, so it's often a question of managing rather than curing the condition.

FACT There are many things you as an owner can do to reduce the allergen load – and many natural remedies and supplements that can help as well as veterinary medications.

NOTE: Food allergies and intolerances are dealt with in **Chapter 6. Feeding a Beagle.**

Types of Allergies

"Canine dermatitis" means inflammation of a dog's skin and it can be triggered by numerous things, but the most common is allergies. Vets estimate that as many as one in four dogs they see has some kind of allergy. Symptoms are (your dog may have one or more of these):

- Chewing, most commonly the feet or belly
- Itchy ears, head shaking
- Rubbing her face on the floor
- Scratching

- 🐾 Scratching or biting the anus
- 🐾 Hair loss
- 🐾 Flaky or greasy skin, perhaps with sore or discoloured patches or hot spots
- 🐾 The skin can smell of corn chips

Beagles who are allergic to something show it through skin problems and itching; your vet may call this *"pruritus."* It may seem logical that if Beagles are allergic to something inhaled, like certain pollen grains, their nose will run; if allergic to something eaten, they may vomit, or if allergic to an insect bite, they may develop a swelling. But in practice this is seldom the case.

Dogs with allergies often chew their feet until they are sore and red. You may see yours rubbing her face on the carpet or couch, or scratching her belly and flanks. Because the ear glands produce too much wax in response to the allergy, ear infections can occur - with bacteria and yeast (which is a fungus) often thriving in the excessive wax and debris.

Digestive health can play an important role. Holistic vet Dr Jodie Gruenstern says: "It's estimated that up to 80% of the immune system resides within the gastrointestinal system; building a healthy gut supports a more appropriate immune response. The importance of choosing fresh proteins and healthy fats over processed, starchy diets (such as kibble) can't be overemphasized. Grains and other starches have a negative impact on gut health, creating insulin resistance and inflammation."

Allergic dogs may cause skin lesions or **hot spots** by constant chewing and scratching. Sometimes they will lose hair, which can be patchy, leaving a mottled appearance, or the coat may change colour. The skin itself may be dry and crusty, reddened, swollen or oily, depending on the dog. It is common to get secondary bacterial skin infections due to these self-inflicted wounds.

An allergic dog's body is reacting to certain molecules called **allergens.** These may come from:

- 🐾 Tree, grass or plant pollens
- 🐾 Flea bites
- 🐾 Grain mites
- 🐾 Specific food or food additives, such as cooked or raw meat or poultry, grains, colourings or preservatives
- 🐾 Milk products
- 🐾 Fabrics, such as wool or nylon
- 🐾 Rubber and plastics
- 🐾 House dust and dust mites
- 🐾 Mould
- 🐾 Chemical products used around the home or garden

 These allergens may be INHALED as the dog breathes, INGESTED as the dog eats, or caused by CONTACT with the dog's body when walking or rolling.

Regardless of how they arrive, they all cause the immune system to produce a protein called IgE, which releases irritating chemicals like histamine inside the skin, hence the scratching.

Managing allergies is all about **REDUCING THE ALLERGEN LOAD.**

One breeder with decades of experience said: "I have found the majority of skin and ear problems in Beagles are actually food allergies - especially when biting at the rectum, tail etc. The feet licking is more inhalant pollen or contact-type allergy. I always look to grain allergy, such as corn, wheat, or soybean, as first suspect - especially if yeasty ear infections are noted."

Inhalant Allergies (Atopy)

Some of the most common allergies affecting Beagles are inhalant and seasonal - at least at first; some allergies may develop and worsen. Substances that can cause an allergic reaction in dogs are similar to those causing problems for humans.

Look at the timing of the reaction. Does it happen all year round? If so, this may be mould, dust or some other permanent trigger. If the reaction is seasonal, then pollens may well be the culprit.

 There is a serum test called **VARL Liquid Gold** widely used in the USA. A simple blood sample is taken and tested for reactions to different types of pollen in your area, other environmental triggers and food. VARL claims it's at least as effective as the more intrusive **intradermal skin testing** (around 75%), which involves sedating the dog, injecting a small amount of antigen into the skin and then inspecting it for an allergic reaction.

They say a further advantage is that it does not give false positives. Depending on the results, treatment may involve avoidance or an immunotherapy programme consisting of a series of injections or tablets. One breeder involved in this book has used the Liquid Gold test on a Beagle with sensitivities to good effect; it highlighted reactions to many allergens.

A similar serum test called **Avacta** is used by vets in the UK.

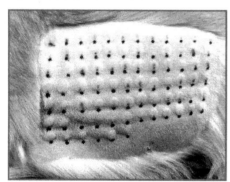 *Our photo shows a Golden Retriever that has undergone intradermal skin testing.*

Other blood tests work by checking for antibodies caused by antigens. The two standard tests are **RAST** and **ELISA**. Many vets feel that the ELISA test gives more accurate results, although both can give false positives.

Some owners of dogs with allergies consider changing to an unprocessed diet (raw or cooked) and natural alternatives to long-term use of steroids, which can cause other health issues.

Environmental or Contact Irritations

These are a direct reaction to something the dog physically comes into contact with, and the triggers are similar to inhalant allergies. If grass or pollen is the issue, the allergies are often seasonal. An affected dog may be given treatments such as tablets, shampoo or localised cortisone spray for spring and summer – with a steroid injection to control a flare-up - but be perfectly fine the rest of the year. This was the case with our dog with allergies.

 If you suspect your Beagle has outdoor contact allergies, hose her down after walks. Washing her feet and belly will get rid of some of the pollen and other allergens, which in turn reduces scratching and biting.

The problem may be localised - such as the paws or belly. Symptoms are a general skin irritation or specific hotspots - itching (pruritus) and sometimes hair loss. Readers of our website sometimes report that their dog will incessantly lick one part of the body, often the paws, anus, belly or back.

Flea Bite Allergy

This is a common allergy affecting lots of dogs. It's typically seasonal, worse during summer and autumn - peak time for fleas - and in warmer climates where fleas are prevalent. Unfortunately, some dogs with a flea allergy also have inhalant allergies.

This allergy is not to the flea itself, but to proteins in flea saliva left under the dog's skin when the insect feeds. Just one bite to an allergic dog will cause red, crusty bumps *(pictured)* and intense itching.

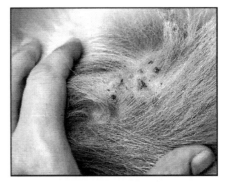

Affected dogs usually have a rash at the base of their tails and rear legs, and will bite and scratch the area. Much of the skin damage is done by the dog's scratching, rather than the flea bite, and can result in hair falling out or skin abrasions. Some dogs also develop hot spots, often along the base of the tail and back.

A vet can make a diagnosis with a simple blood test. If fleas are the cause, you'll also have to make sure her bedding and your home are flea-free zones. Most flea bite allergies can be treated with medication, but they can only be totally prevented by keeping all fleas away from the dog. Various flea prevention treatments are available – see the section on **Parasites.**

 A few dogs can have an adverse reaction to topical (on-the-skin) chemical flea treatments. If so, consider tablets or holistic remedies as an alternative.

Acute Moist Dermatitis (Hot Spots)

A hot spot can appear suddenly and is a raw, inflamed and often bleeding area of skin. The area becomes moist and painful and begins spreading due to continual licking and chewing. They can become large, red, irritated lesions in a short pace of time. The cause is often a local reaction to an insect bite.

 Some owners have had good results after dabbing hot spots, interdigital cysts and other skin irritations with an equal mixture of the amber-coloured Original Listerine *(pictured),* baby oil and water. US owners have also reported success with Gold Bond Powder.

Once diagnosed and with the right treatment for the underlying cause, hot spots often disappear as soon as they appeared. Treatments may come in the form of injections, tablets or creams – or a combination of all three. The affected area is clipped and cleaned by the vet to help the effectiveness of any spray or ointment.

The dog may also have to wear an E-collar, which is stressful for everybody, as you watch your Beagle bumping into door frames and furniture. Some dogs can be resistant to the *"Cone of Shame"* - they may slump down like you've hung a 10-ton weight on their neck or sink into a depression. Fortunately, they don't usually have to wear them for more than a few days. One alternative is an *inflatable comfy collar, pictured.*

Bacterial infection (Pyoderma)

Pyoderma literally means *pus in the skin* (yuk)! The offending bacteria is staphylococcus, and the condition may also be referred to as a *staph infection.* Early signs are itchy red spots filled with yellow pus, similar to pimples or spots in humans. They can sometimes develop into red, ulcerated skin with dry and crusty patches. Fortunately, the condition is not contagious.

Pyoderma is caused by several things: a broken skin surface, a skin wound due to chronic exposure to moisture, altered skin bacteria, or poor blood flow to the skin.

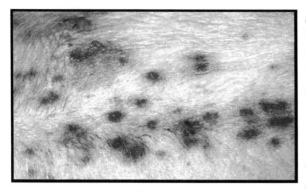

Allergies to fleas, food, parasites, yeast or fungal skin infections, thyroid disease, hormonal imbalances, heredity and some medications can all increase the risk. One of the biggest causes is a dog with a skin disorder excessively licking or biting an itchy patch.

Puppies can develop **puppy pyoderma** in thinly-haired areas, such as the groin and underarms. If you notice symptoms, get to the vet quickly before the condition develops from **superficial pyoderma** into **severe pyoderma**, which is very unpleasant and takes a lot longer to treat.

Superficial and puppy pyoderma are usually successfully treated with a two to six-week course of antibiotic tablets or ointment. Severe or recurring pyoderma looks awful, causes your dog some distress and can take months to completely cure.

Medicated shampoos and regular bathing, as instructed by your vet, are also part of the treatment. It's also important to ensure your dog has clean, dry, padded bedding. Bacterial infection, no matter how bad it may look, usually responds well to medical treatment.

Malassezia Dermatitis and Yeast Infections

Malassezia Dermatitis is a specific type of yeast infection that affects many dogs. **Malassezia** is a yeast, or fungus, that gets into the surface layers of the skin. These organisms cause no harm to the vast majority of animals, but cause inflammation in some dogs when numbers multiply.

Like all yeast infections, they like humid conditions - so climate can be a factor – and especially warm, damp areas on a dog's body like ear canals and skin folds. One trigger is saliva with repetitive licking – which explains why feet are often stained and itchy; saliva stains them and Malassezia grows. Beagles that already have poor skin condition, allergies or a hormonal disorder are more prone to Malassezia infection. Symptoms are:

- 🐾 Itchy, flaky skin at inflamed areas around the lips, ear canals, neck and armpits, between the toes and in skin folds on the face
- 🐾 Greasy or flaky skin
- 🐾 Unpleasant smell
- 🐾 In long-term cases, the skin becomes thicker and darker
- 🐾 Reddish-brown discolouration of the claws

The condition is easily diagnosed with a skin scraping and is often effectively treated with anti-fungal shampoos, wipes and creams, or tablets. If another skin disorder is causing the Malassezia to spread, this will have to be addressed to rid the dog of the problem.

Interdigital Cysts

If your Beagle gets a fleshy red lump between the toes that looks like an ulcerated sore or a hairless bump, then it's probably an interdigital cyst - or **interdigital furuncle**. These can be very difficult to cure as they are often not the main problem, but a symptom of some other ailment.

They are not cysts, but the result of **furunculosis**, a skin condition that clogs hair follicles and creates chronic infection. Causes include allergies, obesity, poor foot conformation, mites, yeast infections, ingrowing hairs or other foreign bodies.

 **FACT** Bulldogs are the most susceptible breed, but any dog can get them - often the dog also has allergies.

These nasty-looking bumps are painful, will probably cause a limp and can be a nightmare to get rid of. Vets might recommend a whole range of treatments to get to the root cause, and it can be very expensive to have a barrage of tests or biopsies - even then you're not guaranteed to find the underlying cause.

The vet might recommend an E-collar. If your dog is resistant, try putting socks on the affected foot or feet instead. This works well while they sleep, but you have to watch them like a hawk when awake to stop them licking the affected areas.

Here are some remedies your vet may suggest:

- 🐾 Antibiotics and/or steroids and/or mite killers
- 🐾 Soaking the feet in Epsom salts
- 🐾 Testing for allergies or thyroid problems
- 🐾 Starting a food trial if food allergies are suspected
- 🐾 Shampooing the feet
- 🐾 Cleaning between the toes with medicated (benzoyl peroxide) wipes
- 🐾 A referral to a veterinary dermatologist
- 🐾 Surgery (this is a last-resort option)

If you suspect your Beagle has an interdigital cyst, get to the vet for a correct diagnosis and then discuss the various options. A course of antibiotics may be suggested initially, along with switching to a hypoallergenic diet if a food allergy is suspected. If the condition persists, many owners get discouraged, especially when treatment continues for several weeks.

 Be wary of agreeing to a series of steroid injections or repeated courses of antibiotics, as this means that the underlying cause of the furuncle has not been diagnosed. In such cases, it is worth exploring natural diets and remedies – and trying to lower the overall allergen load on your dog.

Before you resort to any drastic action, first try soaking your Beagle's affected paw in Epsom salts for five or 10 minutes twice a day. After the soaking, clean the area with medicated wipes, which are antiseptic and control inflammation.

Surgery is a drastic option. Although it can be effective in solving the immediate issue, it doesn't deal with the underlying problem.

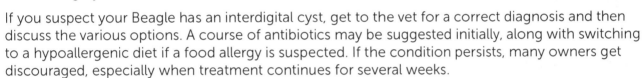

Post-surgery healing is slow and difficult, and the dog does not have the same foot as before. Future orthopaedic issues and more interdigital cysts are a couple of problems that can occur afterwards.

All that said, your vet will understand that interdigital cysts are not simple to deal with, but they are always treatable. *Get the right diagnosis as soon as possible.*

Parasites

Demodectic Mange (Demodex)

Also known as red mange, follicular mange or puppy mange, this skin disease is caused by the tiny mite Demodex canis, **pictured.** The mites actually live inside the hair follicles on the bodies of virtually every adult dog and most humans without causing any harm or irritation.

 In humans, the mites are found in the skin, eyelids and the creases of the nose...try not to think about that!

The mite spends its entire life on the host dog. Eggs hatch and mature from larvae to nymphs to adults in 20 to 35 days and the mites are transferred directly from the mother to the puppies within the first week of life by direct physical contact.

Demodectic mange is not a disease of poorly kept or dirty kennels. It is generally a disease of young dogs with inadequate or poorly developed immune systems - or older dogs suffering from a suppressed immune system.

Virtually every mother carries and transfers mites to her puppies, and most are immune to the mite's effects, but a few puppies are not and they develop full-blown mange. They may have a few (less than five) isolated lesions and this is known as *localised mange* – often around the head.

Puppy Mange is quite common, usually mild and often disappears on its own.

Generalised mange is more serious and covers the entire body or region of the body.

Bald patches are usually the first sign, usually accompanied by crusty, red skin which sometimes appears greasy or wet. Usually hair loss begins around the muzzle, eyes and other areas on the head. The sores may or may not itch.

In localised mange a few circular crusty areas appear, most frequently on the head and front legs of three to six-month-old puppies. Most self-heal as the puppy becomes older and develops her own immunity, but a persistent problem should be treated.

With generalised mange there are bald patches over the entire coat, including the head, neck, body, legs, and feet. The skin on the head, side and back is crusty, often inflamed and oozes a clear fluid. The skin itself will often be oily to touch and there is usually a secondary bacterial infection. Some puppies can become quite ill and can develop a fever, lose their appetites and become lethargic.

If you suspect your puppy has generalised demodectic mange, get her to a vet straight away.

There is also a condition called *pododermatitis*, when the mange affects a puppy's paws. It can cause bacterial infections and be very uncomfortable, even painful. Symptoms include hair loss on the paws, swelling of the paws (especially around the nail beds) and red, hot or inflamed areas which are often infected. Treatment is always recommended, and it can take several rounds to clear it up.

Diagnosis and Treatment – The vet will make a diagnosis after he or she has taken a skin scraping or biopsy, in which case the mites can be seen with a microscope. As these mites are present on every dog, they do not mean that the dog necessarily has mange. Only when they are coupled with lesions will a diagnosis of mange be made. Treatment usually involves topical (on the skin) medication and sometimes tablets.

One common treatment for Demodex is the FDA-approved heartworm drug Ivermectin, given at a higher dose. Treatment, thought to be 80%-85% effective, is given as a tablet or liquid. For dogs that don't tolerate Ivermectin, including herding breeds, other treatments include another heartworm medication, Milbemycin.

Another option, sometimes a last resort, is the anti-parasitic dip Mitaban every two weeks. Owners should always wear rubber gloves when treating their dog, and it should be applied in an area with adequate ventilation. Most dogs need from six to 14 dips every two weeks.

After the first three or four dips, your vet will probably take another skin scraping to check that the mites have gone. Dips continue for one month after the mites have disappeared, but dogs shouldn't be considered cured until a year after the last treatment.

FACT All of these treatments can have side effects. Some dogs, especially Toy breeds, don't respond well to Mitaban as it can make them nauseous. Discuss treatment and other options fully with your vet.

Veterinarian Dr Samantha Goldberg, of Beagle Health (UK) added: "One very effective treatment for Demodex is Bravecto, recently licensed for this, and now the best one available."

Dogs with generalised mange may have underlying skin infections, so antibiotics are often given for the first several weeks of treatment. Because the mite flourishes on dogs with suppressed immune systems, try to get to the root cause of immune system disease, especially if your Beagle is older when she develops demodectic mange.

Sarcoptic Mange (Scabies)

Also known as canine scabies, this is caused by the parasite *Sarcoptes scabiei.* This microscopic mite can cause a range of skin problems, the most common of which is hair loss and severe itching.

The mites can infect other animals such as foxes, cats and even humans, but prefer to live their short lives on dogs. Fortunately, there are several good treatments and it can be easily controlled.

In cool, moist environments, the mites live for up to 22 days. At normal room temperature they live from two to six days, preferring to live on parts of the dog with less hair. Diagnosing canine scabies can be somewhat difficult, and it is often mistaken for inhalant allergies.

The vet will take a skin scraping to make a diagnosis and there are a number of effective treatments, including selamectin (Revolution – again, some dogs can have a reaction to this), an on-the-skin solution applied once a month which also provides heartworm prevention, flea control and some tick protection. Various Frontline products are also effective – check with your vet for the correct ones.

One product used by some breeders is the **Seresto Flea Collar,** *pictured,* which provides full body protection for up to eight months against all fleas, ticks, sarcoptic mange, lice and other bloodsucking critters! The collar is waterproof. There are also holistic remedies for many skin conditions.

Because your dog does not have to come into direct contact with an infected dog to catch scabies, it is difficult to completely protect her. Foxes and their environment can also transmit the mite.

> **FACT: Beagles are more susceptible to epilepsy than many other breeds.**
> Chemical flea and parasite treatments, such as Seresto, Bravecto Comfortis, Nexgard, Frontline, Advantix, Trifexix, etc. can trigger epilespy, other disorders or strange behaviour in a very small percentage of dogs.
> Do your research, talk to your vet and consider all options, including natural alternatives.

Fleas

When you see your dog scratching and biting, your first thought is probably: *"She's got fleas!"* and you may well be right. Fleas don't fly, but they do have very strong back legs and they will take any opportunity to jump from the ground or another animal into your Beagle's lovely, warm coat. You can sometimes see the fleas if you part your dog's hair.

And for every flea that you see on your dog, there is the stomach-churning prospect of hundreds of eggs and larvae in your home.... So, if your dog gets fleas, you'll have to treat your environment as well as the dog in order to completely get rid of them. **The best form of cure is prevention.**

Vets recommend giving dogs a preventative flea treatment every four to eight weeks – although the Seresto Flea Collar lasts for eight months. If you do give a regular skin treatment, the frequency depends on your climate, the season - fleas do not breed as quickly in the cold - and how much time your Beagle spends outdoors.

To apply topical insecticides like Frontline and Advantix, part the skin and apply drops of the liquid on to a small area on your dog's back, usually near the neck. Some kill fleas and ticks, and others just kill fleas - check the details.

It is worth spending the money on a quality treatment, as cheap brands may not rid your Beagle completely of fleas, ticks and other parasites. There are also holistic and natural alternatives to insecticides, discussed later in this chapter.

Some breeders are opposed to chemical flea treatments. One added that when she found a flea, she simply washes all of her dogs, one after the other, and then washes every last piece of bedding.

Ticks

A tick is not an insect, but a member of the arachnid family, like the spider. There are over 850 types, some have a hard shell and some a soft one. Ticks don't have wings, they crawl. They have a sensor called Haller's organ that detects smell, heat and humidity to help them locate food, which in some cases is a Beagle. A tick's diet consists of one thing and one thing only – blood! They climb up onto tall grass and when they sense an animal is close, crawl on.

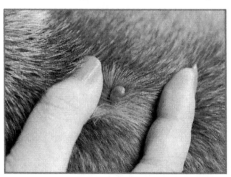

Ticks can pass on a number of diseases to animals and humans, the most well-known of which is **Lyme Disease**, a serious condition that causes lameness and other problems. Dogs that spend a lot of time outdoors in high-risk areas, such as woods, can have a vaccination against Lime Disease.

One breeder said: "We get ticks from sand dunes sometimes and, if removed quickly, they're not harmful. We use a tick tool which has instructions in the packet. You put the forked end either side of the tick and twist it till it comes out."

If you do find a tick on your Beagle's coat and are not sure how to get it out, have it removed by a vet or other expert. Inexpertly pulling it out yourself and leaving a bit of the tick behind can be detrimental to your dog's health. Tick prevention treatments are similar to those for fleas. If your Beagle has sensitive skin or allergies, she may well do better with a natural flea or tick remedy.

Heartworm

Although heartworm does not affect the skin, we have included it in this section as it is a parasite. Heartworm is a serious and potentially fatal disease affecting pets in North America and many other parts of the world, but not the UK. However, it is present in Mediterranean countries, so your Beagle may need protection on holiday there. (**Leishmaniasis** is another parasitic disease that UK dogs can pick up in Europe. It's transmitted by a biting sand flea and causes skin lesions or organ infection).

The foot-long heartworms live in the heart, lungs and blood vessels of affected animals, causing severe lung disease, heart failure and damage to organs. The dog is a natural host for heartworms, enabling the worms living inside a dog to mature into adults, mate and produce offspring. If untreated, their numbers can increase; dogs have been known to harbour several hundred worms in their bodies.

Untreated heartworm disease causes lasting damage to the heart, lungs and arteries, and can affect the dog's health and quality of life long after the parasites are gone. For this reason, **prevention is by far the best option** and treatment - when needed - should be administered as early as possible.

When a mosquito (**pictured**) bites and takes a blood meal from an infected dog, it picks up baby worms that develop and mature into **infective-stage** larvae over 10 to 14 days. Then, when it bites another dog, it spreads the disease.

Once inside a dog, it takes about six months for the larvae to develop into adult heartworms, which can then live for five to seven years in a dog. In the early stages, many dogs show few or no symptoms. The longer the infection persists, the more likely symptoms will develop, including:

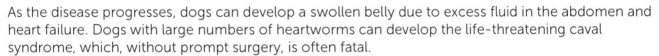

- 🐾 A mild persistent cough
- 🐾 Reluctance to exercise
- 🐾 Tiredness after normal activity
- 🐾 Decreased appetite and weight loss

As the disease progresses, dogs can develop a swollen belly due to excess fluid in the abdomen and heart failure. Dogs with large numbers of heartworms can develop the life-threatening caval syndrome, which, without prompt surgery, is often fatal.

Although more common in the south eastern US, heartworm disease has been diagnosed in all 50 states. The American Heartworm Society recommends that you get your dog tested every year and give your dog heartworm preventive treatment for all 12 months of the year.

If you live in a risk area, check that your tick and flea medication also prevents heartworm. In the UK, heartworm has only been found in imported dogs.

....

Ringworm

This is not actually a worm, but a fungus and is most commonly seen in puppies and young dogs. It is highly infectious and often found on the face, ears, paws or tail. This fungus is most prevalent in hot, humid climates but, surprisingly, most cases occur in autumn and winter. But it is not that common; in one study of dogs with active skin problems, less than 3% had ringworm, **pictured.**

Ringworm is transmitted by spores in the soil and by contact with the infected hair of dogs and cats, typically found on carpets, brushes, combs, toys and furniture. Spores from infected animals can be shed into the environment and live for over 18 months, but most healthy adult dogs have some resistance and never develop symptoms. The fungi live in dead skin, hairs and nails - and the head and legs are the most common areas affected.

Tell-tale signs are bald patches with a roughly circular shape. Ringworm is relatively easy to treat with fungicidal shampoos or antibiotics from a vet.

FACT Humans can catch ringworm from pets, and vice versa. Children are especially susceptible, as are adults with suppressed immune systems and those undergoing chemotherapy. Hygiene is extremely important.

If your dog has ringworm, wear gloves when handling her and wash your hands well afterwards. And if a member of your family catches ringworm, make sure they use separate towels from everyone else or the fungus may spread. As a teenager, I caught ringworm from horses at the local stables where I worked at weekends - much to my mother's horror - and was treated like a leper by the rest of the family until it cleared up!

Ear Infections

One of the most attractive features of Beagles is their beautiful faces with the trademark velvety, floppy ears. All scent hounds have floppy (pendant) ears; they help them to trap a scent. However, they also make these breeds more susceptible to ear infections than dogs with pricked-up ears that allow air to circulate inside more easily.

FACT The fact that a dog has recurring ear infections does NOT necessarily mean that the ears are the issue – although they might be. They may also be due to allergies or low thyroid function (hypothyroidism). The underlying problem must be treated or the dog will continue to have ear infections.

The ears themselves can be the cause – a dog's ear canal can be a warm, damp environment much loved by home-hunting bacteria.

Tell-tale signs of an ear infection include your dog shaking her head, scratching or rubbing her ears a lot, or an unpleasant smell from the ears, which is typical of a yeast infection.

If you look inside the ear, you may notice a reddy brown or yellow discharge. The ear may also be red and inflamed with a lot of wax. Sometimes a dog may appear depressed or irritable; ear infections are painful. In severe cases, the inside of her ears may become crusty or thickened. Treatment depends on the cause and what – if any - other conditions your dog may have.

Antibiotics are used to treat bacterial infections and antifungals for yeast infections. Glucocorticoids, such as dexamethasone, are often included in these medications to reduce the inflammation in the ear. Your vet may also flush out and clean the ear with special drops, something you may have to do daily at home until the infection clears.

A dog's ear canal is L-shaped, which means it can be difficult to get medication into the lower, or horizontal, part of the ear. The best method is to hold the dog's ear flap with one hand and put the ointment or drops in with the other, if possible tilting the dog's head away from you so the liquid flows downwards **with gravity**.

Hold the ear flap down and massage the medication into the horizontal canal before letting go of your dog, as the first thing she will do is shake her head – and if the ointment or drops aren't massaged in, they will fly out. Nearly all ear infections can be successfully managed if properly diagnosed and treated. But if an underlying problem remains undiagnosed, the ears will continue to become infected.

 Ear infections are notoriously difficult to get rid of once your dog's had one, so prevention is better than cure. Check your Beagle's ears weekly when grooming, dry them after swimming and get the vet to check inside on routine visits.

As Beagles have short coats, plucking hairs out of the inside of the ears is not usually necessary, but get into the habit of checking and, if your Beagle is prone to ear infections, cleaning them every week. Be very careful not to put anything too far inside and DO NOT use cotton buds; they are too small and can cause injury. Canine ear cleaning solution is widely available, or you can use a mixture of water and white vinegar.

Use a large piece of cotton wool soaked in the solution and be sure to dry your dog's ears afterwards. Any dampness will only encourage yeast and other bacteria. Visit YouTube to see how to clean ears without injuring them.

If your dog appears to be in pain, has smelly ears, or if the inside of her ear looks red or sore, contact your vet straight away before the infection has a chance to become entrenched or recurring. If you can nip the first infection in the bud, you reduce the risk of it returning.

Some Allergy Treatments

Treatments and success rates vary tremendously from dog to dog and from one allergy to another, which is why it is so important to consult a vet at the outset. <u>Earlier diagnosis is more likely to lead to a successful treatment.</u>

Some owners of dogs with recurring skin issues find that a course of antibiotics or steroids works wonders for their dog's sore skin and itching. However, the scratching starts all over again shortly after the treatment stops.

Food allergies require patience, a change or several changes of diet and maybe even a food trial, and the specific trigger is notoriously difficult to isolate – unless you are lucky and hit on the culprit straight away.

With inhalant and contact allergies, blood and skin tests are available, followed by hyposensitisation treatment. However, these are expensive and often the specific trigger for many dogs remains unknown. So, the reality for many owners of Beagles with allergies is that they manage the condition, rather than curing it completely.

FACT While a single steroid injection is often highly effective in calming down symptoms almost immediately, frequent or long-term steroid use is not a good option as it can lead to serious side effects.

Our Experience With Max

According to our vet, Graham, more and more dogs are appearing in his waiting room with various types of allergies. Whether this is connected to how we breed or feed our dogs remains to be seen.

Our dog, Max, was perfectly fine until he was about two years old, when he began to scratch a lot. He scratched more in spring and summer, which meant that his allergies were almost certainly

FACT inhalant or contact-based and related to pollens, grasses or other outdoor triggers. We decided not to have a lot of tests, not because of the cost, but because the vet said it was highly likely that he was allergic to pollens. Max was an active dog and if we'd had pollen allergy confirmed, we were not going to stop taking him out for thrice-daily walks.

 If your dog is scratching and you suspect outdoor allergies, hose her down or wash her paws and belly after each walk. This will definitely help to reduce the overall allergen load, leading to less itching.

Regarding medications, Max was at first put on to a tiny dose of Piriton *(pictured)*, a cheap antihistamine manufactured in the millions for canine and human hay fever sufferers. For the first few springs and summers, this worked well. Allergies can change and a dog can build up a tolerance to a treatment, which is why they can be so difficult to treat. Max's symptoms changed from season to season, although the main ones were: general scratching, paw biting and ear infections.

One year he bit the skin under his tail a lot— he would jump around like he had been stung by a bee and bite frenetically. This was treated effectively with a single steroid injection, followed by spraying the area with cortisone once a day at home for a period. Localised spray can be very effective if the itchy area is small, but no good for spraying all over a dog's body.

Over the years we tried a number of treatments, all of which worked for a while, before he came off the medication in October when pollen levels fell. He was perfectly fine the rest of the year without any treatment at all.

Not every owner wants to treat his or her dog with chemicals, nor feed a diet that includes preservatives, which is why this book includes alternatives. Also, 15 years ago, when we were starting out on the *"Allergy Trail,"* there were far fewer options than there are now.

We fed Max a high quality hypoallergenic dry food. If we were starting again from scratch, knowing what we know now, I'd look into a raw or home-cooked diet (which is what he was fed towards the end of his life), if necessary, in combination with holistic remedies.

One spring the vet put him on a short course of steroids, which were effective for a season, but steroids are not a long-term solution. Another year we were prescribed the non-steroid Atopica. The active ingredient is **cyclosporine**, which suppresses the immune system - some dogs can get side effects, although ours didn't.

The daily tablet was expensive, but initially extremely effective – so much so that we thought we had cured the problem completely. However, after a couple of seasons on cyclosporine he developed a tolerance to the drug and started scratching again. A few years ago, he went back on the antihistamine Piriton, a higher dose than when he was two years old, and this was effective.

Other Options

In 2013 the FDA approved **Apoquel** (oclacitinib) *– pictured -* to control itching and inflammation in allergic dogs. Like most allergy drugs, it acts by suppressing the immune system, rather than addressing the root cause.

It has, however, proved to be highly effective in treating countless thousands of dogs with allergies. We used Apoquel with excellent results. There was some initial tweaking to get the daily dose right, but it proved highly effective. The tablets are administered according to body weight – it's not cheap, but Apoquel can be a miracle worker for some dogs, including ours.

Side effects have been reported in some dogs, and holistic practitioners, Dogs Naturally magazine and others believe it can be harmful to the dog. Do your research.

Cytopoint is another recent option that's proved to be highly effective for many dogs. It is given as an injection every four to eight weeks and starts working almost immediately. Dogs with seasonal allergies may only need the injections for part of the year.

One added advantage of Cytopoint is that it is a biological therapy, not pharmaceutical, and does not suppress the dog's immune system. It contains engineered antibodies, similar to a dog's natural antibodies, which fight viruses and bacteria. These antibodies have been specifically designed to target and neutralise a protein that sends itch signals to a dog's brain. This in turn helps to minimise scratching, giving the irritated skin chance to heal.

Allergies are often complex and difficult to treat; you should weigh up the pros and cons in the best interests of your own dog. Max's allergies were manageable; he loved his food, was full of energy and otherwise healthy, and lived a happy life to the age of 13. The Apoquel definitely helped him, but it's not for every dog.

Add fish oils, which contain Omega-3 fatty acids, to a daily feed to keep your dog's skin and coat healthy all year round – whether or not she has problems. A liquid supplement called Yuderm, *pictured,* (formerly Yumove Itchy Dog), which contains Omegas 3 and 6, golden flax and borage, is a good choice to add to your dog's daily feeds all year round.

When the scratching got particularly bad, we also bathed Max in an antiseborrheic shampoo called Malaseb twice a week for a limited time. This helped, although was not necessary once on Apoquel. Here are some other suggestions from owners:

Use an astringent such as witch hazel or alcohol on affected areas. We have heard of zinc oxide cream being used to some effect on dogs as well as babies' bottoms! In the human world, this is rubbed on to mild skin abrasions and acts as a protective coating. Zinc oxide works as a mild astringent and has some antiseptic properties and is safe to use on dogs, *as long as you do not allow the dog to lick it off!*

Vitamins A and E also help to make a dog's skin healthy, and lots of owners have tried coconut oil with some success. Here is a link to an article on the benefits of coconut oils and fish oils, check with your vet first: www.dogsnaturallymagazine.com/the-health-benefits-of-coconut-oil

One breeder added: "A couple of mine tend to have itchy legs and feet. I feed them a grain-free food and use anti-itch herbal remedies."

Massage

Anybody can do it – we do – and your Beagle will love the attention! There are many videos on YouTube explaining techniques and showing very relaxed Beagles enjoying a massage from their owners.

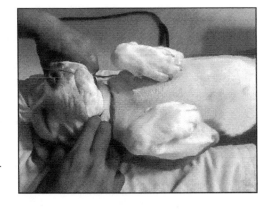

Tip **Massage can stimulate your dog's immune system and help to prevent or reduce allergies. It's also good for improving your dog's circulation and flexibility, reducing muscle and arthritis pain and other age-related problems.**

Holistic practitioners also believe that *acupressure* can specifically help dogs with allergies. Type *"Acupressure for Dogs"* into Google to learn about the theory behind it and how to apply pressure at specific points on your dog's body.

Acupressure can also help nervous and elderly dogs.

The Holistic Approach

Many owners of dogs with sensitivities find that their dog does well for a time with injections or medication, but then the symptoms slowly start to reappear. More owners are now considering natural foods and remedies. A holistic practitioner looks at finding and treating the root cause of the problem, rather than just treating the symptoms.

Dr Sara Skiwski is an American holistic vet. She writes here about canine environmental allergies: "Here in California, with our mild weather and no hard freeze in Winter, environmental allergens can build up and cause nearly year-round issues for our beloved pets.

"Also, seasonal allergies, when left unaddressed, can lead to year-round allergies. Unlike humans, whose allergy symptoms seem to affect mostly the respiratory tract, seasonal allergies in dogs often take the form of skin irritation/inflammation.

"Allergic reactions are produced by the immune system. The way the immune system functions is a result of both genetics and the environment: Nature versus Nurture. Let's look at a typical case. A puppy starts showing mild seasonal allergy symptoms, for instance a red tummy and mild itching in Spring. Off to the vet!

"The treatment prescribed is symptomatic to provide relief, such as a topical spray. The next year when the weather warms up, the patient is back again - same symptoms but more severe this time.

"This time the dog has very itchy skin. Again, the treatment is symptomatic - antibiotics, topical spray (hopefully no steroids), until the symptoms resolve with the season change. Fast forward to another Spring...on the third year, the patient is back again but this time the symptoms last longer, (not just Spring but also through most of Summer and into Fall).

"By Year Five, all the symptoms are significantly worse and are occurring year-round. This is what happens with seasonal environmental allergies. The more your pet is exposed to the allergens they are sensitive to, the more the immune system over-reacts and the more intense and long-lasting the allergic response becomes. What to do?

"In my practice, I like to address the potential root cause at the very first sign of an allergic response, which is normally seen between the ages of six to nine months old. I do this to circumvent the escalating response year after year. Since the allergen load your environmentally-sensitive dog is most susceptible to is much heavier outdoors, I recommend two essential steps in managing the condition. They are vigilance in foot care as well as hair care.

"What does this mean? A wipe down of feet and hair, especially the tummy, to remove any pollens or allergens is key. This can be done with a damp cloth, but my favorite method is to get a spray bottle filled with Witch Hazel and spray these areas.

"First, spray the feet then wipe them off with a cloth, and then spray and wipe down the tummy and sides. This is best done right after the pup has been outside playing or walking. This will help keep your pet from tracking the environmental allergens into the home and into their beds. If the feet end up still being itchy, I suggest adding foot soaks in Epsom salts."

Dr Sara also stresses the importance of keeping the immune system healthy by avoiding unnecessary vaccinations or drugs: "The vaccine stimulates the immune system, which is the last thing your pet with seasonal environmental allergies needs.

"I also will move the pet to an anti-inflammatory diet. Foods that create or worsen inflammation are high in carbohydrates. An allergic pet's diet should be very low in carbohydrates, especially grains. Research has shown that 'leaky gut,' or dysbiosis, is a root cause of immune system overreactions in both dog and cats (and some humans).

"Feed a diet that is not processed, or minimally processed; one that doesn't have grain and takes a little longer to get absorbed and assimilated through the gut. Slowing the assimilation assures that there are not large spikes of nutrients and proteins that come into the body all at once and overtax the pancreas and liver, creating inflammation.

"A lot of commercial diets are too high in grains and carbohydrates. These foods create inflammation that overtaxes the body and leads not just to skin inflammation, but also to other inflammatory conditions, such as colitis, pancreatitis, arthritis, inflammatory bowel disease and ear infections. Also, these diets are too low in protein, which is needed to make blood. This causes a decreased blood reserve in the body and in some of these animals this can lead to the skin not being properly nourished, starting a cycle of chronic skin infections which produce more itching."

After looking at diet, check that your dog is free from fleas and then these are some of Dr Sara's suggested supplements:

✓ **Raw (Unpasteurised) Local Honey** - an alkaline-forming food containing natural vitamins, enzymes, powerful antioxidants and other important natural nutrients, which are destroyed during the heating and pasteurisation processes.

Raw honey has anti-viral, anti-bacterial and anti-fungal properties. It promotes body and digestive health, is a powerful antioxidant, strengthens the immune system, eliminates allergies, and is an excellent remedy for skin wounds and all types of infections. Bees collect pollen from local plants and their honey often acts as an immune booster for dogs living in the locality.

Dr Sara says: "It may seem odd that straight exposure to pollen often triggers allergies, but that exposure to pollen in the honey usually has the opposite effect. But this is typically what we see. In honey, the allergens are delivered in small, manageable doses and the effect over time is very much like that from undergoing a whole series of allergy immunology injections."

✓ **Mushrooms** - make sure you choose the non-poisonous ones! Dogs don't like the taste, so you may have to mask it with another food. Medicinal mushrooms are used to treat and prevent a wide array of illnesses through their use as immune stimulants and modulators, and antioxidants. The most well-known and researched are reishi, maitake, cordyceps, blazei, split-gill, turkey tail and shiitake. Histamine is what causes much of the inflammation, redness and irritation in allergies. By helping to control histamine production, the mushrooms can moderate the effects of inflammation and even help prevent allergies in the first place.

WARNING! Mushrooms can interact with some over-the-counter and prescription drugs, so do your research as well as checking with your vet first.

✓ **Stinging Nettles -** contain biologically active compounds that reduce inflammation. Nettles can reduce the amount of histamine the body produces in response to an allergen. Nettle tea or extract can help with itching. Nettles not only help directly to decrease the itch, but also work overtime to desensitise the body to allergens.

✓ **Quercetin** – is an over-the-counter supplement with anti-inflammatory properties. It is a strong antioxidant and reduces the body's production of histamines.

✓ **Omega-3 Fatty Acids** - these help decrease inflammation throughout the body. Adding them into the diet of all pets - particularly those struggling with seasonal environmental allergies – is very beneficial. If your dog has more itching along the top of their back and on their sides, add in a fish oil supplement. Fish oil helps to decrease the itch and heal skin lesions. The best sources of Omega 3s are krill oil *(pictured)*, salmon oil, tuna oil, anchovy oil and other fish body oils, as well as raw organic egg yolks. If using an oil alone, it is important to give a vitamin B complex supplement.

✓ **Coconut Oil** - contains lauric acid, which helps decrease the production of yeast, a common opportunistic infection. Using a fish body oil combined with coconut oil before inflammation flares up can help moderate or even suppress your dog's inflammatory response.

Dr Sara adds: "Above are but a few of the over-the-counter remedies I like. In non-responsive cases, Chinese herbs can be used to work with the body to help to decrease the allergy threshold even more than with diet and supplements alone. Most of the animals I work with are on a program of Chinese herbs, diet change and acupuncture.

"So, the next time Fido is showing symptoms of seasonal allergies, consider rethinking your strategy to treat the root cause instead of the symptom."

With thanks to Dr Sara Skiwski, of the Western Dragon Integrated Veterinary Services, San Jose, California, for her kind permission to use her writings as the basis for *The Holistic Approach*.

....

Remember:

🐾 A high-quality diet

🐾 Maintaining a healthy weight

🐾 Regular grooming and check-overs, and

🐾 Attention to cleanliness

All go a long way in preventing or managing skin problems in Beagles.

If your Beagle does have a skin issue, seek a professional diagnosis as soon as possible before attempting to treat it yourself and it becomes entrenched.

Even if a skin condition cannot be completely cured, almost all can be successfully managed, allowing your dog to live a happy, pain-free life.

13. Grooming

Although Beagles can be high input when it comes to teaching the Recall and obedience, the good news is that they are relatively low maintenance on the grooming front. That doesn't mean they don't need grooming; they do - but compared to many breeds and crossbreeds, the Beagle is a breeze.

Although they are shedders, the plus side is that, unlike with "non-shedding" dogs, you do not have to visit the grooming parlour every few weeks as you can do all or most of the required maintenance yourself at home.

The Beagle has a short double coat. The undercoat is soft and dense and the outer coat has tougher, fine hairs that are somewhat water repellent. The coat sheds throughout the year, but during Spring and Autumn (Fall), the shedding is at its heaviest. As well as seasons, other factors affecting shedding are:

- Bloodlines
- Age
- Sudden changes in temperature
- Nutrition
- Allergies
- Whether the dog has been spayed (if so, she will probably shed more)

A healthy Beagle's coat has a sheen to it and is a joy to behold; it's one of the breed's many attractive features. Regular brushing (once or twice a week normally, every other day in shedding season) helps to keep the coat in tiptop condition and reduce shedding.

It also removes dirt and dead hair, stimulates blood circulation - which in turn helps to keep the skin healthy - and spreads natural oils throughout the coat.

A high-quality diet also helps, and some owners have found that feeding hypoallergenic kibble, or a raw or home-cooked diet improves skin and reduces shedding. Adding a once-daily squirt or spoonful of Omega 3 oil to a feed is also beneficial.

Beagles love to be outdoors following a scent, getting dirty and rolling in all manner of stinky wildlife deposits! A Beagle who regularly runs free will naturally get muddy or dusty and is therefore not a dog for the very houseproud.

Living the dream! Photo of nine-month-old Copper (Kelcardi Keep the Heid) courtesy of Kelly Diamond.

If brushed regularly, your dog shouldn't need a bath more than once or twice a year, unless he has a skin condition or is particularly smelly.

Time spent grooming is also time spent bonding with your Beagle. It is this physical and emotional inter-reliance which brings us closer to our dogs. Routine grooming sessions also allow you to examine your Beagle's ears, tail, teeth, eyes, paws and nails for signs of problems. Older Beagles may need more regular personal attention and checks from their owners.

 Beagles can be stubborn and it's important to get your puppy used to being handled; a wilful adult will not take kindly to being groomed if he's not used to it. And some Beagles are notorious howlers when it comes to nail trimming, so start early.

NOTE: If you do notice an unpleasant smell (in addition to your Beagle's normal odour and gassy emissions) and he hasn't been rolling in something unmentionable, then he may have a yeast infection or his anal glands may need squeezing.

Beagle Coat Colours

Beagles actually come in a wide range of colours and patterns. In fact, several different coloured puppies can be born in the same litter.

 Coat colours are all about genetics and a purebred Beagle cannot be just one colour as the breed does not have the solid colour gene. Beagles have "hound colouring," meaning they have at least two colours in their coat.

The US Breed Standard states: "Any true hound color," while National Beagle Club Visualization states: "'Any true hound color' includes traditional black/tan/white tri, or blue tri. The tri-colored Beagle can be either richly and deeply colored or faded (the blanket containing more tan than black or blue hairs).

"Other, equally acceptable colors, are tan/white, lemon/white, red/white and chocolate, as well as variations and dilutes of these colors. While ticking on a Beagle is fine, grizzle or brindling are not acceptable."

The UK Breed Standard recognises 10 colours:

- 🐾 Tri-colour (black, tan and white)
- 🐾 Blue
- 🐾 White and tan
- 🐾 Badger pied (mix of black, silver and fawn)
- 🐾 Hare pied (more tan than black and white, resembling a hare)
- 🐾 Lemon pied (mainly lemon or cream hairs intermingling with black and white)
- 🐾 Lemon and white
- 🐾 Red and white
- 🐾 Tan and white
- 🐾 Black and white
- 🐾 All white (rarely, if ever, seen)

There are also coat patterns, such as *Ticked* (called *"Mottle"* in the UK). These dogs have little spots of colour in the whites, such as those seen on Coonhounds and roan Cocker Spaniels. So, you get dogs described as "Tri-Colour Ticked/Mottle," "Lemon Ticked/Mottle," "Tan Ticked/Mottle" or "Red Ticked/Mottle."

Two recessive genes that can also affect colour are the B (Brown) and D (Dilution-Blue) genes which result in blue and isabella (lilac) Beagles. Although these are purebred Beagles, they have very light eyes, and these dogs are not accepted in shows run under Kennel Club rules.

NOTE: There is no such thing as a *Brindle* (Tiger Striped) or *Merle* Beagle. The Beagle does not carry the gene for brindle or merle, so another breed has been introduced somewhere along the line.

 Some colours are genetically rarer than others and command a higher price. If you have set your heart on a colour, make sure you've checked the health certificates for the parents as well.

Beagles love to sunbathe. However, they also have a short coat, so keep an eye on your dog for signs of sunburn on areas where the hair is non-existent or sparse – particularly if they have a light-coloured coat.

Limit your Beagle's sunbathing or buy a canine sunscreen (not a human one as these can contain substances poisonous to dogs). Apply it to the areas most exposed to the sun: nose, ear tips, lips, groin, inner thighs and anywhere else where there is little or no hair and pigmentation is light. Stick around for 10 minutes or so to make sure he doesn't lick it all off.

Grooming Tips

Brush options include a bristle brush, a slicker brush (with metal pins, some with rubber ends) or a rubber brush. A Beagle favourite is the hound glove, or rubber grooming mitten, which means they get stroked at the same time!

The Kong Zoom Groom is a useful tool, *as demonstrated here by Wilbur and London breeder Karen Simkin.*

Widely available online, it does a good job of removing loose hair. It stimulates capillaries and natural oil production for healthy skin and coat and can also be used when shampooing your Beagle.

A bristle brush is easy to use and good for breeds with short, shiny coats like the Beagle. It glides over the top coat to smooth fur and stimulate the even distribution of a dog's natural oils.

Bristle brushes are a good way to finish off your grooming routine after you've got rid of loose hair and dead skin.

One widely-advertised de-shedding tool you may come across is the Furminator. It removes the undercoat and loose hair without cutting the topcoat on double-coated dogs, but should not be used on sensitive areas like the face, ears, legs or tail.

 If you are intending to show your Beagle, a Furminator is not suitable as it can affect the quality of the top coat. A Kong Zoom Groom, *pictured,* is a better choice.

When grooming, brush your dog in the opposite direction a few times to loosen dead hair, then brush from neck to tail, and do the sides from front to back. Don't press too hard with the brush.

Gently brush the chest, belly and underneath the neck and unfurl the tail. If you rub your dog down with a damp chamois leather afterwards it will grab any loose hairs. A few things to look out for when grooming are:

Ears – see **Ear Cleaning** section of this chapter.

Eyes - These should be clean and clear. Cloudy eyes, particularly in an older dog, could be early signs of cataracts. Red or swollen tissue in the corner(s) could be a symptom of Cherry Eye, which can affect all breeds. Ingrowing eyelashes is another issue which causes red, watery eyes.

If your dog has an issue, gently bathe the outer eye(s) with warm water and gauze or cotton cloth - never use anything sharp; your dog can suddenly jump forwards or backwards, causing injury. If the eye is red or watering for a few days or more, get it checked out by a vet.

Dry Skin - A dog's skin can dry out, especially with artificial heat in the winter months. If you spot any dry patches, for example on the inner thighs or armpits, or a cracked nose, massage a little petroleum jelly or baby oil into the dry patch.

Acne - Little red pimples on a dog's face and chin means he has got acne. A dog can get acne at any age, not just as an adolescent. Plastic bowls can also trigger the condition, which is why stainless steel ones are better. Daily washing followed by an application of an antibiotic cream is usually enough to get rid of the problem.

Bathing

Too much bathing can rid the coat of its natural oils, so don't bathe your Beagle unless it's necessary. However, if a Beagle's coat and skin get too dirty it can cause irritation, leading to scratching and excessive shedding - it's all a question of getting the balance right.

Frequency depends on how much outdoor exercise your Beagle gets, what sort of areas he's walking or playing in and what his natural skin condition is like.

A Beagle getting lots of off-lead exercise will naturally pick up more dirt than one that's mostly kept on a lead.

Often a hose down outside is enough to wash the dirt out of a Beagle.

FACT ❯ If you decide your Beagle needs a proper bath, only use a canine shampoo. A dog's coat has a different pH to human hair and shampoos made for humans can cause skin irritation.

If your Beagle has skin problems or allergies, select a medicated shampoo with antibacterial, antifungal or anti-itching (which contains antihistamines) properties as it will help to get rid of bacteria and fungi without damaging the coat. Your vet will be able to recommend a suitable shampoo. They are also widely available in pet stores and online.

Tip To prevent ear infections, towel dry the inside of the ears after bathing. Another option is to put cotton wool in each ear. Do it gently and don't force the cotton wool into the ear canal – don't forget to remove them afterwards or your Beagle will be even deafer than usual to your commands!

You also have to be extremely careful with the eyes. Some owners recommend putting a drop or two of artificial tears in each eye to offer some limited protection against soap or chemicals in the shampoo.

There is a wide variation on how your dog will react to having a bath – some Beagles love the attention, while others hate the water. Make sure you get everything ready before you start and keep your dog's collar on so you have something to hold on to.

You can wash your Beagle outdoors or in the family bath with a non-slip mat in the bottom. Don't use the sink, a Beagle can easily jump out.

Photo courtesy of Charlie Anna Reeve, Charlie's Pawfect Angels Dog Grooming, Watford, UK.

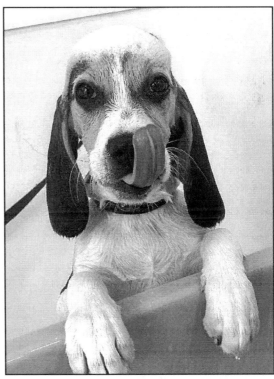

Use **lukewarm** water and spray it from the neck down to the tail until the coat is completely soaked, avoid wetting the face if you can, but gently wash the ear flaps without getting water in the ear canals.

Work the shampoo into your dog's body and legs, not forgetting the underneath, and if it's a medicated shampoo, you may have to leave it on for a few minutes.

This is not easy with an energetic, aquaphobic Beagle, so keep a firm hold or better still, have an accomplice hold the dog. It does get better as they get more used to it – especially if they get a treat at the end of the ordeal.

Rinse your dog thoroughly on top, underneath, on the legs, etc., making sure that all of the soap is out of the coat. Use your hand to squeegee excess water off the coat before putting him on an old towel on the floor and towelling him dry - again, be careful with the eyes.

Then stand back as he gets his revenge by shaking and soaking you too! Dry the coat as much as possible, a double-coated dog takes a while to dry naturally. You may want to put the heating on to help him dry out or find him a sunny spot. Don't forget to remove the cotton wool.

One not uncommon reaction after a bath is for a Beagle to run around like a lunatic afterwards, as though they have just miraculously escaped the most horrific death by drowning in two inches of water!

Nail Trimming

If your Beagle is regularly exercised on grass or other soft surfaces, his nails may not be getting worn down sufficiently, so they may require clipping or filing.

FACT ▶ Nails should be kept short for the paws to remain healthy. Overly-long nails interfere with a dog's gait, making walking awkward or painful and putting stress on elbows, shoulder and back. They can also break easily, usually at the base of the nail where blood vessels and nerves are located.

Be prepared: many Beagles dislike having their nails trimmed – especially if they are not used to it - so it requires patience and persistence if you do it yourself.

Get your dog used to having his paws inspected from puppyhood; it's also a good opportunity to check for other problems, such as cracked pads or interdigital cysts. (These are swellings between the toes, often due to a bacterial infection).

Photo courtesy of Sally Kimber, Coachbarn Beagles, Kent.

To trim your dog's nails, use a specially designed clipper. Most have safety guards to prevent you cutting the nails too short. Do it before they get too long.

 If you can hear the nails clicking on a hard surface, they're too long.

You want to trim only the ends, before *"the quick,"* which is a blood vessel inside the nail. You can see where the quick ends on a white nail, but not on a dark nail.

Clip only the hook-like part of the nail that turns down. Start trimming gently, a nail or two at a time, and your dog will learn that you're not going to hurt him. If you accidentally cut the quick, stop the bleeding with some styptic powder.

Another option is to file your dog's nails with a nail grinder tool, also called a Dremel, *pictured.* Some Beagles have tough nails that are harder to trim and this may be a less stressful method for your dog, with less chance of pain or bleeding. The grinder is like an electric nail file and only removes a small amount of nail at a time.

Some owners prefer to use one as there is less chance of cutting the quick, and many dogs prefer them to a clipper. Introduce your dog to the grinder gradually - the noise and vibration take some getting used to.

If you find it impossible to clip your dog's nails, or you are at all worried about doing it, take him to a vet or groomer and have it done as part of a routine visit - and get your Beagle's anal sacs squeezed, or "expressed," while he's there!

Anal Glands

While we're discussing the less appealing end of your Beagle, let's dive straight in and talk about anal sacs. Sometimes called scent glands, these are a pair of glands located inside your dog's anus that give off a scent when he has a bowel movement. You won't want to hear this, but problems with impacted anal glands are not uncommon in dogs!

When a dog passes firm stools, the glands normally empty themselves, but soft poop or diarrhoea can mean that not enough pressure is exerted to empty the glands, causing discomfort.

If they get infected, they become swollen and painful. In extreme cases, one or both anal glands can be removed – we had a dog that lived happily for many years with one anal gland.

If your dog drags himself along on his rear end – *"scooting"* - or tries to lick or scratch his anus, he could well have impacted anal glands that need squeezing, either by you if you know how to do it, your vet or a groomer. (Scooting is also a sign of worms). Either way, it pays to keep an eye on both ends of your dog!

Ear Cleaning

Floppy ears create a warm, moist haven for bacteria and infection. Any dog can get an ear infection, particularly if they suffer from allergies, or have dense hair inside the ear.

Ear infections are notorious for recurring once they have taken hold. They are painful and can even cause deafness in very severe cases. So it pays to check your dog's ears regularly while grooming.

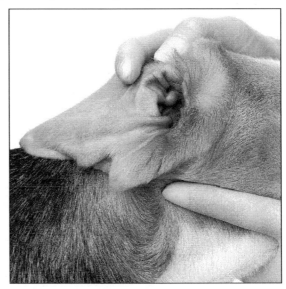

Many Beagles enjoy swimming or paddling. A good habit to get into is to towel dry the ears afterwards or use an ear-drying powder, as ear infections can develop if the ear remains wet.

Keep an eye out for redness or inflammation at the inner base of the ear, or a build-up of dark wax.

 Never put anything sharp or narrow - like a cotton bud – inside your dog's ears, as you can cause damage.

Typical signs of an ear infection are the dog:

- 🐾 Shaking his head a lot
- 🐾 Scratching his ears
- 🐾 Rubbing his ears on the floor
- 🐾 An unpleasant smell coming from the ears, which is a sign of a yeast infection

If your dog exhibits any of these signs, consult your vet ASAP, as simple routine cleaning won't solve the problem.

Teeth Cleaning

Veterinary studies show that by the age of three, 80% of dogs show signs of gum or dental disease. Symptoms include yellow and brown build-up of tartar along the gum line, red inflamed gums and persistent bad breath (halitosis). And if your dog suddenly stops eating his food, check his mouth and teeth.

Many owners keep their dogs' teeth clean by giving them an occasional raw bone (not chicken as it splinters), or regularly feeding bully sticks, Nylabones, Dentastix, etc.

However, it is important to take time to take care of your Beagle's teeth – regular dental care greatly reduces the onset of gum and tooth decay and infection. If left, problems can quickly escalate.

Without cleaning, plaque coats teeth and within a few days this starts to harden into tartar, often turning into gingivitis (inflammation of the gums). Gingivitis is regularly accompanied by periodontal disease (infections around the teeth).

This can be serious as, in the worst cases, it can lead to infections of the vital organs, such as heart, liver and kidneys. Even if the infection doesn't spread beyond the mouth, bad teeth are very unpleasant for a dog, just as with a human, causing painful toothache and difficulty chewing.

Some owners book their dog in for a professional clean at the local veterinary clinic every year. However, if your Beagle needs a deep clean, remedial work or teeth removing, he will have to be anaesthetised, a procedure which is to be avoided unless it is absolutely necessary. Prevention is better than cure.

 If your dog has to be anaesthetised for something else, ask the vet to check and clean your dog's teeth while he's under.

One option is to brush your dog's teeth. There are also various tools owners can buy to control plaque, such as dental picks and scrapers.

Start while still a puppy and take things slowly in the beginning, giving lots of praise. Once used to the process, many dogs love the attention - especially if they like the flavour of the toothpaste!

Use a pet toothpaste, as the human variety can upset a canine's stomach.

The real benefit comes from the actual action of the brush on the teeth, and various brushes, sponges and pads are available for dogs - the choice depends on factors such as the health of your dog's gums, the size of his mouth and how good you are at teeth cleaning.

Get him used to the toothpaste by letting him lick some off your finger when he is young. If he doesn't like the flavour, try a different one. Continue this until he enjoys licking the paste - it might be instant or it might take days.

Put a small amount on your finger and gently rub it on one of the big canine teeth at the front of his mouth. Then get him used to the toothbrush or dental sponge for several days - praise him when he licks it. The next step is to actually start brushing.

Lift his upper lip gently and place the brush at a 45° angle to the gum line. Gently move the brush backwards and forwards. Start just with his front teeth and then gradually do a few more.

Do the top ones first. Regular brushing shouldn't take more than five minutes - well worth the time and effort when it spares your Beagle the pain and misery of serious dental or gum disease.

Breeders on Grooming

Darlene Stewart, Aladar Beagles, Alabama: "Beagles DO shed!! I brush every week, teeth brush daily, and nail trim every two weeks. I check the ears every week and clean if needed. Baths depend on the weather, environment etc. - when they get smelly dirty they get a bath.

"I also check anal glands during the bath and empty if necessary. The average owner may not be able to do this - due to lack of training and uncooperative Beagle!

"With teeth cleaning, I start my pups with me just using a tasty dog toothpaste such as Sentry Petrodex Veterinary Strength Dog Toothpaste.

"Once they are used to me giving it to them and rubbing their teeth with my fingers, I then start using a soft toothbrush. I now have some dogs that I can use an electric tooth brush on."

Lori Norman, Lokavi Beagles, Florida: "I don't bathe mine unless they need a bath; bathing too frequently can dry their skin and coat, and they need the natural oils for them to be protected by their coat.

"Beagles have a nose that controls them, so if there is anything dead or stinky, they will love to roll in it until totally covered with it — that's always a perfect time to bathe them!

"When grooming a Beagle, always remember the ears. The long ears cover the ear canal and prevent good ventilation, which makes them susceptible to ear infection, usually yeast. Get a good ear cleaner and clean the ears frequently using a cotton ball.

"When the ears are not sore is the time to do preventative cleaning. When the ears get sore, they won't want you messing with them. Additionally, I always make sure the anal glands are emptied, so on your vet visits it is always a good idea to ask for that to be done."

Photo of this handsome puppy courtesy of Lori.

Georgina Armour-Langham, Robentot Beagles, Leicester, UK: "I don't bathe mine, they are only washed down; they love fox poo!"

Peter Sievwright, Mattily Beagles, Renfrewshire: "We leave it up to the dogs to clean themselves; the only time we intervene is when one of the dogs has rolled in bird mess or dog, cattle or sheep dung, or if they have a medical issue. We find the dogs do a perfectly good job of keeping themselves clean and tidy with minimal help from us.

"What we do do is back comb the dogs to release some of the loose hair when it is casting. This is done outside approximately every two weeks so we don't have a house covered in loose dog hair."

Sharon Hardisty, Blunderhall Beagles, Lancashire: "I bath a lot due to showing most weekends, but in general Beagles are a low maintenance breed for grooming. A hound glove, rubber curry comb and soft brush are sufficient.

"When bathing always take care to make sure the tail is dry and that when the dog shakes there is nothing around for it to injure the tail on. Beagles are prone to a condition called *"beagle tail"* (see **Chapter 11. Beagle Health**) which causes a painful condition that results in a temporary drooping of the tail if the tail is banged when wet."

Debbie Tantrum, Debles Beagles, Shropshire: "Ours are sometimes bathed two or three times weekly depending on the weather, often it's just a quick hose down with the hose pipe.

"They have short coats that need brushing twice weekly as they shed their coat all year round, eyes and ears need to be cleaned at least twice weekly, as they can get infections, teeth cleaned if possible - ours sometimes eat the paste - and nails need to be kept trimmed."

Kelly Diamond, Kelcardi Beagles, Fife: "Beagles have low grooming requirements, around once per week, some times more when losing old coat. Personally, mine may get one bath a year on a nice hot sunny day or if they have rolled in something, otherwise they won't get one. None of them smell and they all have wonderful shiny coats."

Sarah Porter, Puddlehill Beagles, Norfolk: "Beagles are designed to be rough and ready and a self-cleaning machine. My dog walker often marvels how she can put them in her transport dirty and, by the time they get home, they are clean again. Regularly bathing strips their coats of the natural oils.

"Beagles have a dual coat to protect from the elements, so this helps. I cannot remember the last time I bathed any of mine – I don't think my 11-month-old has ever been bathed, the eldest two probably in the summer. My show dog was obviously bathed more regularly primarily before a show. They go to a groomer every six weeks to have their nails cut."

Karen Simkin, Simeldaka Beagles, London: "As I show my dogs, I bath the day before show. Brush them daily, you build a bond and can feel anything that shouldn't be there. I always show my pup buyers how to clean teeth and remove something from their mouth that should not be there!"

14. The Facts of Life

Judging by the number of questions our website receives, there is a lot of confusion about the canine facts of life. Some ask if, and at what age, they should have their dog spayed or neutered, while others want to know whether they should breed their dog.

Owners of females ask when and how often she will come on heat and how long this will last. Sometimes they want to know how you can tell if a female is pregnant or how long a pregnancy lasts. So here, in a nutshell, is a chapter on the birds and bees as far as Beagles are concerned.

....

Females and Heat

Just like all other female mammals, including humans, a female Beagle has a menstrual cycle - or to be more accurate, an oestrus cycle (*estrus* in the US). This is when she is ready (and willing!) for mating and is more commonly called **heat**, being **in heat**, **on heat** or **in season**.

A Beagle can have her first cycle any time between six months and 20 months old. Generally, smaller breeds mature faster than large breeds. We asked some of our breeders when their females typically had their first heat and they said: 10-11 months, 10-14 months, around 14 months, 14-16 months, 6-20 months with current average around 14 months.

Sharon Hardisty: "I personally find they are quite late! I have only had one come in season at seven months and the rest have been around one year old and over. I currently have one at 16 months who has not been in season."

Sally Kimber: "In nearly 50 years of breeding Beagles, my bitches have always come into season (on heat) between seven and 12 months. I think across the board, Beagle bitches usually come into season between six and 18 months."

Tip Females often follow the patterns of their mother, so ask the breeder at what age the dam had her first heat and then how often they occur.

A female typically has a heat cycle every six to nine or 10 months, Beagles tend to be towards the longer end of the cycle. Peter Sievwright: "I find that generally my girls are every 32 weeks. This can be quite rigid sometimes, they follow a 32-week pattern, although sometimes there is a slight blip in the cycle."

Lori Norman added: "I think they vary from other breeds that tend to do the six-month cycle. I tend to see every eight to 10 months."

There is no time of the year that corresponds to a breeding season, so the heat could occur during any month. When a young bitch comes in season, it is normal for her cycles to be somewhat irregular - it can take up to two years for regular cycles to develop. The timescale also becomes more erratic with older, unspayed females.

A heat cycle normally lasts 18 to 21 days, the last days might be lighter in terms of blood loss - you might not even know that she is still in heat.

FACT ❯ Unlike women, female dogs do not stop menstruating when they reach middle age, although the heat becomes shorter and lighter. However, a litter takes a heavy toll on older females. NOTE: Women cannot get pregnant during their period, while female dogs can ONLY get pregnant during their heat.

There are four stages of the heat cycle:

Proestrus – this is when the bleeding starts and lasts around nine days. Male dogs are attracted to her, but she is not yet interested, so she may hold her tail close to her body. You will notice that her vulva (external sex organ, or pink bit under her tail) becomes swollen.

If you're not sure if she's in heat, hold a tissue against her vulva – does it turn pink or red? She will lick the area a lot, which may be your first sign that she is coming into season. The blood is usually light red or brown, turning more straw-coloured after a week or so. She may also urinate more frequently.

Oestrus - this is when eggs are released from ovaries and the optimum time for breeding. Males are extremely interested in her - and the feelings are very much reciprocated. Her hormones are raging and she definitely wants sex! If there is a male around she may stand for him and *"flag"* her tail (or move it to one side) to allow him to mount her. Oestrus is the time when a female CAN get pregnant and usually lasts a further nine days.

Dioestrus – this is the two-month stage when her body produces the hormone progesterone whether or not she is pregnant. All the hormones are present; even if she hasn't conceived. This can sometimes lead to what is known as a *"false pregnancy."* During this stage she is no longer interested in males.

Anoestrus – this the period of rest when reproductive organs are inactive. It is the longest stage of the cycle and lasts around five-and-a-half months. If she normally lives with a male dog, they can return to living together again - neither will be interested in mating and she cannot get pregnant.

The canine heat cycle is a complex mix of hormonal, behavioural, and physical changes. Each dog is different. Some show behavioural changes, such as becoming more clingy or irritable, going off their food, shedding hair, mounting other dogs or your leg, or sulking in their beds.

The amount of blood varies from one female to another; some clean themselves regularly, while others are less scrupulous on the personal hygiene front.

If your girl is a heavy menstruater and on and off your furniture, one option to reduce staining is to put her in doggie pants for her heaviest days, *pictured.*

Even with pants on, leakages occasionally occur and a few females will even take advantage and eliminate in them! And one breeder added: "I have one that can get out of them by rubbing on the carpet or underneath a chair in about two seconds! Please also tell owners that those panties are not chastity belts!"

FACT ❯ When a female is on heat, she produces pheromones that attract male dogs. Because dogs have a sense of smell several hundred times stronger than ours, your girl on heat is a magnet for all the neighbourhood males. It is believed that they can detect the scent of a female on heat up to two miles away!

They may congregate around your house or follow you around the park - if you are brave or foolish enough to venture out there while she is in season - waiting for their chance to prove their manhood (or mutthood in their case).

It is amazing the lengths some entire (uncastrated) males will go to impregnate a female on heat. Travelling great distances to follow her scent, digging under fences, jumping over barriers, chewing through doors or walls and sneaking through hedges are just some of the tactics employed by canine Casanovas on the loose.

Love is a powerful thing - and canine lust even more so. A dog living in the same house as a female in heat has even been known to mate with her through the bars of a crate!

To avoid an unwanted pregnancy, you must keep a close eye on her throughout her heat and not allow her to wander unsupervised - and that includes the garden or yard unless you 100% know it is safe. Determined male dogs can jump and scramble over high fences.

Keep her on a lead if you go out on walks and whatever you do, don't let her run free anywhere that you might come across other dogs. If you have a large garden or yard, you may wish to restrict her to that during her heat. You can compensate for the restrictions by playing more games at home to keep her mentally and physically active.

 The instinct to mate will trump all of her training. Her hormones are raging and, during her most fertile days (the Oestrus), she is ready, able and ... VERY willing! If you do have an entire male, you need to physically keep him in a separate place or kennel.

The desire to mate is all-consuming and can be accompanied by howling or "marking" (urinating) indoors from a frustrated Romeo.

You can also buy a spray that masks the natural oestrus scent. Marketed under such attractive names as "**Bitch Spray,**" these lessen, but don't eliminate, the scent. They may reduce the amount of unwanted attention, but are not a complete deterrent.

There is no canine contraceptive, so if your female is unspayed, you need to keep her under supervision during her heat cycle - which may be up to three or four weeks.

If your female is accidentally mated (a **"mis-mating"),** there is an injection available in the UK called Alizin which blocks progesterone production. It is used any time from the end of the season up to 45 days after the mis-mating. It is given as two injections 24 hours apart and has a low risk if used early on. If used late it causes abortion.

Neutering - Pros and Cons

This is currently a hot potato in the dog world. Dogs kept purely as pets – i.e. not for showing, breeding or working – are often spayed or neutered. There is also the life-threatening risk of *Pyometra* in unspayed middle-aged females.

There is already too much indiscriminate breeding of dogs in the world. However, there's also mounting scientific evidence that early spay/neuter can have a detrimental effect on dogs of all breeds.

As you will read in **Chapter 15. Beagle Rescue**, it is estimated that 1,000 dogs are put to sleep every hour in the USA alone. Rescue organisations in North America, the UK and Australia routinely neuter all dogs that they rehome. The RSPCA, along with most UK vets, also promotes the benefits of neutering; it's estimated that more than half of all dogs in the UK are spayed or castrated.

Another point is that you may not have a choice. Some breeders' Puppy Contracts may stipulate that, except in special circumstances, you agree to neuter your Beagle as a Condition of Sale. Others may state that you need the breeder's permission to breed your dog.

While early spay/neuter has been traditionally recommended, there is scientific evidence that it is better to wait until the dog is through puberty – whatever your vet might recommend.

The Science

Dr Samantha Goldberg, Beagle breeder, vet and Kennel Club Health Co-ordinator for UK Beagle Clubs, has written a paper on Beagles and early spay/neuter.

Regardless of how big young Beagles look, their skeletons take a full 12 months to mature, and Dr Goldberg strongly recommends **waiting until Beagles are at least 12 months old before considering spaying or neutering.**

This is because we now realise that the sex hormones play an important role in normal growth and development. Dr Goldberg says: "Testosterone and oestrogen are involved in some of the long bone formations in the body, so removing this too early can affect correct growth leading to prolonged growth and poorer quality bone with abnormal mechanical behaviours of the joints.

"Early neutering – i.e. before skeletal growth has finished - results in taller, leggier hounds as the closure of the plates in the long bones is helped by release of puberty hormones. There is also increased risk of cranial cruciate rupture, intervertebral disc disease, hip dysplasia and patella luxation being cited in some breeds. The number of breeds listed as affected is likely to increase as we know more.

"Bitches may be sexually mature before the body has finished developing physically and mentally. Although they may be able to come into season, they have not finished growing if under 12 months and will certainly not have finished maturing mentally.

"It is best to be patient and not just neuter to suit the human family. The season is only three weeks and a well-crate trained Beagle can cope with plenty of chews and walks on a lead where the number of other dogs is low.

"Many vets will try to influence owners to spay their bitch at six months and often before a season."

"Beagles are a breed bred to think for themselves whilst out hunting. Thus they may be harder to recall and often get distracted when off-lead - making yourself more interesting than a hare is difficult!

"Neutering will not alter this! In male beagles one of the commonest things I hear is: "He runs off, I think he is looking for bitches." Actually, it is highly likely that the dog is also hunting and this is not driven by testosterone. A heedless teenage Beagle is best trained first and then neutered.

"Teenage Beagles generally need consistent guidance on how they fit in the family pack. If they are neutered too young that behaviour can become fixed as they need to come out of puberty to be mentally mature. There is a lot of work looking at behavioural issues with dogs in rescues and when they were neutered. So far it seems likely that more dogs ending up in rescue with behavioural issues were neutered early – i.e. under 12 months.

"Neutering reduces metabolic rate and this means they need fewer calories or more exercise to balance it. Often neutering is carried out without the vet warning the owner of this. Thus we hear "she is overweight because she is spayed. Actually not true - being overweight is caused by eating more calories than are expended.

"Overweight dogs have higher risks from many health conditions, e.g. Diabetes Mellitus and joint issues...and obvious things such as heart disease due to increased workload.

"Neutering male dogs directly reduces risks of increased prostate size due to testosterone (not the same as tumours) and in bitches removes the risk of Pyometra, a life-threatening uterine condition, and ovarian cancers. These effects are very positive.

"To summarise: Neutering should be carried out at the correct time to maximize health in your dog and afterwards their lifestyle may be changed a little, e.g. calorie control. Neuter to reduce risks of many health conditions, but do it at the right time to maximize the lifespan of your Beagle."

Spaying

Spaying is the term traditionally used to describe the sterilisation of a female dog so that she cannot become pregnant. This is normally done by a procedure called an *"ovariohysterectomy"* and involves the removal of the ovaries and uterus, or womb. Although this is a routine operation, it is major abdominal surgery and she has to be anaesthetised.

One less invasive option offered by some vets is an *"ovariectomy,"* which removes the ovaries, but leaves the womb intact. It requires only a small incision and can even be carried out by laparoscopy, or keyhole surgery. The dog is anaesthetised for a shorter time and there is less risk of infection or excess bleeding during surgery.

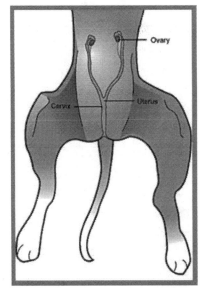

One major reason often given for not opting for an ovariectomy is that the female still runs the risk of **Pyometra** later in life. However, there is currently little or no scientific evidence of females that have undergone an ovariectomy contracting Pyometra afterwards. Traditional spaying considerably reduces the risk of Pyometra.

FACT Spaying is a much more serious operation for females than neutering is for males. It involves an internal abdominal operation, whereas the neutering procedure is carried out on the male's testicles, which are outside his abdomen.

As with any major procedure, there are pros and cons.

Pros:

- Spaying prevents infections, cancer and other diseases of the uterus and ovaries. A spayed female will have a greatly reduced risk of mammary cancer

- Spaying eliminates the risk of Pyometra, which results from hormonal changes in the female's reproductive tract. It also reduces hormonal changes that can interfere with the treatment of diseases like diabetes or epilepsy

- You no longer have to cope with any potential mess caused by bleeding inside the house during heat cycles
- You don't have to guard your female against unwanted attention from males
- Spaying can reduce behaviour problems, such as roaming, aggression towards other dogs, anxiety or fear (not all canine experts agree)
- A spayed dog does not contribute to the pet overpopulation problem

Cons:

- Complications can occur, including an abnormal reaction to the anaesthetic, bleeding, stitches breaking and infections; these are not common
- Occasionally there can be long-term effects connected to hormonal changes. These include weight gain or less stamina, which can occur years after spaying
- Cost. This can range from £100 to £250 in the UK, more for keyhole spaying, and anything from $150 to over $1,000 at a vet's clinic in the USA, or from around $50 at a low-cost clinic, for those that qualify
- Early spay can lead to an increased risk of joint and other diseases
- Urinary incontinence is more common in neutered females

One breeder added: "Spaying too early or during a heat cycle can cause life-long incontinence in female puppies."

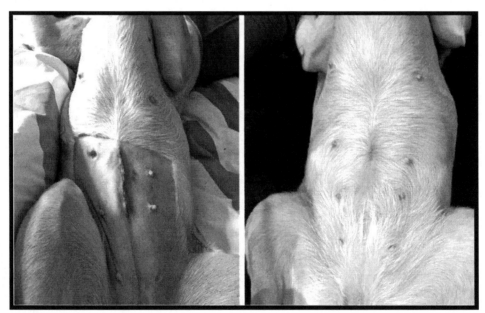

These photographs are reproduced courtesy of Guy Bunce and Chloe Spencer, of Dizzywaltz Labrador Retrievers, Berkshire, England. The left image shows four-year-old Disney shortly after a full spay (ovariohysterectomy). The right one shows Disney several weeks later.

Neutering

Neutering male dogs involves castration, or the removal of the testicles. This can be a difficult decision for some owners, as it causes a drop in the pet's testosterone levels, which some humans – men in particular! - feel affects the quality of their dog's life. Fortunately, dogs do not think like people, and male dogs do not miss their testicles or the loss of sex.

Dogs working in the Services or for charities are often neutered and this does not impair their ability to perform any of their duties. NOTE: Male show dogs are all unneutered (entire).

Technically, neutering can be carried out at any age over eight weeks provided both testicles have descended. However, recent scientific studies, are undoubtedly coming down on the side of waiting until the dog is one year or older.

Surgery is relatively straightforward, and complications are less common and less severe than with spaying. Although he will feel tender afterwards, your dog should return to his normal self within a couple of days. When a dog comes out of surgery, his scrotum, or sacs that held the testicles, will be swollen and it may look like nothing has been done. It is normal for these to shrink slowly in the days following surgery. Here are the main pros and cons:

Pros:

- Castration is a simple procedure, and dogs usually make a swift recovery afterwards
- Unwanted sexual behaviour, such as mounting people or objects, is usually reduced or eliminated
- Behaviour problems such as aggression, marking and roaming can be reduced
- Testicular problems such as infections, cancer and torsion (painful rotation of the testicle) are eradicated
- Prostate disease, common in older male dogs, is less likely to occur
- A submissive intact male dog may be targeted by other dogs. After he has been neutered, he will no longer produce testosterone and so will not be regarded as much of a threat by the other males, so he is less likely to be bullied
- A neutered dog is not fathering unwanted puppies

Cons:

- Studies indicate that Beagles neutered before one year old are more likely to get IVDD than those neutered after two years
- As with any surgery, there can be bleeding afterwards; you should keep an eye on your dog after the procedure. Infections can also occur, generally caused by the dog licking the wound, so try and prevent him doing this. If he persists, use an E-collar. In the **vast majority** of cases, these problems do not occur

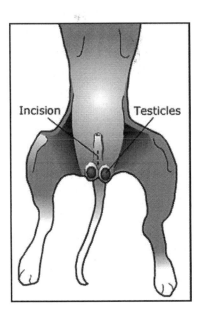

Incision / Testicles

- Some dogs' coats may be affected; this also applies to spaying. Supplementing the diet with fish oil can compensate for this
- Cost - this starts at around £80 in the UK. In the USA this might cost anything from $100 to $1,000 at a private veterinary clinic, depending on your state, or $50-$100 at a low cost or Humane Society clinic

New Techniques

Two other phrases you may hear are *"tubal ligation"* or *"vasectomy."* *Tubal ligation* is the tying of a female's Fallopian tubes and a **vasectomy** is the clamping shut of the sperm ducts from the male's testicles. Many veterinary papers have been written on these topics, but as yet, not many vets offer them as options.

In both cases, unlike with spaying and neutering, the dog continues to produce hormones, but is unable to get pregnant or father puppies. With further evidence of the positive effects of hormones, these operations could become more common in the future – although more vets will first have to be trained.

There's a new non-surgical procedure to sterilise male dogs called *"Zeutering."* It involves injecting zinc gluconate into the dog's testicles. Dogs are lightly sedated, but not anaesthetised. It's inexpensive, there's little recovery time and no stitches. However, studies show that Zeutering is only 99% effective, and its long-term effects are still being researched. And while it makes dogs sterile, they still retain some of their testosterone.

Therefore, habits that usually disappear with traditional castration, such as marking, following females on heat and aggression towards other males, remain. Zeutering isn't for every dog, but worth discussing with your vet.

Urban Myths

Neutering or spaying will spoil the dog's character - There is no evidence that any of the positive characteristics of your dog will be altered. He or she will be just as obedient, playful and loyal as before. Neutering may reduce aggression or roaming in male dogs, because they are no longer competing to mate with a female.

A female needs to have at least one litter - There is no proven physical or mental benefit to a female having a litter.

Mating is natural and necessary - We tend to ascribe human emotions to our dogs, but they do not think emotionally about sex or having and raising a family. Unlike humans, their desire to mate or breed is entirely physical, triggered by the chemicals called hormones within their body. Without these hormones – i.e. after neutering or spaying – the desire disappears or is greatly reduced.

Male dogs will behave better if they can mate - This is simply not true; sex does not make a dog behave better. In fact, it can have the opposite effect. Having mated once, a male may show an increased interest in females. He may also consider his status elevated, which may make him harder to control or call back.

 Do your own research. Many vets still promote early spay and neuter.

Pregnancy

Regardless of how big or small the dog is, a canine pregnancy lasts for 58 to 65 days; 63 days is average. This is true of all breeds of dog from the Chihuahua to the Great Dane. Sometimes pregnancy is referred to as *"the gestation period."*

Photo of Honey with her five-day-old litter courtesy of Kelly Diamond, Kelcardi Beagles, Fife, Scotland.

A female should have a pre-natal check-up after mating. The vet should answer any questions about type of food, supplements and extra care needed, as well as informing the owner about any physical changes likely to occur in your female.

There is a blood test available that measures levels of *relaxin*. This is a hormone produced by the ovary and the developing placenta, and pregnancy can be

detected by monitoring relaxin levels as early as 22 to 27 days after mating. The levels are high throughout pregnancy and then decline rapidly after the female has given birth.

A vet can usually see the puppies (but not how many) using Ultrasound from around the same time. X-rays carried out seven to eight or so weeks into the pregnancy show the puppies' skeletons and give the breeder a good idea of the number of puppies. They can also help to give the vet more information, which is particularly useful if the female has had previous whelping problems.

Signs of pregnancy are:

- After mating, many females become more affectionate. However, a few may become uncharacteristically irritable and maybe even a little aggressive!

- She may produce a slight mucous-like discharge from her vagina one month after mating

- Three or four weeks after mating, some females experience morning sickness – if this is the case, feed little and often. She may seem more tired than usual

- She may seem slightly depressed or show a drop in appetite. These signs can also mean there are other problems, so you should consult your vet

- Her teats will become more prominent, pink and erect 25 to 30 days into the pregnancy. Later on, you may notice a fluid coming from them. This first milk (colostrum) is the most important milk a puppy gets on Day One as it contains the mother's immunity.

- Her body weight will noticeably increase about 35 days after mating

- Her abdomen will become noticeably larger from around Day 40, although first-time mums and females carrying few puppies may not show as much

- Many pregnant females' appetite will increase in the second half of pregnancy

- Her nesting instincts will kick in as the delivery date approaches. She may seem restless or scratch her bed or the floor - she may even rip and shred items like your comforter, curtains or carpeting!

- During the last week of pregnancy, females often start to look for a safe place for whelping. Some seem to become confused, wanting to be with their owners and at the same time wanting to prepare their nest. If the female is having a C-section, she should still be allowed to nest in a whelping box with layers of newspaper, which she will scratch and dig as the time approaches

⊘ *If your female Beagle becomes pregnant – either by design or accident - your first step should be to consult a vet.*

Our breeders have had anything from two to 12 puppies in a litter, although five to eight is the average. The number depends on factors such as bloodlines, the age of the dam and sire (young and older dogs have smaller litters), health and diet of the dam, and the size of the gene pool; the lower the genetic diversity, the smaller the litter.

False Pregnancies

Occasionally, unspayed females may display signs of a false pregnancy. Before dogs were domesticated, it was common for female dogs to have false pregnancies and to lactate (produce milk). She would then nourish puppies of the Alpha bitch or puppies who had lost their mother in the pack.

False pregnancies occur 60 to 80 days after the female was in heat - about the time she would have given birth – and are generally nothing to worry about for an owner. The exact cause is unknown; however, hormonal imbalances are thought to play an important role. Some dogs have shown symptoms within three to four days of spaying; these include:

-  Making a nest
- Mothering or adopting toys and other objects
- Producing milk (lactating)
- Appetite fluctuations
- Barking or whining a lot
- Restlessness, depression or anxiety
- Swollen abdomen
- She might even appear to go into labour

Under no circumstances should you restrict your Beagle's water supply to try and prevent her from producing milk. This is dangerous as she can become dehydrated.

Occasionally, an unspayed female may have a false pregnancy with each heat cycle. Spaying during a false pregnancy may actually prolong the condition, so better to wait until it is over to have her spayed.

FACT ❯ False pregnancy is not a disease, but an exaggerated response to normal hormonal changes. Even if left untreated, it almost always resolves itself.

However, if your dog appears physically ill or the behavioural changes are severe enough to worry about, visit your vet. He or she may prescribe *Galastop*, which stops milk production and quickly returns the hormones to normal. In rare cases, hormone treatment may be necessary.

Generally, dogs experiencing false pregnancies do not have serious long-term problems, as the behaviour disappears when the hormones return to their normal levels in two to three weeks.

Pyometra

One exception is *Pyometra,* a serious and potentially deadly infection of the womb, caused by a hormonal abnormality. It normally follows a heat cycle in which fertilisation did not occur and the dog typically starts showing symptoms within two to four months. It occurs most often in middle-aged females.

Commonly referred to as *"pyo,"* there are **open** and **closed** forms of the disease. Open pyo is usually easy to identify with a smelly discharge, so prompt treatment is easy.

Closed pyo is often harder to identify and you may not even notice anything until your girl becomes feverish and lethargic. When this happens, it is very serious and time is of the essence. Typically, vets will recommend immediate spaying in an effort to save her life.

Typical signs of Pyometra are excessive drinking and urination, vomiting and depression, with the female trying to lick a white discharge from her vagina. She may also have a slight temperature. If the condition becomes severe, her back legs will become weak, possibly to the point where she can no longer get up without help.

Pyometra can be fatal. It needs to be dealt with promptly by a vet, who will give the dog intravenous fluids and antibiotics for several days. In most cases this is followed by spaying.

Should I Breed From My Beagle?

The short and very simple answer is: **NO!** Not unless you do a lot of research, find a mentor for expert advice and then a good vet, preferably experienced with Beagles.

Breeding healthy Beagle puppies with good temperaments is an expensive, time-consuming and complex process, and should not be approached lightly.

The risk of breeding puppies with health issues is very real if you don't know what you are doing. Today's responsible breeders are continually looking at ways of improving the health of the Beagle through selective breeding. See **Chapter 11. Beagle Health** for a list of recommended health tests.

FACT ❯❯ According to an in-depth UK study involving 36,000 dogs from 170 breeds published in the Journal of Small Animal Practice, over 21% of Beagle litters were born by Caesarean, or C-Section.

Typical veterinary fees for a C-section are in four figures and are not covered by normal pet insurance - and even then a good outcome is not guaranteed. I know of a Beagle owner who lost her beloved female after a C-section only last month.

Beagle genetics are a complicated business that cover a multitude of traits, including health, colour coat, temperament and natural instinct. Well-bred Beagle puppies fetch four-figure sums. But despite this, you may be surprised to hear that many dedicated Beagle breeders make little money from the practice, due to the high costs of veterinary fees, health screening, stud fees and expensive special nutrition and care for the female and her pups.

Responsible breeding is backed up by genetic information and screening as well as a thorough knowledge of the desired traits of the Beagle. It is definitely not an occupation for the amateur hobbyist.

ⓧ **Breeding is not just about the look or colour of the puppies; health and temperament are at least as important.**

Many dog lovers do not realise that the single most important factor governing health and certain temperament traits is genetics. Top breeders have years of experience in selecting the right pair for mating after they have considered the ancestry, health, temperament, coat, size and physical characteristics of the two dogs involved.

Photo of Ruby and her litter courtesy of Sharon Hardisty, Blunderhall Beagles, Lancashire.

They may travel hundreds of miles to find the right mate for their dog. Some of them also show their dogs.

Anyone breeding from their Beagle must first consider these questions:

- 🐾 **Did you get your Beagle from a good, ethical breeder?** Dogs sold in pet stores and on general sales websites are seldom good specimens and can be unhealthy

- 🐾 **Does your dog conform to the Breed Standard?** Do not breed from a Beagle that is not an excellent specimen in all respects, hoping that somehow the puppies will turn out better.

They won't. Talk with experienced breeders and ask them for an honest assessment of your dog

- 🐾 **Do you understand COI and its implications?** COI stands for Coefficient of Inbreeding. It measures the common ancestors of a dam and sire and indicates the probability of how genetically similar they are

- 🐾 **Have your dog and its mate both been screened** for MLS, Lafora and other Beagle health issues that can be passed on to the puppies?

- 🐾 **Have you researched his or her lineage** to make sure there are no problems lurking in the background? Puppies inherit traits from their grandparents and great-grandparents as well as from their mother and father

- 🐾 **Are you 100% sure that your dog has no temperament issues** which could be inherited by the puppies?

- 🐾 **Are you positive that the same can be said for the dog you are planning on breeding yours with?**

- 🐾 **Do you have the finances** to keep the mother healthy through pregnancy, whelping, and care of her and the puppies after birth – even if complications occur?

- 🐾 **Is your female two years old or older and at least in her second heat cycle?** Female Beagles should not be bred until they are physically mature, have had their joints screened, and are robust enough to whelp and care for a litter. Even then, not all females are suitable

- 🐾 **Giving birth takes a lot out of a female Beagle - are you prepared to put yours through that?** And, as you've read, it's not without risk

- 🐾 **Some Beagles are poor mothers,** which means that you have to look after the puppies 24/7. Even if they are not, they need daily help from the owner to rear their young

- 🐾 **Can you care for up to eight lively puppies if you can't find homes for them?**

- 🐾 **Will you be able to find good homes for all the puppies?** Good breeders do not let their precious puppies go to just any home. They want to be sure that the new owners will take good care of their dogs for their lifetime

- 🐾 **Would you take back, or help to rehome, one of your dogs if circumstances change?**

Having said that, experts are not born, they learn their trade over many years. Anyone who is seriously considering getting into the specialised art of breeding Beagles should first spend time researching the breed and its genetics.

Make sure you are going into Beagle breeding for the right reasons and not primarily to make money - ask yourself how you intend to improve the breed. Visit dog shows and make contact with established breeders. Find yourself a mentor, somebody who is already very familiar with the breed.

To find a good breeder:

✓ **In the UK**, find a member of a breed club in your area. Visit www.thebeagleclub.org or The Beagle Association at http://beagleassociation.org.uk/puppies.html or the Kennel Club website and find a Kennel Club **Assured Breeder** in your county.

✓ **In the USA,** search their online Breeder Directory of The National Beagle Club of America for details of members near you at https://www.nationalbeagleclub.org/Breeders Visit the AKC website for a **Breeder of Merit,** or one who is a member of the **Bred with H.E.A.R.T.** programme.

If you are determined to breed from your Beagle - and breed properly - do your research. Read as much as you can; one useful resource is *"Book of the Bitch"* by J. M. Evans and Kay White.

You may have the most wonderful Beagle in the world, but don't enter the world of dog breeding without knowledge and ethics. Don't do it for the money or the cute factor – or to show the kids "The Miracle of Birth!"

Breeding poor examples only brings heartache in the long run when health or temperament issues develop. Our strong advice is: When it comes to Beagles, leave it to the experts – or set out to become one yourself.

15. Beagle Rescue

Not everyone who wants a Beagle gets one as a puppy from a breeder. Some people prefer to give a rescue dog a second chance for a happy life.

What could be kinder and more rewarding than giving a poor, abandoned dog a loving home for the rest of his life?

Not much really; adoption saves lives and gives unfortunate dogs a second chance of happiness. The problem of homeless dogs is truly depressing. It's a big issue in Britain, but even worse in the US, where the sheer numbers in kill shelters are hard to comprehend. In *"Don't Dump The Dog,"* Randy Grim states that 1,000 dogs are being put to sleep every hour in the States.

Reasons for Rescue

If you're thinking of adopting a Beagle, you'll need patience and commitment. They are active dogs

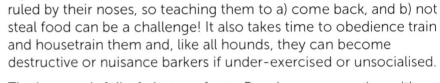

ruled by their noses, so teaching them to a) come back, and b) not steal food can be a challenge! It also takes time to obedience train and housetrain them and, like all hounds, they can become destructive or nuisance barkers if under-exercised or unsocialised.

The internet is full of photos of cute Beagles, some posing with their celebrity owners, like Meghan Markle and Miley Cyrus, and there are more than 12 million posts devoted to *#Beagle* on Instagram.

That gorgeous little Snoopy puppy with the beautiful big eyes looks so cute. And people rush out in their droves to buy them, with scant regard to the health or nature of the Beagle puppy they are buying.

Many expect a lapdog and realise too late what they've actually got is a hound! By then, the dog may have become too stubborn, anxious or vocal, due to his needs not being met.

Nigel Wright, Chairman of the UK's Beagle Welfare, told us: "While there are many reasons for Beagles being surrendered to Beagle Welfare, the ones which are cited most often include a change in circumstances, such as returning to work, or an increase in work commitments.

"A Beagle left on their own for long periods of time – particularly if they've been used to having a lot of human company - can be a noisy and destructive creature prone to separation anxiety.

"Other reasons are the arrival of a new baby, leaving little time for an attention-seeking hound, or simply that the time commitment required to fully train and occupy a Beagle has become too much for an owner.

"True to their hunting roots, Beagles like to have a job or purpose, and, without the right level of training and exercise, a Beagle can quickly become too much to manage for the novice owner."

Linda Forrest is founder of SOS Beagle Rescue and for the last 30 years has devoted her life to rehoming as many Beagles as she can in eastern USA. She says: "Most of the dogs we pull into recue have been strays found running at large, with a heavy intake at the end of hunting season in Tennessee.

"Owner give-ups are usually due to the bad health of the owner, moving to a new apartment that doesn't allow pets, or the people were just clueless as to the energy and stubbornness of a hound.

"We do get calls from people who want to surrender dogs with bite histories, but for liability reasons we can't accept them.

"The biggest thing we emphasize with rescue Beagles is how stubborn they can be - I compare them to a three-year-old child who doesn't want to do what Mom and Dad ask.

"Owners need to know that a Beagle doesn't usually make a good walking companion because their nose is constantly working, that they can't be trusted off-leash unless in a fenced-area, and they are as smart as a fox but stubborn as a mule!"

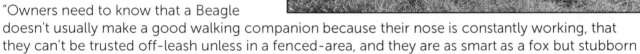

Consider This..

Here are some things to consider from SOS Beagle Rescue and Beagle Welfare.

SOS Beagle Rescue: "If you are thinking of adding a Beagle to your family, make sure it's the right breed for you.

"The Beagle's small size, adorable looks, and friendly and loving personality make it a very popular family pet. But the decision to purchase or adopt a Beagle (or any pet for that matter) should be made only with careful consideration and planning.

"Ask yourself the following questions:

- 🐾 Are you ready to care for a Beagle for the rest of his or her life? Beagles live on average 12-15 years. Be sure you're ready to make a lifelong commitment to your pet

- 🐾 Are you financially prepared to support a Beagle? The cost of purchasing or adopting a dog is only the start. Don't forget dog food, toys, treats, bedding, routine and emergency veterinary care, and kennel expenses if no one will be able to care for your dog when you go away

- 🐾 Will you be able to exercise your Beagle once or twice a day? Beagles are high energy dogs and need daily exercise to burn off that excess energy. And, being scent hounds, they need to "get out and sniff"

- 🐾 Are you prepared to train your Beagle so she or he will be a well-behaved family member? Beagles are very clever, but they are inherently stubborn and can be mischievous or even destructive when it comes to acquiring food (Beagles are notorious "chowhounds"). But they respond well to diligent and consistent training, particularly if a positive approach with food rewards is used. This is true for puppies as well as adult dogs

- 🐾 If you're a parent, do you want a Beagle just as much as your children do, and are you prepared to provide the majority of its care? Don't make the mistake of getting a dog "for the kids" and assuming they will take care of it. You will have the ultimate responsibility

♣ And if your children are toddlers, are you prepared to supervise all interaction between them? This is an absolute necessity in order to prevent accidental nipping, or worse. And if your children are older, chances are that they will be at home for only part of your Beagle's lifetime. Many people give up their dogs when the kids leave home. Don't be one of them!

"Now let's talk about puppies versus adult Beagles. While Beagle puppies are adorably cute, they don't remain that tiny ball of fur for very long, and they require much effort and training during the first year. Puppies need to be housebroken...make sure your work and family schedule can accommodate his or her needs.

"Puppies are little whirlwinds of energy when they're awake and they need to be watched constantly so they don't get in trouble. It's like following a two-year-old around. If puppy care isn't for you, then consider adopting an older Beagle.

"Now let me discuss a few of the negatives. First, when Beagles are outside, they must always be either on a leash or in a securely fenced area. If they are loose, they will run away. While they are busy tracking whatever scent gets their interest, they will not pay any attention to cars.

"Next, most Beagles will bark and howl on occasion, and this can be a great source of annoyance for neighbors. And lastly, Beagles shed a lot. This is how all short-haired dogs maintain their coat length. If you have allergies or consider yourself a "neat freak," beware!

"If you've read this far, you might be saying to yourself, "Gee, is there anything good about Beagles?" Of course there is! I have three Beagles of my own whom I love dearly.

"They are cute, funny, loving, and a constant source of delight to my husband and me. And don't just take my word for it! Visit some of the Beagles on the web in the pack or the kennel to see how they enrich the lives of their owners - but make the right decision! Make sure that a Beagle is the right dog for you.

"We also make sure they understand that with strays, it may look like a Beagle, bay like a Beagle, act like a Beagle, but a DNA test may show other breeds in its ancestry - we had someone accuse us of misleading them when a DNA test didn't come back 100% Beagle on a stray dog.

"We strongly suggest a secure physically fenced yard, although we'll make exceptions for committed owners in apartments or condos with no young children (they might inadvertently open the door and let the dog out).

"We advise constant supervision of the dog and child interaction in homes with children under the age of eight to be sure there is no teasing that might provoke a bite, and warn seniors (like me) that puppies are TONS of work and may outlive a 70 to 80-year-old adopter, so we always ask for a back-up person who will accept responsibility for the dog.

"A good rescue will always place the dog spayed or neutered, up to date on shots and heartworm preventative, with a contract that requires the adopter to notify the rescue if ever they are unable to keep the dog. All good rescues would take the dog back if the group was still in existence."

Nigel added: "As with any rescued dog, it's important for prospective adopters to understand that a pre-loved Beagle will inevitably come with baggage. It's a very different experience to purchasing an eight-week-old puppy which comes with a blank canvas.

"The most common behavioural issues which Beagle Welfare sees in surrendered dogs are resource guarding, separation anxiety, and reacting to other dogs on a lead. Anyone interested in adopting a dog which has been identified with one or more of these issues is made fully aware of the implications, and how to manage it, before an adoption can proceed."

Beagle Welfare advises UK adopters: "A Beagle needs a home with a garden, which needs to be fenced with "Colditz" in mind! Beagles can dig as well as jump, so five to six-foot-high fencing is recommended. They can squeeze through small spaces, such as trellis work or wrought iron gates, so you'll need to make sure you have the right sort of fencing as well as making sure it is high and deep enough.

"Remember that your hound will need to be exercised for at least an hour each day and part of that time should, if possible, be free running in a safe area away from traffic or livestock. Never forget that the Beagle was bred to hunt, it is instinctive and will show up in its behaviour on walks."

On the positive side they add: "The Beagle is full of fun, enthusiastic and always ready for any sort of activity. They are easy to feed, too easy sometimes as he will put on weight easily if allowed.

"They have an appetite for all sorts of disgusting things and will welcome the opportunity to raid next door's bins! Beagles are easy to keep clean which is just as well, given their delight in rolling in bad smells. Health surveys have shown the Beagle to be a very healthy breed."

The Dog's Point of View...

If you are serious about adopting a Beagle, do so with the right motives and with your eyes wide open. If you're expecting a perfect dog, you could be in for a shock. Rescue Beagles can and do become wonderful companions, but much depends on you and how much effort you are prepared to put in.

Many Beagles do not do well in noisy, busy, crowded rescue centres. If you can, look for a rescue organisation specialising in Beagles – and preferably one where the dog has been fostered out. If a dog has bad habits, the foster parents have probably started to work on some of them.

Beagles are extremely loyal to their owners. Sometimes those that end up in rescue centres are traumatised, others may have behaviour or health problems. They don't understand why they have been abandoned, neglected or badly treated by their owners and may arrive at your home with "baggage" of their own until they adjust to being part of a loving family again.

This may take time. Patience is the key to help the dog to adjust to new surroundings and family and to learn to love and trust again. Ask yourself a few questions before you take the plunge and fill in the adoption forms:

- Are you prepared to accept and deal with any problems - such as bad behaviour, aggression, timidity, chewing, jumping up or eliminating in the house - that a rescue dog may display when initially arriving in your home?
- Just how much time do you have to spend with your new Beagle to help him integrate back into normal family life?
- Are you prepared to take on a new addition to your family that may live for another decade?
- Will you guarantee that dog a home for life - even if he develops health issues later?

What could be worse for the unlucky dog than to be abandoned again if things don't work out between you?

Other Considerations

Adopting a rescue dog is a big commitment for all involved. It is not a cheap way of getting a Beagle. It could cost you several hundred pounds – or dollars.

Depending on the adoption centre, you may have to pay adoption fees, vaccination and veterinary bills, as well as worm and flea medication and spaying or neutering. Make sure you're aware of the full cost before committing.

Many rescue dogs are older and some may have health or temperament issues. You may even have to wait a while until a suitable dog comes up. One way of finding out if you are suitable is to become a foster home for a rescue centre. Fosters offer temporary homes until a forever home comes along. It's shorter-term, but still requires commitment and patience.

And it's not just the dogs that are screened! Rescue groups make sure that prospective adopters are suitable. They also want to make the right match - placing a high-energy Beagle with an elderly couple, or an anxious dog in a noisy household - would be storing up trouble. It would be a tragedy for the dog if things did not work out.

Most rescue groups ask a raft of personal questions - some of which may seem intrusive. But you'll have to answer them if you are serious about adopting. Here are some typical questions:

- Name, address, age
- Details, including ages, of all people living in your home
- Type of property you live in
- Size of your garden or yard and height of the fence around it
- Extensive details of any other pets
- Your work hours and amount of time spent away from the home each day
- Whether you have any previous experience with dogs or Beagles
- Your reasons for wanting to adopt
- Whether you have any experience dealing with canine behaviour or health issues
- Details of your vet
- If you are prepared for aggression/destructive behaviour/chewing/fear and timidity/soiling inside the house/medical issues

- Whether you are willing to housetrain and obedience train the dog
- Your views on dog training methods
- Whether you are prepared for the financial costs of dog ownership
- Where your dog will sleep at night
- Whether you are prepared to accept a Beagle cross
- Two personal references

If you go out to work, it is useful to know that UK rescue organisations will not place dogs in homes where they will be left alone for more than four to five hours at a stretch.

After you've filled in the adoption form, a chat with a representative from the charity usually follows. There will also be a home inspection visit - and even your vet may be vetted! If all goes well, you will be approved to adopt and when the right match comes along, a meeting will be arranged with all family members and the dog. You then pay the adoption fee and become the proud new owner of a Beagle.

It might seem like a lot of red tape, but the rescue groups have to be as sure as they can that you will provide a loving, forever home for the dog. It would be terrible if things didn't work out and the dog had to be placed back in rescue again.

All rescue organisations will neuter the dog or, if he or she is too young, specify in the adoption contract that the dog must be neutered and may not be used for breeding. Some Beagle rescue organisations have a lifetime rescue back-up policy, which means that if things don't work out, the dog must be returned to them.

Training a Rescue Dog

Some Beagles are in rescue because of behavioural problems, which often develop due to lack of training and attention from the previous owner.

As one rescue group put it: **"Rescue dogs are not damaged dogs; they have just been let down by humans, so take a little while to unpack their bags and get familiar with their new owners and surroundings before they settle in."**

If you approach rescue with your eyes wide open, if you're prepared to be patient and devote plenty of time to your new arrival, then rescuing a Beagle is incredibly rewarding. They are such affectionate and loyal dogs, you'll have a friend for life.

Organisations with experience of Beagles are more likely to be able to assess the dog and give you an idea of what you might be letting yourself in for. Often, lack of training or exercise is the root cause of any issues – but how this manifests itself varies from one dog to another.

 Ask as many questions as you can about the background of the dog, his natural temperament and any issues likely to arise. You are better having an honest appraisal than simply being told the dog is wonderful and in need of a home.

Training methods for a rescue Beagle are similar to those for any adult Beagle, but it may take longer as the dog first has to unlearn any bad habits.

If the dog you are interested in has a particular issue, such as indiscriminate barking or lack of housetraining, it is best to start right back at the beginning with training.

Don't presume the dog knows anything and take each step slowly. See **Chapter 8. Basic Training** for more information.

Tips

🐾 Start training the day you arrive home, not once he has settled in

🐾 He needs your attention, but, importantly, he also needs his own space where he can chill out. Put his bed or crate in a quiet place; you want your dog to learn to relax. The more relaxed he is, the fewer hang-ups he will have

🐾 Show him his sleeping and feeding areas, but allow him to explore these and the rest of his space in his own time

🐾 Using a crate may help speed up training, but it's important he first learns to regard the crate as a safe place, and not a prison. See **Chapter 5.** for the best way of achieving this

🐾 If you have children or other animals, introduce them quietly and NEVER leave them alone with the dog for the first few months – you don't know what his triggers are

🐾 Maintain a calm environment at home

🐾 Never shout at the dog – even if he has made a mess in the house - it will only stress him and make things worse

🐾 Don't give treats because you feel sorry for him. Only give him a treat when he has carried out a command. This will help him to learn quicker and you to establish leadership

🐾 Set him up to SUCCEED and build confidence – don't ask him to do things he can't yet do

🐾 Socialisation is extremely important – introduce him to new places and situations gradually and don't over-face him. You want him to grow in confidence, not be frightened by new things. Talk reassuringly throughout any new experience

🐾 Mental stimulation as well as physical exercise is important for Beagles, so have games, toys or challenges to keep your new dog's mind occupied

🐾 Don't introduce him to other dogs until you are confident he will behave well – and then not while he is on a lead (leash), when the *"fight or flight"* instinct might kick in

🐾 Getting an understanding of your dog will help to train him quicker – is he by nature submissive or dominant, anxious or outgoing, fearful or bold, aggressive or timid? If he shows aggressive tendencies, such as barking, growling or even biting, he is not necessarily bold. His aggression may be rooted in fear, anxiety or lack of confidence

 The aim of training a rescue Beagle is to have a relaxed dog, comfortable in his surroundings, who respects your authority and responds well to your positive training methods.

Rescue Organisations

Rescue organisations are usually run by volunteers who give up their time to help dogs in distress. They often have a network of foster homes, where a Beagle is placed until a permanent new home can be found. There are also online Beagle forums where people sometimes post information about a dog that needs a new home.

UK - Beagle Welfare www.beaglewelfare.org.uk

USA - SOS Beagle Rescue covers the NJ, Eastern PA, and parts of NY, with a chapter in Knoxville, TN. There is a list of Beagle rescues for the USA and Canada at **Beagles on The Web** www.beagles-on-the-web.com/adopt

If you visit these websites, you cannot presume that all descriptions are 100% accurate. They are given in good faith, but ideas of what constitutes a "lively" or "challenging" dog may vary.

Some dogs advertised may have other breeds in their genetic make-up. It does not mean that these are worse dogs, but if you are attracted to the Beagle for its handsome looks, temperament, quirky character and other assets, make sure you are looking at a Beagle.

DON'T get a dog from Craig's List, Gumtree or any of the other general advertising websites that sell golf clubs, jewellery, old cars, washing machines, etc.

You might think you are getting a bargain Beagle, but in the long run you will pay the price. Good breeders with healthy dogs do not advertise on these websites - or sell to pet shops.

You may be storing up a whole load of trouble for yourselves in terms of health or temperament issues, due to poor genetics and/or environment.

If you haven't been put off with all of the above... **Congratulations**, you may be just the person that poor homeless Beagle is looking for!

If you can't spare the time to adopt - and adoption means forever - you might consider fostering. Or you could help by becoming a home inspector or fundraiser to help keep these very worthy rescue groups providing such a wonderful service.

How ever you decide to get involved, Good Luck!

With thanks to Beagle Welfare UK and SOS Beagle Rescue for help with this article.

....

Saving one dog will not change the world,
But it will change the world for one dog

16. Caring for Older Beagles

Beagles live longer than many other breeds. If all goes well, you can expect your puppy to reach 10 to 12 years, or even more. Several of our breeders have had dogs who lived into their teens.

Lifespan is influenced by genetics and also by owners; how you feed, exercise and generally look after your dog will all have an impact on his life. Beagles can remain fit and active well into old age. But eventually all dogs – even Beagles – slow down.

Approaching Old Age

After having got up at the crack of dawn as a puppy, you may find that they now like to have a lie-in in the morning. They may be even less keen to go out in the rain. Physically, joints may become stiffer, and organs, such as heart or liver, may not function quite as effectively. On the mental side - just as with humans - your dog's memory, ability to learn and awareness will all start to dim.

Your faithful companion might become a bit grumpier, stubborn or a little less tolerant of lively dogs and children. You may also notice that they don't see or hear as well as they used to.

On the other hand, our old friends might not be hard of hearing at all. They might have developed that affliction common to many older dogs of *"selective hearing."*

Our 12-year-old Max had bionic hearing when it came to the word *"Dinnertime"* whispered from 20 paces, yet seemed strangely unable to hear the commands *"Come"* or *"Down"* when we were right in front of him!

Pictured enjoying life is Dotti (Ch Aladars Just Enchant'N), aged 11½, top, and 15, bottom. Photo courtesy of Darlene Stewart, Aladar Beagles, Alabama.

You can help ease mature dogs into old age gracefully by keeping an eye on them, noticing the changes and taking action to help them as much as possible. This might involve:

- Slowly reducing the amount of daily exercise
- A change of diet
- Modifying your dog's environment
- A visit to the vet for supplements and/or medications

Ageing varies greatly from dog to dog and bloodline to bloodline. Just as with humans, a Beagle of ideal weight that has been active and stimulated all of his life is likely to age slower than an overweight couch potato!

Keeping Beagles at an optimum weight as they get older is very important. Their metabolisms slow down, making it even easier than normal for them to pile on the pounds - particularly spayed females. Extra weight places additional, unwanted stress on the joints, back and organs, making them all have to work harder than they should.

FACT ❯ A dog is classed as a "Veteran" at seven years old in the show ring. Our breeders generally agreed that Beagles typically start to show signs of ageing at around eight, maybe seven, years old.

Physical and Mental Signs of Ageing

Here are some signs that your Beagle's body is feeling its age – an old dog may have a few or more of these symptoms:

- They generally slow down and are no longer as keen to go out on walks, or don't want to go as far. They are happy pottering and sniffing - and often take forever to inspect a single clump of grass! Some refuse to go outside in bad weather – but they still need their outdoor exercise

- They get up from lying down and move more slowly; all signs that joints are stiffening

- Grey hairs are appearing, particularly around the muzzle and coat colour fades

- They have put on a bit of weight

- They may have the occasional "accident" (incontinence) inside the house

- They urinate more frequently

- They drink more water

- They have bouts of constipation or diarrhoea

- They shed more hair

- The foot pads thicken and nails may become more brittle

- One or more lumps or fatty deposits (lipomas) develop on the body. One of our old dogs developed two small bumps on top of his head aged 10 and we took him straight to the vet, who performed minor surgery to remove them. They were benign (harmless), but always get the first one(s) checked out ASAP in case they are an early form of cancer - they can also grow quite rapidly, even if benign

- They can't regulate body temperature like they used to and so feel the cold and heat more

- Hearing deteriorates

- Eyesight may also deteriorate – if eyes appear cloudy they may be developing cataracts, so see your vet if you notice the signs. Most older dogs live quite well with failing eyesight, particularly as Beagles have an incredible sense of smell

- Bad breath (halitosis), which could be a sign of dental or gum disease. If the bad breath persists, get his checked out by a vet

- If inactive, they may develop callouses on the elbows, especially if lying on hard surfaces

It's not just your dog's body that deteriorates; his mind may too. Your dog may display some, all or none of these signs of *Canine Cognitive Dysfunction:*

- 🐾 Sleep patterns change; older dogs may be more restless at night and sleepy during the day. They may start wandering around the house at odd times, causing you sleepless nights

- 🐾 They bark more, sometimes at nothing or open spaces

- 🐾 They stare at objects, such as walls, hide in a corner, or wander aimlessly around the house or garden

- 🐾 Increased anxiety, separation anxiety or aggression

- 🐾 Forgetting or ignoring commands or habits they once knew well, such as the Recall and sometimes toilet training

- 🐾 Some dogs may become clingier and more dependent, often resulting in separation anxiety. They may seek reassurance that you are near as faculties fade and they become a bit less confident and independent. Others may become a bit disengaged and less interested in human contact

Understanding the changes happening to your dog and acting on them compassionately and effectively will help ease your dog's passage through his senior years.

Your dog has given you so much pleasure over the years, now they need you to give that bit of extra care for a happy, healthy old age. You can help your Beagle to stay mentally active by playing gentle games and getting new toys to stimulate interest.

Helping Your Dog Age Gracefully

There are many things you can do to ease your dog's passage into his declining years.

As dogs age they need fewer calories and less protein, so many owners feeding kibble switch to one specially formulated for older dogs. These are labelled *Senior, Ageing* or *Mature.*

Check the labelling; some are specifically for dogs aged over eight, others may be for 10 or 12-year-olds.

If you are not sure if a Senior diet is necessary for your Beagle, talk to your vet on your next visit. Remember, if you do change brand or switch to a wet food, do it gradually over a week or so. Unlike with humans, a dog's digestive system cannot cope with sudden changes of diet.

Years of eating the same food, coupled with less sensitive taste buds can result in some dogs going off their food as they age. If you feed a dry food, try mixing a bit of gravy with it; this works well for us, as has feeding two different feeds: a morning one of kibble with gravy and the second tea-time feed of home-cooked rice and boiled chicken or fish. Rice, white fish and chicken – all cooked – can be particularly good if your old dog has a sensitive stomach.

If you are considering a daily supplement, Omega-3 fatty acids are good for the brain and coat, and glucosamine and various other supplements help joints. Yumega Omega 3, Yumove and Joint Aid are used by lots of breeders with older dogs.

We had one dog that became very sensitive to loud noises as he got older and the lead up to Bonfire Night was a nightmare. (November 5th in the UK, when the skies are filled with fireworks and loud bangs). Some dogs may also become more stressed by grooming or trips to the vet as they get older.

 There are medications, homeopathic remedies, such as melatonin, and various DAP (dog appeasing pheromone) products that can help relieve anxiety. Check with your vet before introducing any new medicines.

One of the most important things throughout your Beagle's life is **dental care** - either by regular tooth brushing or feeding bones, bully sticks or antlers, etc. to gnaw on. Not only is toothache painful and unpleasant, it can be traumatic for dogs to have teeth removed under anaesthetic after they lose weight due to being unable to eat properly.

If your old friend has started to ignore your verbal commands when out on a walk – either through *"switching off"* or deafness - try a whistle to attract his attention and then use an exaggerated hand signal for the Recall. Once your dog is looking at you, hold your arm out, palm down, at 90 degrees to your body and bring it down, keeping your arm straight, until your fingers point to your toes.

Hand signals worked very effectively with our old Max. He looked, understood ... and then decided if he was going to come or not - but at least he knew what he should be doing! More often than not he did come back, especially if the visual signal was repeated while he was still making up his mind.

Weight - no matter how old your Beagle is, he still needs a waist! Maintaining a healthy weight with a balanced diet and regular, gentler exercise are two of the most important things you can do for your dog.

Environment - Make sure your dog has a nice soft place to rest his old bones, which may mean adding an extra blanket to his bed.

This should be in a place that is not too hot or cold, as he may not be able to regulate his body temperature as well as when he was younger.

He also needs plenty of undisturbed sleep and should not be pestered and/or bullied by younger dogs, other animals or young children.

If his eyesight is failing, move obstacles out of his way or use pet barriers to reduce the chance of injuries.

Jumping on and off furniture or in or out of the car should definitely NOT be allowed. It's high impact for old joints and bones. He will need a helping hand on to/into the couch, bed or car - or a ramp.

We bought an expensive plastic ramp to get one old dog into the car, but it proved to be a complete waste of money as he didn't like the feel of the non-slip surface under his paws.

After a few tentative attempts, he steadfastly refused to set a paw on it and we donated the ramp to a canine charity! I have heard of breeders carpeting ramps to (successfully) persuade their dogs to use them.

Exercise - Take the lead from your dog, if he doesn't want to walk as far, then don't. But if your dog doesn't want to go out at all, you will have to coax him out.

ALL old dogs need exercise, not only to keep their joints moving, but also to keep their heart, lungs and joints exercised, and their minds engaged with different places, scents, etc.

Ears – Sometimes older dogs produce more ear wax, so check inside the ears regularly. Keeping the hair under the ear flap short and clean allows good air circulation, reduces moisture in the ear and lessens the wax and yeast build-up.

If necessary, use clean damp cotton wool to clean out the inner ear and pluck extra ear hair if it's getting waxy.

Coat – Some Beagles' coats thicken with age and they require more regular grooming.

....

Time to Get Checked Out

If your dog is showing any of these signs, get them checked out by a vet:

- Excessive increased urination or drinking, which can be a sign of reduced liver or kidney function, Cushing's disease or diabetes

- Constipation or not urinating regularly, a possible symptom of a digestive system or organ disorder

- Incontinence, which could be a sign of a mental or physical problem

- Cloudy eyes, possibly cataracts

- Decreased appetite – often one of the first signs of an underlying problem

- Lumps or bumps on the body - often benign, but can occasionally be malignant (cancerous)

- Excessive sleeping or a lack of interest in you and his surroundings

- Diarrhoea or vomiting

- A darkening and dryness of skin that never seems to get any better, which can be a sign of hypothyroidism

- Any other out-of-the-ordinary behaviour for your dog. A change in patterns or behaviour is often your dog's way of telling you that all is not well

....

What the Experts Say

Veterinarian Dr Samantha Goldberg, Molesend Beagles, County Durham: "In terms of health I would say Beagles slow down a little at eight plus and sleep a bit more, but until 10 they are not really that senior.

"I feed the same, but a bit less Adult food mixed with raw, and I give Yumove joint supplement to mine when they reach around eight or nine, depending on the individual. They do get stiffer when laid down for a while, such as a car journey.

"I'm aware they may not want to walk so far, but we keep the daily exercise the same unless I have a really old dog. I watch out for the old girl as she doesn't always realise when we finish a walk - we walk in a field we own with two horses in it. My oldest Beagle is 12 and she has gone deaf, but can still run at speed when she wants. The oldest I've come across was a rescue from a research breeding facility in the UK who was 20.

"Older Beagles sleep more, but seem more demanding at meal times! They are perhaps a bit less tolerant of the youngsters. I have only had one with dementia, but she lived to 17. They seem to shed their coats less easily and I groom more at moulting season. I am also more aware of them getting cold or wet. Mine live together and coats or jackets would probably get pulled off, but I do towel them off very well when they get older.

"My tips are: Be aware they may not be as able to hold their bladder all night and may need letting our more often. Also, be mindful of any weight changes, up or down, and work out why they happen. Keep an eye on teeth and anything which is not normal for seniors."

Sharon Hardisty, Blunderhall Beagles, Lancashire: "I would say that Beagles are like people; some age better than others.

"I have a seven-year-old boy who's no different now than when he was three. Whereas my nine-year-old definitely shows signs of age, notably a little stiffer, more prone to weight and faded/greyer in the coat - but can still act like a puppy!

"I do put them on a senior food. I have my own range of complete dog food so the one I use has joint care supplements added and is lower in calories to help prevent weight gain. In terms of exercise, my nine-year-old doesn't have the same stamina she used to, so I don't overdo it with her.

"When I give them a bath, I also give them a good massage, which they love. All our oldies live in the house and are pampered!"

Photo: Lola celebrating her ninth birthday, courtesy of Sharon.

Specialist Beagle trainer Kellie Wynn: "I'd say Beagles often start to age at seven to eight years old. Some start to go a little white in the face, like my Daisy, and others don't really show signs of slowing down until 10 years old.

"My two are seven in the next 12 months, but you would never know it. They bounce around those fields like they are puppies Once they hit seven, I'll start giving them Yumove and cod liver oil for their joints and bones.

"Older Beagles sleep a lot more. They go back to their puppy days and can sleep 18-20 hours a day. They can also get grumpy if moved because, as their joints start to stiffen with age, it can hurt to get up out of a comfy spot. They may become less tolerant of children and young dogs. My tip for older Beagles is to watch their weight."

Sarah Porter, Puddlehill Beagles, Norfolk: "My oldest beagle is Yoda, aged nine. The signs of ageing he shows are enjoying his sleep more, wanting more alone time and sniffing more on walks. He also seems a bit more fearful, and can be a bit grumpy. I make sure he has a bit more alone time due to the youngsters in the house, although he does like rough and tumble with them still, and we continue with our same exercise regime.

"I feed raw and will continue to do so. I feed supplements such as cod liver oil throughout their lives - even from puppyhood. From about six or seven I have also given Yoda glucosamine and chondroitin."

Sarah is a canine myotherapist, which is a type of remedial massage therapist. All her dogs have regular massage therapy, even the young ones. She says: "Massage throughout a dog's life keeps the muscles pliable. You are bringing oxygenated nutrient-rich blood to the muscles which improves mobility and suppleness of joints, as well as muscle tone. This in turn improves gait and weight bearing while maintaining mobility and flexibility.

"Regular massage keeps the overall blood circulation where it should be and encourages lymph drainage, which is important. By keeping the muscles in the best possible health, there will be quicker recovery in times of injury, illness or post-surgery. Massage also has the added benefits of promoting skin and coat health."

Karen Simkin, Simeldaka Beagles, London: "In the show ring, the dogs enter Veteran class at seven years, but some give the youngsters a run for their money and move so well! Signs of ageing are fading coat colour and stiffness. I feed Royal Canin Beagle dry food, so that continues, but there are formulas for senior dogs. If they seem stiff in the limbs, I give them glucosamine."

"Mine seem to get a thicker coat, I call them 'teddy bears' when they get older. Therefore you will get more loose hairs, so groom regularly."

Karen's "once in a lifetime" dog Clarence (Simeldaka Balluta Boy), aged 13, has 40 winks in the sunshine.

She added: "I've noticed they can be quieter and sleep more - but not all Beagles; my Nala was still charging around at 13! If necessary, walk a bit slower and shorter distances when they age, but Beagles generally will still walk a long way - even in old age.

"My tips are: be aware they may not remember to toilet outside or hold themselves overnight, especially if they're spayed. Watch their weight, make sure nails are trimmed and check for any lumps or swellings."

Nigel Wright, Huntshill Beagles, Gwent: "My oldest Beagle lived to 17. When they get to 10 years of age, they are sleeping more and develop aches and pains, very much like ourselves - although some hang on to youth into later life.

"I don't change to a senior diet, but change to feeding several times a day, making the food easier to digest. I sometimes add glucosamine to help with mobility. Older Beagles sometimes need some time away from younger dogs.

"Their coat seems to get thicker and more brushing is needed - although they seem to be able to self-groom by rolling on your carpets and rubbing against you when you put on black trousers! My advice is to keep to the same routine; Beagles love routine."

Peter Sievwright, Mattily Beagles, Renfrewshire: "Personally I think Beagles become seniors around the age of seven to nine. They start slowing down and becoming stiff, more so in the mornings after a good night's sleep, but also after their afternoon naps. It takes them longer to get up and they look slightly bent over and just that little bit older, with grey eyebrows and facial features.

"I tend to feed the older dogs puppy food just to give them those extra vitamins and minerals to keep them plodding along. Sometimes I may give them a multivitamin, but not that often.

"They are less excited and bouncy and they get shorter and quieter walks. I do tend to stroke the older dogs more as they tend to be around me and sitting with me more than the younger dogs.

"As for caring for older Beagles, they are like old people - they need lots of love, care and attention. They need the temperature slightly higher to prevent stiffness and the cold creeping in, as they are less active. They just need a bit more TLC."

The Last Lap

Huge advances in veterinary science have meant that there are countless procedures and medications that can prolong the life of your dog, and this is a good thing. But there comes a time when you do have to let go.

If your dog is showing all the signs of ageing, has an ongoing medical condition from which they cannot recover, is showing signs of pain, anxiety or distress and there is no hope of improvement, then the dreaded time has come to say goodbye.

You owe it to your Beagle.

There is no point keeping an old dog alive if all that lies ahead is pain and death. We have their lives in our hands and we can give them the gift of passing away peacefully and humanely at the end when the time is right.

Losing our beloved companion, our best friend, a member of the family, is truly heart-breaking. But one of the things we realise at the back of our minds when we got that gorgeous, lively little puppy that bounded up to meet us like we were the best person in the whole wide world is the pain that comes with it.

We know we will live longer than them and that we'll probably have to make this most painful of decisions at some time in the future.

It's the worst thing about being a dog owner.

If your Beagle has had a long and happy life, then you could not have done any more. You were a great owner and your dog was lucky to have you. Remember all the good times you had together.

Try not to rush out and buy another dog straight away. Assess your current life and lifestyle and, if your situation is right, only then consider getting another dog and all that that entails in terms of time, commitment and expense over the next decade and more.

Whatever you decide to do, put the dog first.

Happy Family. Pictured are four generations of Beagles bred by Sally Kimber.
Left to right: UK Champion Coachbarn Cobweb (aged 14), Barrvale Krafty of Coachbarn (10),
Coachbarn Castor (8) and Coachbarn Coda (5).

Contributing Breeders

UK

Dr Samantha Goldberg, BVSc MRCVS, Kennel Club Health Coordinator, UK Beagle Clubs. Molesend Beagles, County Durham www.molesend.co.uk

Nigel Wright, Chairman, Beagle Welfare, Huntshill Beagles, Caldicott, Gwent, Wales

Sharon Hardisty, Blunderhall Beagles, Saddleworth, Lancashire www.blunderhallbeagles.co.uk

Karen Simkin, Simeldaka Beagles, London karenjsimkin@yahoo.co.uk

Kelly Diamond, Kelcardi Beagles, Fife, Scotland www.facebook.com/kelcardibeagles

Georgina Armour-Langham, Robentot Beagles, Leicester

Debbie Tantrum, Debles Beagles, Lydbury North, Shropshire www.facebook.com/deblesbeagles

Sarah and Ben Porter, Puddlehill Beagles, Norfolk www.puddlehillbeagles.co.uk

Peter Sievwright, Mattily Beagles, Renfrewshire, Scotland

Sally Kimber, Coachbarn Beagles, Kent

and

"Beagles As Pets," originally compiled by S. Kimber and P. Carmichael, with contributions by A. D'Arcy and many others, for Beagle Welfare and the Beagle Association.

USA

Ruth Darlene Stewart, Chairperson, Health and Genetics Committee, National Beagle Club of America. Aladar Beagles, Mobile, Alabama www.aladarbeagles.com

Lori Norman, Lokavi Beagles, Bonita Springs, Florida www.Lokavi.com

and

Linda Forrest, Founder, SOS Beagle Rescue, Atco, NJ www.sosbeagles.org

Dr Sara Skiwski, Western Dragon holistic veterinary practice, San Jose, California www.thewesterndragon.com

Useful Contacts

National Beagle Club of America www.nationalbeagleclub.org

The Beagle Association (UK) www.beagleassociation.org.uk

The Beagle Club (UK) www.thebeagleclub.org

AKC (American Kennel Club) www.akc.org/dog-breeds/beagle

Kennel Club (UK) Assured Breeders www.thekennelclub.org.uk/search/find-an-assured-breeder

Aladar Beagles - a treasure trove of Beagle info: care, training, health, colours, etc. http://www.aladarbeagles.com/toc.html

The most up-to-date information on Beagle health www.beaglehealth.info

Beagle Welfare (UK-wide rescue) www.beaglewelfare.org.uk/

RSPCA Puppy Contract https://puppycontract.rspca.org.uk/home

AKC Preparing a Puppy Contract www.akc.org/expert-advice/dog-breeding/preparing-a-contract-for-puppy-buyers

AKC Canine Good Citizen www.akc.org/products-services/training-programs/canine-good-citizen

KC Good Citizen Scheme www.thekennelclub.org.uk/training/good-citizen-dog-training-scheme

Specialist Beagle trainer Kellie Wynn www.thebeaglelady.com

Association of Pet Dog Trainers UK www.apdt.co.uk

Association of Pet Dog Trainers US www.apdt.com

Canadian Association of Professional Pet Dog Trainers www.cappdt.ca

Useful info on dog foods (US) www.dogfoodadvisor.com (UK) www.allaboutdogfood.co.uk

Helps find lost or stolen dogs in the US: register your dog's microchip at www.akcreunite.org and www.petmicrochiplookup.com to trace a registered microchip

Beagle internet forums and Facebook groups are also a good source of information from other owners.

Disclaimer

This book has been written to provide helpful information on Beagles. It is not meant to be used, nor should it be used, to diagnose or treat any medical condition. For diagnosis or treatment of any animal medical problem, consult a qualified veterinarian.

The author is not responsible for any specific health or allergy conditions that may require medical supervision and is not liable for any damages or negative consequences from any treatment, action, application or preparation, to any animal or to any person reading or following the information in this book.

The views expressed by contributors to this book are solely personal and do not necessarily represent those of the author. References are provided for informational purposes only and do not constitute endorsement of any websites or other sources.

Pet Care Tracker

Vet's Name: _ _ _ _ _ _ _ _ _ _ _	Groomer's Name: _ _ _ _ _ _ _ _ _ _ _
Vet's Phone: _ _ _ _ _ _ _ _ _ _	Groomer's Phone: _ _ _ _ _ _ _ _ _ _
Day Care: _ _ _ _ _ _ _ _ _ _ _	Holiday Sitter: _ _ _ _ _ _ _ _ _ _ _

Pet's Name	Date	Vet Visit	Groomer	NOTES

Made in the USA
Monee, IL
02 August 2022

10768041R00127